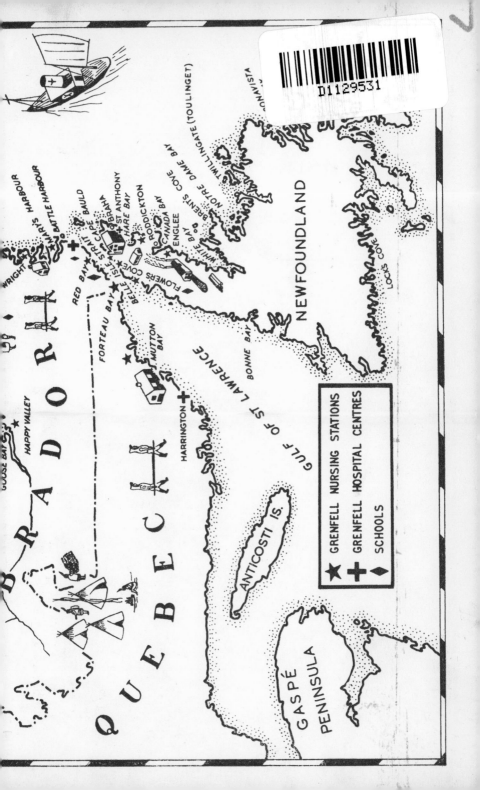

WILFRED GRENFELL: HIS
LIFE AND WORK

SIR WILFRED GRENFELL

WILFRED GRENFELL
His Life and Work

By

J. LENNOX KERR

With a Foreword by

LORD GRENFELL OF KILVEY

President, the Grenfell Association of Great Britain and Ireland

THE RYERSON PRESS — TORONTO

First published in Canada
by THE RYERSON PRESS, TORONTO

© *The Grenfell Association of*
Great Britain and Ireland 1959

D4611

Composed in Linotype Granjon type and printed by
Western Printing Services Ltd, Bristol
Made in Great Britain

Foreword

by

Lord Grenfell of Kilvey

To-day, close on twenty years after the death of Sir Wilfred Grenfell, the Mission he founded for the physical and spiritual welfare of the people of Labrador and Northern Newfoundland, and for the fishermen who work on these dangerous coasts, has grown to a size and usefulness unique in the history of privately conducted and voluntarily supported missions. The work of the Grenfell Mission, so ably continued under the devoted care of Dr Charles Curtis, now covers the welfare of all those who work and live on some two thousand miles of coastline, in Labrador from Cape Chidley, at the entrance to Hudson Bay, to the Quebec boundary, and along the northern and part of the eastern coasts of Newfoundland.

Seven doctors, twenty-six nurses, and a great many helpers are engaged permanently and throughout the year to man four hospitals with from twenty to eighty beds and equipped to perform every sort of operation or treatment, as well as eight nursing stations. At St Anthony, in Northern Newfoundland, the Mission buildings form a small town in themselves, where, besides the eighty-bed hospital, there are a children's home for over thirty children, an eighty-bed sanatorium for tubercular patients, an annexe for convalescents, a farm with a large herd of prize cattle, pigs, greenhouses, and poultry, a marine railway for taking and repairing ships up to 500 tons, a handicraft department employing disabled fishermen and the wives of fishermen, and other departments for the maintenance of the Mission's property. Two hospital ships and one aircraft operate from St Anthony, carrying doctors and nurses where they are needed and covering many thousands of miles every year.

The other hospitals and nursing stations give a service only less in degree, and are as well equipped for medical or other work. A second aircraft and another hospital ship operate from North West River, in Hamilton Inlet, to serve the northern part of Labrador, the doctor and nurses attending on Eskimos, Indians, and the rapidly increasing white population in this developing country. Dentists are in attendance at the hospitals and travel the Coast regularly by ship or aircraft. Each summer volunteers come from the United States, Canada, and Great Britain to assist the permanent staff and to undertake every sort of task for the Mission.

The cost of this service is now heavy, though the volunteers work for nothing and the permanent staff give their services for much less than they could earn elsewhere. The money required is donated from endowments held by or subscriptions collected by the supporting associations: the Grenfell Association of America, in New York; the Grenfell Association of Great Britain and Ireland, in London; the Grenfell Association of New England, in Boston; the Grenfell Association of Newfoundland; and the Grenfell Labrador Mission, in Ottawa. To-day the Canadian Government contributes also.

The governing body which handles all finance and Mission policy is the International Grenfell Association, officially based at St John's, in Newfoundland, but conducted mostly from New York and Boston; the members of the Council of this body, like those conducting the several associations, volunteer their services without payment.

Altogether, through its hospitals and nursing stations, and by aircraft, ships, and winter sledges, the Mission doctors and nurses treat some 50,000 patients every year, as well as giving many other non-medical services.

Wilfred Grenfell would be proud of how his great work has been continued and developed and of how his ideal of co-operation between the peoples of nations has been achieved. Members of his family have in the centuries distinguished themselves in various walks of life, but none of them more so than Wilfred Grenfell, whose courage and initiative and faith brought the first hope, spiritual and medical, to the people he made his own and whom the Mission still serves.

This biography, commissioned and sponsored by the Grenfell Association of Great Britain and Ireland, gives a sincere and honest portrait of the Mission's founder and of a man who dedicated himself to Christ and to Christ's people. I acknowledge with gratitude a generous contribution made by an anonymous donor to the costs of its production.

It is a matter of great satisfaction to me that Wilfred's biographer should himself be a man of the sea, sharing Wilfred's love of adventure and admiration for fishermen. I commend the book to its readers in the knowledge that its author, having had access to the family and Grenfell Associations' documents, and having spent some time on the Coast, has given us an accurate and understanding account of the life of one whose name will always be remembered as one of the great missionaries, and wherever the quality of mercy is recognized.

Preface

IN COLLECTING the material for this biography I travelled
not less than ten thousand miles in Great Britain, the United
States, Canada, Labrador, and Newfoundland. I interviewed
several hundreds of men and women who had known or who
had worked with Sir Wilfred Grenfell, and I studied the
records and archives of many associations, Government departments, and commercial concerns, as well as private letters and
papers made available by Sir Wilfred's family and friends. It
would be impossible in a limited space to name all who gave
me information and help, and I can only thank them collec-
tively. The help and kindliness I received in seeking, as I did,
original sources rather than published books was invaluable.

Certain acknowledgments, as well as thanks, are due to the
Council and the Secretary of the Royal National Mission to
Deep Sea Fishermen, who made all their records and copies of
their magazine, *Toilers of the Sea*, available, and who have
permitted me to quote from these papers and the magazine; to
the International Grenfell Association and its directors and
officers both in the United States and in Newfoundland; to the
Grenfell Associations of Great Britain and Ireland, New England, and Newfoundland; to the Hudson's Bay Company and
its archivist; to the Librarian of H.M. Commonwealth Relations Office Library; to the Admiralty Hydrographic Department; and to Yale University, who permitted me the use of
their library to study the Grenfell Papers in their care. I am
deeply grateful to Sir Wilfred's son, Mr Wilfred Grenfell, and
to his daughter and her husband, Mrs and Mr J. Wyman Shaw,
who allowed me to question them and who lent me letters and
family papers, and have permitted the use of their father's
cartoons which are being used as chapter decorations in this
book. Without the sympathetic aid of Dr Charles S. Curtis,
Superintendent of the Grenfell Mission in Labrador and New-

foundland, the book could never have been written. I am deeply grateful to Dr Curtis and to Miss Shirley Smith, Secretary of the New England Grenfell Association.

There are very many others I ought to thank by name—ex-missionaries, nurses, 'Wops,' fishermen on the Labrador and Newfoundland coasts, people in St John's—who all did so much to help me. I can only hope that the completed work falls not too far short of what they hoped I might produce.

J. L. K.

Contents

This life is either a tragedy ending in death
or a field of honour beginning our real life.
SIR WILFRED GRENFELL

1

The Horizon-seeker: Boyhood

FEW schools have been placed so distractingly for their pupils as was Mostyn House School, in Parkgate, on the Cheshire shore of the river Dee. A mere fifty feet of roadway separated its front wall from a revetment of large blocks of red sandstone, Parkgate's often inadequate defences against the sea that at high tide rose against this bulwark as the water spread across the five miles of estuary between the Welsh and English shores, and as many miles up-river to where the land grew inward and seemed to join towards Chester. The contours of both shores, as seen from the school, and the lifting Welsh hills gave the illusion of containing a large and protected lake— an illusion that was destroyed when storms from the westward drove the water up violently from the Irish Sea and Liverpool Bay, and waves, ranked and swelling over the shallows, burst against the sandstone revetment to splatter the school windows, flood the long promenade, enter the houses, and in great gales to tear boats from their moorings and cast them on the roadway.

With the ebb the waters receded, to become a fast-running stream contained in a narrow gut, known as the Deep, that followed close under the Welsh shore until opposite Parkgate, where it wound across the now exposed sands to the English side and passed westward to the sea. At low water the sands extended across the estuary, westward as far as Hilbre Island, seven miles below Parkgate, and up-river to where the remains of a defeated sea-wall marked the entrance to the river Dee itself. By 1865, when the subject of this biography was born at Mostyn House School, the Dee had been silting up steadily for over a hundred years. Chester had long ceased to be the important seaport it had been, and the remnants of its trade, the Irish cross-channel packets, were entirely gone. These smart little vessels, for many hundreds of years the main sea link for passengers between Ireland and England, had sought since the late eighteenth century to continue by shifting their place of departure down-river from Chester, but gradually the encroaching sands had closed each place of retreat, and by the eighteen-twenties the packets had lost the fight and the upstart Mersey had taken over their trade.

The last stand of the Irish passenger vessels had been at Parkgate, and for a brief period the small community of fishermen and their families enjoyed the prosperity that came with the trade. Passengers came by coach from as far as London, lodging at the George Inn, now Mostyn House School, until their ship sailed. This prosperity was increased by Parkgate's popularity as a fashionable sea-bathing resort and as a salubrious locality pleasing to rich Merseysiders living expansively in large country houses; a popularity that declined and then ceased when the famous 'golden sands' became fouled by the crude sewage of the time and recurring outbreaks of cholera and smallpox were blamed on the open wells that supplied the village with its fresh water. With its two short bursts of prosperity gone, the last landlady of the George Inn dramatizing their going by hanging herself from the old pump that still stood in the school's back kitchen, Parkgate returned to what it had been, a small fishing community.

This is what it was when Wilfred Thomason Grenfell, second son of the headmaster and owner, was born in the school on February 28, 1865. A population of some few hundreds won a hard but modestly adequate living from the waters of Liverpool Bay and the estuary. Working with boats up to thirty feet long, Parkgate fishermen trawled and lined for the excellent prime fish in the outer waters. In March and at the end of August, when the salmon were running, they seined from the edge of the sand between tides, and in winter the boats drifted their trawls along the Deep with the flood-tide, or men walked in the shallows with hand-nets to bring home the famous Parkgate shrimps, whose fame spread as the new railways carried them to the cities. Parkgate's mussels were nearly as famous as its shrimps, and barefooted, linsey-skirted, and shawl-clad village women led their pannier-slung donkeys over the sand to bring back the catch their menfolk scooped out of deep pools with rakes at the end of 30-foot-long poles.

It was a fully engaged and picturesque corner of England, and he would have been a dull boy who did not find Parkgate and its sands and sea full of interest and rich for the adventurous. Certainly Wilfred Grenfell, as he passed through his boyhood, found it so. Behind the long, irregular-roofed houses on the promenade, which was the only real street in the place, the Cheshire land rose gently, the rounded hilltops poising windmills against the sky, offering its own sort of beauty and interest to those satisfied with the slow cycle of a countryside. The young Grenfell was little interested in lanes and woodlands. He sought wider horizons, and needed movement faster than the movements of a countryside. The estuary, reassuringly familiar though it was, was never twice the same. Each cloud across the sky was a brush drawing a new colour on sand and sea and the distant Welsh hills. They were gold with the setting sun, cold silver under the moon, and heavy stormclouds darkened them to deep, sombre colour. Each tide moulded the sands to new shapes, demanding exploration, the discovery of pools where fish might have been trapped and could be watched by a budding scientist and keen naturalist, then scooped up and carried home in triumph.

To the young Grenfell the wide, tide-shaped, and rippled sands offered a new experience each day, a new challenge to what was a foolhardy daring. For those who sailed and those who went by foot the estuary could be a trap. A boat grounding on a newly raised ledge or close to the edge of a channel could be toppled on her side as the receding tide drifted the sand from under her. A careless or unwatchful wanderer, a fisherman who waited too long to haul in his salmon-net or to be satisfied with his catch of shrimps, could be caught by the rising tide as it spread at deceptive speed over the banks, or encircled a sand-bank to leave its victim marooned. There had been many caught this way, and Wilfred had watched one man trying vainly to anchor himself with his net-pole as the tide gathered him up and bore him away. This man had been saved by his friends hauling a heavy boat over the sand to float it and reach him, but others had been less fortunate. The Rev. Charles Kingsley, Canon of Chester Cathedral, famous poet and author, and a relative of the young Grenfell's by marriage to his father's cousin, had written:

> The western tide crept up along the sand,
> And o'er and o'er the sand,
> And round and round the sand,
> As far as eye could see.
> The rolling mist came down and hid the land,

in his poem telling of one victim, a herd girl, caught on the Sands of Dee.

The young Grenfell gave little thought to such dangers. The estuary or the patchwork green of the Welsh hills called him, and he went, sliding from the top of the revetment to the sand in preference to more decorous descent by the steps or slipways along the wall and going outward, searching for a new route each time and testing his hardy body in leaping water-filled guts or racing up newly discovered hillocks. The shallow basin of the estuary teemed with life and interest—in the pools, where the boy could watch water creatures; in the sky, where sea-birds and wintering fowl brightened his hunter's eyes; birds and butterflies in the hills he would reach either by wading naked across the Deep at low water, his clothes held above his head, or by swimming. When—at the early age of twelve—he grew to the responsibility of a gun he brought home trophies from the great flocks of pink-footed geese, as many as three thousand birds in a flight, that came drumming from the northward to winter on Burton marshes, a few miles up-river from Parkgate, oyster-catchers caught strutting the edges of the mussel beds, curlews and green and golden plover and other birds that came to the Dee to find the rich pickings of the sands and marshes. Lacking a dog to retrieve the birds he brought down in the water, Wilfred stripped off and swam to secure his prizes, careless of winter cold and biting wind.

If not on some solitary expedition over the estuary at low water, the boy was with the fishermen. The men liked this friendly, talkative, grey-blue-eyed boy who wanted so much to learn their craft and who so admired them. He was the son of the Big House, his father the principal gentleman of their small world, but the boy never gave this a thought. He was friends equally with his well-born schoolfellows and with the fishermen's sons; he came to their cottages and sat down to share their simple meals as naturally as though he were in his own home, and he took their wives' chiding for coming in soaked and chilled as meekly as did their own sons. The villagers considered both Wilfred and his brother Algernon, two years his senior, foolishly reckless. They built a cranky boat, which they named *Reptile*, and were capsized into the water; Algernon was blinded for two weeks when he overcharged his gun and it blew up in his face; and their escapades were a topic of wonder and worry to the whole village. When Wilfred sailed with the fishermen to Liverpool Bay he had to be watched all the time, for his exuberance and thoughtlessness of danger could be a menace. If he managed to coax the tiller from some soft-hearted fisherman he would sail the boat happily over a dangerous bank in trying a new course and to make a shorter run home, or in experimenting with some new idea of sailing he had just thought of. The fishermen's liking for the boy was often strained; their admiration for his willingness to share their labours and their rough lives turned to oaths and fury when he let go a rope to follow some fancy that had just occurred. He was a likeable lad, the making of a fine man, but a restless shipmate. They taught him what they could in boat-handling and about fishing, but they kept a wary eye on him at sea.

He was permitted a freedom remarkable for those Victorian times, when children were seen but not heard and correct behaviour was a religion. During the school term he had to attend classes like any other lad, and he did certain small chores for his mother, recording carefully in his diary, for the few days

B

each year he kept such a record, the number of eggs he had gathered and errands he had done, but he still managed to get away on his hunting and fishing expeditions, and to make an almost daily visit with his schoolfellows to the "Cocoa Shop" on the promenade. During the school holidays he and Algernon were left completely free, except for what authority a much-tried housekeeper could exercise over them. With the Reverend Algernon and Mrs Grenfell off to their favourite Switzerland, this unfortunate matron had many anxious hours waiting for the boys to return from some new adventure proposed by the over-original Algernon and eagerly taken up by his younger brother.

Mrs Grenfell was the only person who asserted control over Wilfred. His father, high in the clouds of the classical scholarship he tried to instil into his pupils, left a great deal to his wife. She was the business head of the school, seeing to the feeding and care of its fifty or so young boys. Her third son—a fourth had died in childhood—needed a great deal of care, for his mental development had been arrested at an early age, and either his mother or a nurse had to be with him all the time. Mrs Grenfell did not have much time to give to controlling high-spirited sons, and contented herself with always being there when she was needed, to welcome home the wet and cold Wilfred and see that he had good food. She was, by her normality and good sense, a remarkable parent, and Wilfred was to admire her above all others and for all his life. A plumpish, energetic little woman, who grew more and more like Queen Victoria as she got older, she exercised a great influence on her son by letting him develop in his own way, her correction a humorous chiding for her "Hottentot," and earned his gratitude and admiration by the example she set in never failing him or her tasks.

That she did not restrain her son's often reckless daring may have been because she was happy to see him fearless. She was a soldier's daughter and came of a long line of soldiers. The Hutchinsons were an English Border family, and one of them, Colonel John Hutchinson, was one of Cromwell's officers and a signator of Charles II's death-warrant. Hutchinsons had served with the British Army in India since the eighteenth century, and Mrs Grenfell's father had been a colonel in the Royal

Engineers there. It was to be Wilfred's pride to tell how no fewer than forty-eight of his cousins, all either soldiers or members of the Indian Civil Service, met at the first Delhi Durbar.

With such an ancestry Mrs Grenfell would value courage and not wish to discipline her son to timidity from her own fears for his safety. Yet, from the evidence of his life and accomplishment and the stories told of his deeds, it would seem that it was not the stolid, balanced courage of the soldier-Hutchinsons the boy had inherited, but the more impulsive and less reasoning daring of his father's family, the Grenfells. Along the history of that many-branched family, the Granvilles, who came to England with William the Conqueror and became a famous West Country family, individuals flare up at intervals with deeds strongly reminiscent of many of Wilfred Grenfell's future actions. Deeds such as Sir Richard Grenville's defiance of a whole Spanish fleet at the Azores in 1591, where reason disappeared in the heat of a proud and obstinate refusal to yield to an opponent, no matter how hopeless the odds.

The branch of this family, whose name had taken several different forms, as Grenville, Grenfell, Greenfield, that was to produce Grenfell of Mostyn House School had few professional warriors. It can be traced to St Just in Cornwall, and to a Pascoe Grenfell who was a tin merchant in Penzance at the end of the seventeenth century. Pascoe prospered, and his family moved nearer to London, the line continuing as successful merchants, churchmen, and Members of Parliament. At the beginning of the nineteenth century the family daring flared out in a colourful sailor of fortune, John Pascoe Grenfell, Wilfred's great-uncle. This Grenfell began his sea career as a midshipman with the East India Company at the age of eleven, and in 1819 became one of that band of able and reckless young British officers who followed the disgraced Admiral Lord Cochrane into the service of the Chilean Navy. In the cutting out of the *Esmeralda* at Callao in 1820, an exploit that was to be considered Cochrane's greatest action and was to cripple Spanish naval power in South America, the young Grenfell distinguished himself with the boarding parties, but, like his leader, was seriously wounded. With their independence won, the Chileans showed neither gratitude nor generosity to the foreigners who had led their forces, and Cochrane transferred his services to the Emperor of Brazil. Grenfell followed him, and rose to high rank in the war with Portugal, losing his right arm in one of the many actions he fought. When Cochrane moved again and took charge of the Greek Navy during the Greek rebellion against Turkey Grenfell stayed with the Brazilians and rose to the rank of rear-admiral. He was Consul-General for Brazil in London in 1846, and ultimately retired to Liverpool. He died in 1869, when Wilfred was four years old. It is certain that the boy met his great-uncle, whose qualities he was to possess but direct into more humane, though often enough as turbulent, channels.

Except for a love of climbing in the Swiss Alps, Wilfred's father showed no sign of the Grenfell daring, and was far from being warlike. His eldest son, Algernon, would have made a brilliant if original warrior, but he was to direct his originality into gay escapades and practical jokes, and his energy into building Mostyn House into the most successful preparatory school in the North of England. Wilfred himself seems never to have considered becoming either soldier or fighting sailor, finding enough scope on the Dee estuary and with boats during his boyhood. He records no boyish ambitions. There is the rare child who knows his direction from an early age, but Wilfred Grenfell was not that sort of boy. He was too busy enjoying himself, in learning the ways of a bird in the air, a boat on the water, and relishing the companionship of his schoolfellows and the fishermen of Parkgate, and in pitting his strong body and keen wits against the waters and living things of the Dee estuary.

He was to miss this wonderful playground when in 1879, at the age of fourteen and a half, he went off to be a Founder Scholar at Marlborough College, in Wiltshire. At this famous school, founded earlier in the century for the education of the sons of clergymen, he made little mark and was far from happy. To a boy who had been allowed the freedom he was allowed at home, where he could wear any old comfortable garment and wander off by himself barefooted and do much what he liked once his school work was done, to be confined by the discipline of a well-organized public school was irksome. He did assert himself on his first day at Marlborough by fighting another new

boy for the possession of a bed under a window in the long,
L-shaped dormitory where he slept, earning himself the nickname of "the Beast" for this exploit and for his mass of untidy
brown hair. But, except for being remembered as a "cheerful,
somewhat red-headed boy who liked his own way and a rag,"
the impression he made at Marlborough was slight.

There was little scope for Grenfell's particular kind of high
spirits and energy at this school. The bolder among the boys
climbed out of the dormitory windows at night, to creep
through the masters' garden and have illicit bathing parties in
the bathing-pool that had been shaped out of the moat of
Marlborough Castle, the home of the Dukes of Somerset before
they built what was to become an inn and then the college. But
this was tame stuff to a boy who was an expert swimmer and
whose favourite water game at home had been to throw himself
into the Deep where the tide ran fastest and eddies swirled dan-
gerously, to test his skill and strength by getting back to the
shore. Grenfell confesses to sneaking into the near-by Saver-
nake Forest on Sundays, a hand-net concealed under his coat,
to catch butterflies—a poor substitute for lying in a hollow at
the edge of Burton marshes in the grey dawn, waiting for the
sanderlings to chirp a warning of the approaching geese and
duck, and spending nights in a pitching fishing-boat in Liverpool Bay.

Early in his second year at Marlborough Wilfred developed
a cough that worried his teachers and parents, and he was sent
to stay with his mother's sister in the South of France. He spent
a congenial few months, hunting the woods for butterflies and
moths, which he mounted to add to his collection of birds he
had shot and stuffed and other trophies of his growing interest
in nature and its creatures. He returned to the school, presenting
the Museum with "Five examples of nests of trapdoor spiders
from France" and to take up the routine of a pupil's life. He
was happier now, for at last he had found an outlet for his restless energy and love of challenge. Sport and exercises were a
substitute for the Dee sands, and his energy could be worked off
in the gymnasium or the football field. He became a good and
skilful boxer, but Rugby football was his new-found delight.
He was an aggressive, energetic player, and that year he played
for his house. He was not a big boy—he was five feet one when

he entered Marlborough—but was exceptionally fast-moving and muscular.

On his return from France, and after his few months' absence, he was held back in a lower form, and his father objected to this. Wilfred was never the brilliant scholar his father and his brother Algernon were, but he learned quickly and easily, and his father had taught him well in the two main subjects at Marlborough, Latin and Greek. When he arrived there he had been more advanced in these subjects than most of his classmates, and now it seemed unfair that he should be held back. When his father protested the boy was moved into a higher form. The form master, forced to accept the boy, showed his displeasure by ignoring what good work he did, and Wilfred was entirely unhappy outside his games and on Sundays, when each week the boys of Marlborough College sang through the whole of Handel's *Messiah*. Wilfred was completely tone-deaf, but he loved to sing, and he bawled out happily every Sunday in the oratorio, the manuscript of which had been lying still unpublished in its composer's baggage when, years before, Handel had lodged at the George Inn at Parkgate, awaiting a ship to Ireland. But neither sport nor singing the *Messiah* advanced the boy's education, and at the end of his second year there Wilfred was taken away from Marlborough.

He came home to Parkgate after a far from happy last term at his public school, his boyish vanity soothed by his mother's loving care and the welcome of his fishermen friends. The freedom to wander over the estuary was doubly sweet after the restrictions of school life, and as it was winter when he arrived home he had the extra pleasure of shooting. For almost a year Wilfred had a very happy and carefree time.

But a change was coming in his life. Wilfred Grenfell never really explained why his father decided to abandon a pleasant and comfortable life as owner and headmaster of a private school to become chaplain of a large hospital in what was then the most foul and poverty-stricken place in England, the East End of London. The Reverend Algernon did make this change in his life; in November 1882 he was appointed chaplain of the London Hospital, in Whitechapel Road, his duties to commence on December 30 that year. This was a momentous decision for a man like Wilfred's father to make. He had been ordained, but had never practised as a clergyman, leaving Oxford to become an assistant master, first at a school in Worcestershire and then at Repton. In 1862 he had married and moved to Mostyn House School, then owned and conducted by its founder, the Reverend Algernon's great-uncle. A year later the great-uncle retired and the young master purchased the school.

His interests seem to have been as much in classical scholarship as in religious teaching. He was a brilliant conversationalist, with a love for argument his son inherited. Wilfred never suggests that the father was a very intense Christian. The family attended church in the village of Neston, near Parkgate, twice every Sunday, and, though Mrs Grenfell was a devout and somewhat narrow worshipper, there seems to have been no exceptional religious emphasis in the home or school. It would seem that something stirred the Reverend Algernon to make him sacrifice the peace and beauty of Parkgate for the ugliness of a London slum, and to give up the pleasant life of a scholar to work among the destitute and diseased. It is fair to speculate on his decision.

Several Grenfells had shown a strong social consciousness. Many were churchmen and politicians, and here and there a member of the family bursts into strong humanitarian action. Wilfred's great-grandfather fought notably in support of William Wilberforce for the abolition of the slave trade. Almost contemporary with the young Wilfred, a Grenfell of Penzance became a famous missionary in Africa, and there were others who gave themselves to the service of their fellowmen. There were also outside influences that might have stirred the Reverend Algernon. Dickens's novels, exposing the conditions of the poor in London, had pricked the consciences of many. Charles Kingsley, while canon at Chester, was a frequent visitor to Mostyn House School, and, though his earlier chartism had mellowed, he was still an outspoken champion of the poor and something of a Christian socialist. He would most probably have declared his views and beliefs to his wife's cousin. There were others, shocking England with disclosures of how the poor lived. The Salvation Army was being formed and was advertising its work, and the first of that company of well-born and gently reared men and women who were to dedicate them-

selves to missionary work in the East End of London at the end
of the nineteenth century were taking up their task. It might
well have seemed to the Reverend Algernon that his Christianity was an empty thing if he did not give himself to helping
those less fortunate. Wilfred Grenfell later wrote: "My father
became anxious to give up teaching and to confine himself more
exclusively to the work of a clergyman." This seems inadequate
recognition of the father's sacrifice. With his family background and the patronage he could have called upon, he could
have become a clergyman in more pleasant places than the
London Hospital. His son was to give the father little uttered
credit as a parent; it was to his mother that he gave most of his
admiration. It would seem that he got from his father the
greatest example of all—self-sacrifice.

The family prepared to leave Parkgate. A deputy was found
to take over the school until the eldest son, Algernon, then at
Oxford, was able to assume control. At the same time the
Reverend Algernon spoke to Wilfred about his future, asking
what he intended to do with his life. This surprised the boy.
It had never occurred to him that his life was other than satis-
factory. He was a member of a class who assumed a right to be
supplied with their needs—the clothes they wore, the food they
ate, a comfortable home. Members of this class took up profes-
sions, not to earn a living, but because it was an established convention and the part they would play in society, or to further an
ambition. Money was not a goal, and, indeed, 'trade' was considered somewhat vulgar. The harsh, driving need to earn their
daily bread was not their lot in life. Their whole upbringing,
their education, detached them from such realities. Wilfred
Grenfell, then, had no knowledge of what poverty meant. He
knew, vaguely, that his mother doled out bowls of soup to
elderly people in the village, but he was more interested in
knowing that the family's dog helped itself to this bounty than
in why the charity was necessary. He did not yet realize that
his fishermen friends had to catch fish and risk their lives from
grim necessity and not for pleasure or excitement. For himself
he was conscious of no needs. He had no extravagant tastes,
and the sands of Dee gave him a full life.

Now that his father had brought up the matter, however,
Wilfred realized that he should have some occupation, and he

knew at once what this should be: he would be a big-game hunter. His home was decorated with the heads of wild animals that had been shot by his uncles and cousins. He would go to India and add to this collection. What his father said to this proposal is not known, but Wilfred was sent to Chester to consult the mother of a friend, the wife of a missionary in China and a most accomplished lady. She explained that big-game hunting was hardly a profession, and suggested that he enter the Church. But being a clergyman did not appeal to the energetic and adventurous boy, so he was sent to another adviser, the local medical practitioner and an old family friend. This was an excellent choice, for Wilfred was fond of the doctor, liking him because he never gave away any of the wilder escapades he knew the Grenfell boys to indulge in during their parents' absences abroad. The doctor had a pretty daughter, who was Wilfred's favourite companion, and also owned several excellent horses, on which he rode "prodigious" distances when covering his large practice. Wilfred Grenfell was later to describe how he decided to become a doctor when his adviser showed him a human brain in pickle. Grenfell says that it had never occurred to him before to think of the human body as a machine; this did suddenly occur to him when he was shown the pickled brain, and he was tremendously impressed. He came away from the interview determined to be a doctor.

This is a nice little story, with just that touch of drama Wilfred Grenfell could never resist using when he recounted an experience. It could be entirely correct. Grenfell was impulsive and given to instant decisions, and he had long been interested in nature and bird-life. The human body was only one step onward. But it is as likely that the boy made his decision because of his liking for his adviser and because riding on good horses along country lanes on mercy bent seemed a most attractive way to live. Whatever the reason, Wilfred told his father he wanted to be a doctor, and his father offered him the choice of taking his degree at Oxford or accompanying the family to London and studying there. Wilfred chose to go to London. He was living there with his parents when he matriculated at London University. He entered London Hospital Medical School on February 5, 1883, a month after his matriculation and within a few weeks of his eighteenth birthday.

2

The Horizon widens: Young Manhood

TRAINING to be a doctor in the eighties was a haphazard and light-hearted business. Already there was a tradition that medical students should 'rag,' drink hard, and absent themselves from as many lectures as they cared to. Some of the instructors appear to have had as little interest in their students as the students had in their instruction, and supervision was practised lightly on the young men. Practical jokes were played in the classrooms, and to be that bit more reckless than anyone else seems to have been the reputation aimed at by the cheerful young men. Tremendous things were happening in medicine at this time, new ideas coming in and new methods being tested; but, if the stories told by doctors who were studying at the time can be accepted, little of this revolution in healing reached the classrooms or inspired the students. Crammers studied the examiners rather than the subject, and were able to pass their protégés through on a knowledge of an examiner's idiosyncrasies and the anticipation of oft-repeated questions. It was a system, or lack of system, that inflicted many dangerous young men on the unfortunate public, and as often 'ploughed' those who had really tried to learn their profession.

The London Hospital School appears to have been no better and no worse than any other medical school of the times. Grenfell confesses in his autobiography that he attended only two botany lectures during his whole course. At the first lecture he attended some joker spilled a solution of carbon disulphide over the professor's platform, and the smell drove every one out of the classroom: at the second lecture some one let loose a couple of pigeons, which were immediately shot at with peashooters. The professor said, "Gentlemen, if you do not wish to learn you are at liberty to leave," and the whole class walked out. In his first year at the school Grenfell seems to have been diligent enough, and his attendance reports are marked either "good" or "all," but his second-year report is less commendable. He attended only four lectures out of a possible sixty in medicine, and his other subjects are only a little less neglected.

His real interests were elsewhere, mainly on London's river and on the Rugby field. His interest in sport, first roused at Marlborough, had now become a passion, and he was making a name for himself in various athletics. He rowed for London University, acting as secretary of the Club and helping to shift the races from the river Lea to the Thames. He helped to start inter-hospital rowing championships, played Rugby for Richmond and the University, and, indeed, lived mostly for his sport. Being the passionate character he was, he had to take this more intensely than anyone else, testing his body to its utmost and toughening himself with exercises. Lacking other facilities, he gathered a group of athletic young students round him and practised weight-throwing on waste ground in the East End, and later, when living in Bayswater, he turned out at crack of dawn to swim in the Serpentine. Hard weather, ice on the pond, merely added zest to his swim. He had scant respect for Park regulations. When the gates were locked he climbed over the railings to reach the water.

If this preoccupation with sport did not further his medical studies, it did keep him away from the heavy drinking and riotous living of many of his fellow-students. In his ambition to excel as an athlete, to preserve and develop his young body, he realized that wild nights in the West End were no sort of training for pulling an oar, diving into a scrum, or lasting ten rounds in the boxing-ring. Fortunately, he had no taste for high and riotous life. Whether he drank at all during those years is not known. His family had no strong prejudices against alcohol, and while at Parkgate his father paid some fisherman half a barrel of beer for digging a trench in the sand, which the sea, he hoped, would deepen and widen, and so preserve a channel to the old jetty.

But what drinking Wilfred Grenfell did in his young manhood would be harmless, and he was soon to become the bitter enemy of drinking-shops and all alcoholic liquors. Drink in the eighties was the curse of England, and of London in particular. There were 14,000 drinking-shops in London alone, and it was reckoned that nineteen out of twenty crimes committed in Great Britain were caused by drink. Every year 20,000 people were arrested for drunkenness in the capital, and that was only a small proportion of those who drank to excess.

Living and working in the East End, Grenfell saw the effect of heavy drinking at its worst and most tragic. Assisting the doctors in the large, bare, stone-coloured Receiving Room of the London Hospital, he saw a procession of miserable creatures, their faces gouged and cut by broken bottles thrust at them in some drunken fight, women who had been ill-treated by drink-maddened husbands or lovers, inhuman creatures who had been women, until drink degraded them, moaning and sobbing, or cursing vilely while doctors tried to sew back the scalps that had been torn half away in a fight with rivals for some sailor's favours. Human wrecks, that had been strong-muscled dock-workers and seamen, writhing in the madness of delirium tremens. London Hospital was close against London's dockland and deep in the worst part of the capital. It was surrounded by foul slums, and the young student-doctors had to go there to attend sufferers who could not walk to the hospital. Grenfell had the tragedies of heavy drinking thrust in front of him.

He was often nauseated by what he saw, but not yet concerned with other people's weaknesses or sins. His main concern was himself, his successes as an athlete. Even his profession was less important than this. Because of his gift for learning quickly he was able to pass his preliminary and intermediate examinations as they came along, but it was not until his instruction included practical experience as assistant to the hospital doctors that he awoke to the drama and challenge of his chosen profession. His awakening came, as was to happen so often in his life, through admiration for some one.

His hero now was Dr Frederick Treves, Surgeon at London Hospital and one of the most brilliant and progressive men in his profession. Only thirty years of age when Grenfell met him, Treves was already well known as a surgeon. He had come into surgery at a time when its methods had remained largely unchanged for a hundred years. Bleeding was still practised, surgeons operated in filthy, blood-caked frockcoats that were the envy of the younger aspiring students and were worn as a robe of distinction, antiseptics were unknown, or unused until Lister gained followers. Patients were held down by husky students while the surgeon hacked and cut with dirty instruments and hardly less dirty hands. Sepsis was the prevailing condition in hospital wards, and practically all major wounds suppurated. In one of his books Treves described how pus was a main topic of conversation among those engaged in surgery, classified according to degrees of vileness. "Laudable" pus was considered rather a fine thing, something to be proud of; "sanious" pus was nasty in appearance and regrettable, and "ichorous" pus the most malignant depths to which matter could descend, its appearance a rather unfair trick to play on a surgeon. Wounds were dressed with a species of cotton waste soaked in oil and named "charpie," a dressing that would "now be discarded by a motor mechanic as too dirty for a machine." The stench in hospital wards was sickening, and in one hospital a whole ward was decimated by infection from the hands of doctors and nurses. Only very few "amputations" lived to leave a hospital, and Treves tells of one woman who, when asked to give permission for an operation to be carried out on her husband, exclaimed, "Oh, it's all very well to talk about consenting, but who is to pay for the funeral?"

Treves fought this filth and brutality, both in the ward and through his clear, incisive writings on surgery. He followed Pasteur's and Lister's teachings, and the young Grenfell was to see him throw a bottle of carbolic out of a hospital window. Himself a scrupulously clean person and something of a dandy in his dress, Treves insisted on absolute cleanliness in his operations, and would tolerate no nurse or student who appeared unwashed or in slovenly dress. His lectures were always well attended, for he had a gift for description, and his language was vivid and racy. He stood no nonsense from the students, or anyone else; and later, when he was Lord Rector of Aberdeen University, he issued a warning through the local Press that if there were the slightest noise while he was delivering his Address he would immediately leave the room.

This was the man Grenfell was now to admire and seek to be like, and who, with another outstanding teacher and practitioner, the physician Sir Andrew Clark, was to instil into the young man a pride in his profession and a progressive attitude to new ways. From Treves he learned surgery, from Clark the art of the physician at its highest, and from both the greater lesson that in choosing this profession he was dedicating himself to the service of humanity. When Grenfell discovered that Treves was also an athlete, an outstanding swimmer and water-polo player, a long-distance cyclist, and a keen yachtsman, his admiration was complete. The older man's influence over Grenfell was to be an important factor in his development and his life.

But it was not Treves who was to awaken Grenfell to a realization that his life was a vain thing while he was concerned only with his own aspirations as sportsman and his progress as a doctor. It was not even the tragedies he saw as he moved through the East End streets and visited patients in their foul and verminous homes. London slums in the eighties were horrifying places. General William Booth, in his book *In Darkest England*, published in 1890, gives some figures. In London alone there were 387,000 very poor people, 222,000 living next door to starvation, 300,000 actually at starvation-level, 33,000 homeless, and 51,000 in workhouses. The majority of these lived in the East End, and it was among them that Grenfell worked; their miserable homes he visited, and their ill-fated children he delivered. He did not feel a call to save them from their fate, or fight the evils that brought them to their degraded state, other than to serve them as a healer and to try to instruct them in cleanliness and hygiene. Grenfell needed something more colourful, with more drama in it, than the whining of a sick woman or the foulness of a drunkard's home.

His awakening came in 1885, though he had been stirred in his conscience two years before then. Grenfell has described what happened.

He was returning one evening from a maternity case, and while passing through the ill-lit and sullen streets of Shadwell he came upon a large tent where a meeting was in progress. The speaker was the evangelist D. L. Moody, and the young man was curious to hear this American whose controversial methods of teaching Christianity had stirred all Britain. In the past ten years, since 1873, Moody and his brother-evangelist, Sankey, had visited Great Britain several times, and with each visit their audiences, drawn from all classes, had increased enormously. The impact on the smug Victorian Church of Moody's rough and outspoken speech and Sankey's robust hymns had roused both criticism and admiration, and their campaigns were argued over in the Press as well as among clergymen and laymen. By the time Grenfell came across the evangelist, Moody had learned to work with the Churches; but he was still a powerful and disturbing attraction. Not to have attended one of his meetings was to lack a social experience and to have missed a contemporary entertainment. The curiosity that sent the young Grenfell into the tent that evening was typical of the times.

Grenfell entered the tent and sat down, only to find himself listening to a long and tedious prayer by one of the speakers. The young man was bored, and was about to rise and leave when another man rose, a large, stout man with a thick black beard, D. L. Moody. Moody called to the audience, "Let us sing a hymn while our brother finishes his prayer"; and Grenfell was so impressed by this practical method of removing a bore that he came away from the meeting deciding to "make religion a real effort as I thought Christ would do in my place as a doctor, or frankly abandon it."

This is typically a Grenfell narration. He sees a dexterous man handling a situation skilfully, and immediately decides he must practise his Christianity in earnest. The story is likely because Grenfell was always impulsive and always a hero-worshipper. His favourite reading as a young man was the lives of great men, and this theme of hero-worship goes through his whole life. He would admire a strong, dominating personality like Moody. However, he did little to carry out his resolution in the next two years and until he was stirred again by an admired personality and another incident with that touch of the dramatic that appealed to him.

Moody's success as an evangelist had been particularly effective among young men in the universities. The cause of this may have been that Britain in those days was sitting back on her laurels, on the performance and profits of having accomplished the Industrial Revolution and built an empire. There were now few new worlds for young and vigorous men to conquer. There had been no wars to fight since the Crimea in the fifties, industry had taken its shape, and the colonies had been pioneered. Young men of the upper class could go and shoot lions in Africa, or they could expend themselves in the West End, where plush and gilt coloured a world of sensual excitement for those who would accept such a substitute for adventure. Young Britain, particularly those sons of the rich who need not strive as their fathers had, needed an outlet, a mission to inspire them.

Moody's thunderous Christianity became this cause, and his success at the universities was tremendous. At Edinburgh he had both professors and undergraduates weeping and coming from their seats to give themselves to Christ. Young men banded themselves into groups and travelled the country as evangelists. Revivals flared up throughout Britain. Brilliant young men abandoned careers and comfort to become missionaries in China and Africa, or went into the East End of London to work in settlements like Oxford House at Bethnal Green, Cambridge House at Camberwell, and the lately started Toynbee Hall.

Inevitably the young Grenfell would be touched by this crusade of his class and age. He had gone through a phase of religious doubt, and even considered abandoning his Christian beliefs. His love and admiration for his mother would save him from this, and, though he mentions this nowhere in his writings, his father's example must have had an influence. The Reverend Algernon had, indeed, made the supreme sacrifice as a Christian minister. The work at London Hospital had proved too much for a far from robust constitution, and he had a recurrence of a mental illness that had shortened his time at

Oxford as a young man. He was placed in a nursing home in North Wales, and died there in 1885. His father's death must have helped Wilfred to realize that life was more than acquiring sporting trophies, that Christianity was a living force and not the mere attending at church services. It was something to do as well as to believe in. Other influences were piling up inside the young man: his work as a doctor among so much human imperfection offending his athlete's ideal of perfection, a growing need for continuity in the pattern of humanity. He could not convince himself that death was complete dissolution. "For my part," he was to write twenty-five years later, "I am very much in love with life, and I enjoy it so much, I want all I can get out of it, I want more of it after the incident called death. . . . Death, corruption, a lifeless world, like the moon, have no attractions for me." He could not accept an end when in himself he felt the splendour of being. He was to find this continuity in Christianity.

Grenfell believed that his discovery of the true Christianity came suddenly. His greatest friend of those days, the late Sir Henry Richards, believed that what happened came from an accumulated growth, a dissatisfaction with the limitations of a life without faith or convictions. It needed, however, a spark to set flaring what was smouldering, and because Grenfell was a hero-worshipper he had to wait until he found some one he could admire who would point the way. He had found no one in the organized Church, and he reacted away from anything where he had to sit and be preached at. "I knew that the right way to use muscles was to use them," he wrote later, "and I argued that a similar treatment was what faith needed." Grenfell was not 'converted' to Christianity, for, except during the brief period of doubt he confesses to, he accepted the Christian faith. It was the living of this faith that he discovered, and because in his strong masculinity he suspected clergymen of being out of touch with the realities and many of them not men whom a muscular young athlete could admire he, often not altogether fairly, scorned parsons.

Moody had seemed a leader such as Grenfell could admire, but he found some one even more ideally suited to his needs and temperament when he attended another of Moody's meetings in 1885. He discovered on the platform a group of young men he knew and admired tremendously, the famous "Cambridge Seven." These seven young men were all either well-known athletes or Army officers, and two of them, the Studd brothers, played cricket for their university and for England. "That was a credential to me," Grenfell was to write, "that it was worth stopping to listen to what was going to be said." And while he listened another of the little dramatic moments that Grenfell loved occurred. One of the speakers asked that those who professed Christ should stand up. Grenfell did not, until he saw a boy in naval uniform rising from among a group of companions, boys from a training-ship. Grenfell was young enough to know how brave an action this was, for the boy would be teased by his companions later. Grenfell stood up to support this young hero.

Grenfell left this meeting, "feeling that I had crossed the Rubicon, and must do something to prove it." The spark that had to come had struck and fired what was awaiting its touch. For Wilfred Grenfell it was a conflagration of every doubt, an illumination of purpose.

3

The Course set: The New Life

GRENFELL did not join Moody's young men. He went, as usual, to his mother for advice on how he should carry out his resolution to live his Christianity, and, orthodox churchgoer that she was, she advised him to see the vicar of the Episcopalian church she had attended while living in the East End. The clergyman offered the young man a small class in his Sunday school, and for a time Grenfell confined his religious work to teaching Gospel texts to a number of boys from the more respectable working-class families of the district.

Sunday-school teaching did not long satisfy the newly awakened young man. He had to have greater scope for his energies than this. As his interest in religion developed he discovered others among his fellow-students who were carrying out missionary work in the East End, and one of these, an Australian named Bobardt, introduced Grenfell to the work going on among the destitute in common lodging-houses and on the streets. With Bobardt, and helping to carry a small harmonium the Australian played, Grenfell went out night after night to preach the Gospel and to find penitents from among the defeated men and women who occupied the foul underground lodging-houses. He stood on the pavements, part of what was one of many groups of evangelists working in the East End every night, urging the human derelicts to come to Christ, gathering an audience of drunken men and women whom gin and beer had made moistly sentimental, sailors who had spent their wages earned over long months of hard toil in sailing-vessels and were now feeling sorry for themselves, and the 'saved' who carried themselves with a proprietary air as they bawled out the Sankey hymns the young man started more energetically than musically. And he entered public-houses to hand out tracts showing the evils of drink, using his boxer's skill and muscles to discourage men who thought that pouring a pint of beer down a teetotaller's throat would be a good joke.

Grenfell enjoyed all this. There was more satisfaction in seeking out converts than in instructing well-behaved boys. He could tell people about his Christianity in his own way and not according to the restraints of a Church. He could sing the sort of hymns he liked, and his voice was better suited to a street than a church hall. He liked going among people, and not having to wait for them to come to him. This was how Christ Himself had carried His message, and he was resolved to live as Christ had lived.

His efforts were purely evangelistic, the carrying of the Gospel to those who needed its comfort and inspiration. He attempted no other 'good works,' though he and Bobardt did dig into their pockets to pay for beds for some of the miserable people who came pleading for help. But this charity had to cease when the young men found that chits they had been giving and which the lodging-house keepers accepted were being forged and that they had to pay out more than they had bargained to give. The young men restricted their work to preaching and tracts.

Grenfell discovered that he could do still more when he got to know the boys of his Sunday-school class better. He learned that these boys were not always the meek and well-scoured models of good behaviour they appeared to be on Sundays, but were a crowd of quick-witted and energetic young East Enders.

They had their heroes, as he had, footballers and boxers mostly, whose careers they followed and over whose skill they argued hotly. They fought, wrestled, and kicked home-made balls round the streets, exhausting their energy as best they could and often getting into trouble because of it. Grenfell decided to direct this energy.

He was then living near the church in Palestine Road, Bethnal Green, where he conducted his Sunday-school class, sharing a house with a number of other athletic students, and he invited the boys there. His sitting-room was turned into a gymnasium, and every Saturday evening the boys were taught boxing and physical exercises. Grenfell believed that to teach the boys to keep their bodies healthy, to accept defeat or victory in the right spirit, was to arouse their self-respect and build them nearer to Christ's image. He had himself been inspired to the Christian way of life by a famous athlete, and he had modelled himself on that example. The boys would find Christ as he had.

The vicar of his church did not agree. He learned of these Saturday-night activities and censured the young man for teaching the boys brutal sports. Grenfell invited the clergyman to see the boys in action, but the minister would not even look at such brutality, and issued an ultimatum: Grenfell must either stop the weekly activities or resign from the Sunday school. Grenfell resigned. He would be denying what was now part of his Christian way of life if he reduced his Christianity to mere preaching, and he was a Grenfell, one of a race who, once decided, yielded to none.

But he had discovered something new and satisfying, an expanding of his Christian life, and he found other boys whom he could teach without interference. Bobardt was helping to run a club on Ratcliff Highway where the boys were neither well scoured nor well behaved, but came in from the streets mainly to break up the furniture and steal what they could find. Grenfell had to teach some of the toughest that Christians were not always meek. He tossed the worst into the street and gained the admiration of the others. He enjoyed himself immensely.

He appears not to have stayed long with this club, and to have returned to the boys of the Sunday school and the weekly instruction at Palestine Road. The records are a little confusing for this period of Grenfell's life, and his own writings do not make them any clearer. In 1887 he is conducting a "Boys' Brigade" attached to St Jude's Episcopalian Church, Bethnal Green, the church whose vicar, the Rev. J. B. Barraclough, disapproved of his methods. The minister is now the Rev. W. H. Davies, and he appears to have been more in sympathy with Grenfell's methods. Grenfell roped in his senior at the hospital, Dr Frederick Treves, as president of his new club, named himself as vice-president, and found a young friend, Mr Henry Richards, to act as secretary. An ex-soldier came in to teach the boys drill, and, although there is no record of Grenfell's ever being an officer of that great movement started in 1882 by Sir William Smith, the boys wore the pill-box hats and belts of the Boys' Brigade and were drilled with old Snider rifles.

This phase in Grenfell's life is important. He was carrying his Christianity beyond the mere preaching of the Gospel, and opening his life to those he instructed. Soon he was removing more barriers which had divided his life into the compartments of his private affairs and his religious practice; he brought these East End boys in to share his dearest pleasures, the sea and the countryside.

He had never lost his love for boats and the sea, and he and his brother Algernon owned a converted fishing-craft, which they sailed in the Irish Sea every summer. When Grenfell returned from his sailing holiday in 1886 he described his adventures to the boys of his club, and their envy and longing was in their eyes. He responded at once, telling the boys to save their pennies and he would take them camping next year. He acted on impulse, but it was the impulse that was to widen his life and shape it permanently.

Eighteen eighty-seven was an important and busy year for Grenfell. It was in that year that he achieved one of his ambitions. He attended for one term at Queen's College, Oxford, and came away with a Blue for Rugby. During his term at Oxford he made something of a figure among the undergraduates as the man who ran a boys' club in the East End and who was going to start a camping holiday for working-class lads, the first such venture ever made, and the forerunner of a great movement. The first camp was held at Llanlliana Bay, in North Wales, that same summer, and at the end of the year

Grenfell took his final examinations and passed these successfully. In February 1888 he was entered as a Member of the Royal College of Surgeons and a Licentiate of the Royal College of Physicians. His record as a student and assistant to Treves and other seniors had not been impressive. His attendance at lectures remained lamentable, and, though he is marked "Good" by a Mr Couper in 1887, Treves, later that year, describes him as "Very Poor," and in another report "Indifferent." However, his gift for acquiring knowledge served him, and he was now Wilfred Grenfell, M.D. He was appointed a house-surgeon under Treves at the London Hospital late in 1888.

Despite Treves's assessment of Grenfell as a surgeon, the two men were now close friends. Outside their profession they had a common interest in the sea and boats, and cruised together in a small yawl, the *Vagabond*, that appears to have been owned jointly. Although Treves does not seem to have been fired by Grenfell's evangelistic fervour, he helped with the boys' club, and invited Grenfell to hold his camp at Lulworth Cove, in Dorset, where Treves had a house. Dorset was nearer than North Wales, and there the boys learned to swim and play water polo under the instruction of the famous surgeon. The camps were an innovation that attracted considerable attention. A long article describing the camps appeared in the *Illustrated London News*, and accompanying sketches showed Treves in the water with the boys. Grenfell and Henry Richards ran the camps strictly enough but with originality. The boys had to take a dip in the sea before being allowed to have breakfast, and, despite Grenfell's claim in his later writings that he did not allow the boys into a boat until they could swim, they were taught to swim by the simple method of being taken some distance offshore in an old lifeboat Grenfell hired from the Royal National Lifeboat Institution and there pushed overboard. Grenfell's methods were often more daring than calculable.

These were happy days for Grenfell; but there was still something irresponsible about the young man. His life still lacked direction. Going into the streets with Bobardt to 'save' the destitute was more of an adventure than a mission, and he was more interested in scoring a try than in doctoring.

He had yet to find something big enough to require all his faculties and all his fine physical qualities.

Treves found such a place and mission for him. The surgeon was Chairman of the Medical Section of the National Mission to Deep Sea Fishermen. This Mission had been established in 1882, mainly through the efforts of a Mr Ebenezer Mather. Mather had been Secretary to the Thames Church Mission, an organization that did evangelistic work among the sailors visiting London's river. He had been approached by the owner of a large fishing fleet, Mr Samuel Hewett, and asked to extend the missionary work to North Sea fishermen. Mather and a clergyman made a voyage on board one of the ships sent to the North Sea to collect fish from the trawlers, and what he saw on the voyage roused Mather so much that he returned and asked his Mission to send missionaries among the fishermen. His Committee did not feel that they could extend their efforts outside the Thames; but when Hewett offered to supply a vessel and equip her for missionary work the Committee agreed to sponsor the venture. Mather assumed responsibility for the vessel, a fifty-ton smack, the *Ensign*, and she sailed from Gorleston, on the East Coast, in July 1882, to the jeers as well as the cheers of fishermen watching from the quays and piers, and with many coarse jests about Holy Joes and their reception by the fishermen at sea.

By then, in 1882, commercial fishing had changed entirely, in character and methods, from what it had been fifty years previously. Single boats owned by those who sailed them still went out for a day or two, fishing with hook and line, or with drift-nets for surface fish like herring; but now these age-old methods brought home only a small share of the fish that were landed. The invention of the beam-trawl early in the nineteenth century had revolutionized fish-catching, and the discovery of the famous Dogger Bank and other places in the North Sea with seemingly inexhaustible supplies of fish, and the use of ice for preserving the fish, had called for an entirely new organization of the industry. Those shrewd enough, and with sufficient capital, built up huge fleets of trawlers, as many as two hundred under the one owner, and these went out as fleets of a hundred or so vessels, working together under the direction of a skilled skipper, who was termed 'Admiral.' There were some half-dozen large companies of trawler-owners whose craft worked in the North Sea, each ship carrying a crew of four, one at least of these being a young lad.

Fishing became an important industry. In 1881 the catch from North Sea trawlers alone was sold at Billingsgate, London's great fish market, for £2,581,000, a figure that does not include fish landed and sold elsewhere round the coast. At all times in any part of the year some twelve to fifteen thousand men were working the smacks in the North Sea, dragging their trawls anywhere between the islands of Texel and Heligoland. The craft remained at sea for from eight to twelve weeks, being relieved by others coming out after a refit or a few days' rest. Except for Sundays, or when the weather stopped it, fishing was continuous, a vast, ever-moving pattern of small sailing-vessels rising and falling to the waves and dragging the heavy trawls over the sea bottom, lifting them every few hours and letting the gleaming fish pour from the cod-end on to the deck, where they were cleaned and packed in boxes. Carriers, fast sailing-, and then steam-vessels, came from London to collect each fleet's catch and hurry it back to market.

To man this armada of small craft labour had been attracted from anywhere it could be found. Boys of twelve years of age were apprenticed from orphanages and reform schools, and crews were made up of men who knew little of fishing or the sea. Army and Navy deserters, ex-convicts, and aimless men from the cities brought to what had been peaceful and God-fearing villages the habits and manners of the towns. The villages grew into large seaports as shoddy houses were raised in long, monotonous rows and public-houses swelled their plate glass at each street-corner. The trawler-owners, shipbuilders, and others who profited most from the industry built themselves large villas on the outskirts of the new towns, shopping centres and offices replaced old thatched cottages, and what had been picturesque little sea-coast villages took on the pattern of any industrial city.

As the new fishing industry grew, shrewd and unscrupulous people discovered the fishermen as a source of profit at sea as well as on shore. Vessels, mostly from Holland and Belgium, came to the fleets working in the North Sea, to offer the men tobacco, alcohol, and sometimes women. There were rich pickings to be had from a fleet of trawlers carrying some five to six hundred men, many of them sick of seeing their own shipmates day after day for months, and eager for any escape from their cramped, ill-kept, and comfortless quarters. They associated drink with enjoyment when on shore, and now it was brought to them at sea. The smacks could not always fish. It needed a good fresh breeze to drive them ahead fast enough to haul the heavy, 30-foot-long wooden beam that held open the mouth of their net and the poke-shaped net itself over the sea bottom, and in light winds fishing stopped. The boats lay swaying to what swell there might be, and the men were idle and bored. Few of them read, and if they did there was nothing to read except a few old newspapers; and, unlike the merchant seamen of those days, fishermen seldom went in for such hobbies as model-building and mat-making.

The 'copers,' as the floating grog-shops were named, were an escape, and provided the companionship of new faces. Boat-loads of men rowed to them, to be greeted with beaming, calculated smiles, handed glasses of throat-burning rum or schnapps that had been doped to stimulate a thirst, and made to feel important. Even those men who had no desire for drink, but wanted to buy tobacco, succumbed to the lure, and after the first free drink stayed on. They sat round the coper's deck, drinking, talking, and singing, the coper always ready with the jar of cheap and dangerous spirits. Men drank themselves to a stupor, or to fighting madness. They argued and fought with their best friends, until they were dropped into their boats and made their way as best they could back to their smacks—smacks often left unattended except for the scared boys, apprehensive of what their shipmates' return would bring, a hearty slap on the back or a beating.

It was to fight the coper that Hewett had asked Mather to send missionaries among the fishermen. The trawler-owner was less concerned with his men's souls than he was with his own property, for when men were hungry for drink they were quite prepared to pay for it with fish and ship's gear. The gear could always be reported lost during bad weather. Smacks were damaged and even lost through the recklessness of drunken skippers, vessels left with only a boy or one man on board were blown far from the fleet when the wind freshened and the crew were enjoying themselves on the coper. Men brought jars of the cheap rum and gin back to their vessels, and fishing stopped until the stuff was consumed and the men recovered from its effects. The coper was to ruin many men and cause much damage to trawler-owners' property.

Mather had seen all this when he made the voyage on a fish-carrier. He had seen the great need for evangelistic work among these hard-living men on the smacks, and he believed, as did many others, that Christian instruction would raise the fishermen above the weaknesses that sent them to the grog-ships. He soon discovered that he had to fight the evil less idealistically, and must compete with the coper's attractions. He asked permission to buy tobacco from bond and sell it at less than the copers charged, but H.M.Customs would not grant the privileges of duty-free stores. The Mission had to purchase tobacco for delivery abroad, and the ships had to sail first to Ostend to take this tobacco on board before calling on the trawlers.

By the time the young Wilfred Grenfell became interested in this work for fishermen the Mission had expanded greatly. Mather had formed it as a separate organization in 1885, with himself as Manager and Secretary, and with a Committee of prominent people. An office was opened in London, and by 1887 seven Mission vessels were at work in the North Sea, all of them secured by a mortgage held by trawler-owners. The work had attracted a great deal of attention, for the scandal of the fishing fleets had been well publicized, commented on by even the Prince of Wales when he read a paper prepared by his brother the Duke of Edinburgh at the opening of the International Fisheries Exhibition in London in 1883. Sea happenings were fully reported in the newspapers of those days, and a trip into the North Sea on board the fish-carriers was a favourite journalistic mission and an attraction for the adventurous and curious. From the publicity and from meetings held throughout the country and addressed by fishermen-converts funds were raised, and little by little the Mission extended its work. To its evangelistic efforts and the sale of tobacco it added a Medical Department; and in 1886 Dr Treves was elected a member of the Mission Committee and became Chairman of the Medical Department.

He knew just how much such a service was needed. The

London Hospital served dockland, and it was to the hospital that the sick and hurt seafarers came. Fishermen were brought in with crushed and broken limbs, suffering from the diseases their work encouraged, and the hospital doctors realized only too well that many lives would have been saved, many broken bodies mended and diseases arrested, had there been medical service on the spot, and the men not had to endure the long voyage in the carriers. From the moment he associated himself with the work Treves decided that its medical service must be improved from the simple first-aid given by the Mission-ship skippers with which it had started. He evolved a scheme for a real medical service, ships equipped as floating hospitals and carrying qualified doctors, and soon after he was appointed to the Committee he outlined his scheme.

The Mission Council approved the suggestion; but there were difficulties. The Mission boats helped to support themselves by fishing when they were not engaged in Mission work, and Treves's suggestion would mean that the boats could no longer be equipped for fishing. The Mission was at this time in financial difficulties, and the expense incurred by the new department would be heavy—though one member of the Council pointed out that the new service would bring in more support and funds. Mather was again making efforts to get duty-free tobacco in England, and if he succeeded one vessel at present fully engaged in carrying tobacco from Ostend to the Mission ships at sea would be released and free for the new service. A resolution was proposed and passed, approving the use of the Mission ship *Clulow* as a hospital ship for a trial period of two months, and adopting the whole scheme, "provided it can be done without incurring any further liabilities, or without interfering in any way with the present evangelistic work of the Mission."

In his speech proposing the hospital ships Treves had said that he would undertake to find doctors for the new service. He mentioned that one gentleman had already volunteered. This was Wilfred Grenfell. The young man had a special place in his heart and thoughts for fishermen, and his boyhood friends had been fishermen's sons. He knew enough about trawling to talk intelligently on the subject, and he aspired to be a seaman himself. Treves realized that, even while he marked Grenfell

"Indifferent" as a doctor, this young man was exactly the sort of person to sail with a hospital ship. But he advised Grenfell to make a trial voyage on board one of the Mission boats, and recommended that this voyage be made during the winter months, when Grenfell would find the North Sea at its least kindly.

4

The Fishermen's Doctor: North Sea

GRENFELL made his first voyage on board a Mission ship in January 1888. He joined the *Thomas Grey* at Gorleston, on the East Coast of England, arriving at the dock where the small sailing-vessel lay on a cold and windy night. The tide was out, and the vessel's deck was far below where the young man stood on the edge of the wharf. "She seemed very small," he wrote later, "only a little larger than our *Roysterer*," the converted fishing-boat he and his brother had owned. He thought of returning to Yarmouth and spending the night in comfort; but when he was hailed from the deck he lowered his bags to the *Thomas Grey*, before leaning out, grasping a stay, and sliding down. The stay had been greased and tarred that day, and Grenfell's clothes suffered. He was greeted by the skipper and taken below, finding the saloon beautifully clean and cosy. He was allotted a small cabin and told that the vessel would be sailing next morning.

The first part of the voyage was to Ostend. By this time, in 1888, the Mission was winning its fight against the copers, and fishermen were preferring the true friendliness of the Mission crews. Only the most hardened drinkers patronized the copers now. They still hung near the fishing fleets, but there were fewer of them. England, France, Holland, Belgium, and other European countries had discussed a pact to drive the now notorious evil from the North Sea; but France refused to ratify the pact when it was presented. France and Russia were England's military and naval rivals in those days, and France, still irritated by the loss of Egypt, considered the pact another British trick to control the near waters. The National Mission to Deep Sea Fishermen had to continue its efforts to clear the copers off the water by augmenting Christian instruction with the more material attractions of comforts in woollen helmets and mittens, carrying libraries, and selling tobacco at half the price it was sold by the copers. H.M.Customs had not yet agreed to the Mission ships carrying duty-free tobacco from England, and the *Thomas Grey* had to go to Ostend to take her supply on board.

The weather was bad all the way. This was to be one of the worst winters in the North Sea for many years, with storms following close on one another and temperatures far below freezing. Grenfell had rather prided himself on being a hard sailing man, but he discovered now that winter sailing in the North Sea was an experience quite different from summer yachting. The little *Thomas Grey* was tossed and swept by heavy seas, the water coming on board freezing on deck and rigging. Grenfell was seasick most of the passage, and wrote to his mother from Ostend: "I wish I were a better sailor, and hope this trip will make me one, as it will be impossible to doctor others if I am ill myself."

Characteristically he fought the weakness by going into the open and running backward and forward as best he could on the tilting and lifting deck. To add to his trials, he could not even keep warm. His tiny cabin was heated by an oil-stove that gave out noisome fumes, to upset his stomach further, and if he put the stove out he awoke in the morning to find icicles hanging from the deck-head. He had all the testing he wanted, or that Treves thought he should have.

The *Thomas Grey* reached Ostend, and was held there for

some time by ice blocking the harbour. Grenfell went sight-seeing, and made friends among the Belgians. They invited him to their homes, and he could be a boisterous guest at times. In one of the many letters he wrote to his mother he describes how he danced a schottische at the home of one of his Flemish friends, using a chair as a partner and bringing down a chandelier. He skated on the frozen harbour, and startled his shipmates by taking a bath on the snow-covered deck every morning and exercising himself over the masthead.

These frolics were probably one reason why it took time for the crew to accept him. In another letter to his mother he said he "was trying to get to know the fishermen," but was finding this "not so easy." This is entirely understandable. Seamen on board their ships have a code of behaviour, and expending energy in unnecessary gymnastics is not part of this. They like to settle into a ship and form a patterned life, and anyone who disturbs or upsets their routine is frowned on. This young man with the inexhaustible energy who must always be up to something, and who talked so much, would be an irritation now and then. And he must have seemed a queer sort of missionary to these fishermen. The missionaries they had met until then had been quite unlike this boisterous, mischievously humorous young man. Even his Christianity seemed more a joyous game than the sober business others made it. Missionaries do not usually challenge sailors to races over the masthead, or douse themselves with salt water while standing naked on a ship's deck. The fishermen would be watchful of this bright young fellow.

With a steamer to break the ice for her, the *Thomas Grey* sailed out of Ostend and headed into the North Sea in search of the fishing fleet she would work with. The weather remained stormy and cold, but Grenfell was beginning to enjoy it all. He was getting over his seasickness, and was soon to write to his mother and tell her proudly: "I am getting my sea legs and able to take my share of salt beef and duff." Clad satisfyingly like his shipmates in fearnought trousers, a thick guernsey, and leather sea-boots, he was beginning to feel himself a real sailor-man. Always active, he helped with the work on deck, and set himself to show these somewhat sceptical fishermen that he was not altogether a landlubber.

In due course the skipper of the Mission ship found the fleet of trawlers, and this was an exciting moment for the young doctor. He was familiar enough with fishing-boats, had sailed in them often, but these were the score or so boats working out of Parkgate or the widely scattered line-fishing craft in the Irish Sea. Now, out of the haze of a North Sea winter day, sail after sail shaped, and the smacks appeared, lifting and falling to the sea, until the sea seemed to be covered with them, each with its trawl-warp slanting from the stern. As the Mission ship moved ahead and came among the smacks loud "Cheer-oh's" hailed her across the water in hearty welcome. The Mission ships were appreciated now, and few mocked the Holy Joes.

No visits were made while the fleet were fishing. A missionary might row across to a smack, but even the most Christian-minded skipper wanted no visitors when trawls were being worked. The *Thomas Grey* streamed her beam and net and became part of the loose formation of the fleet. Grenfell's muscles were welcomed, and he worked with a will. When the 'Admiral' hoisted a flag to tell his craft to haul in, Grenfell manned the capstan bars with his shipmates and walked the warp inboard. With the great beam on the surface, the men lined the low bulwarks and leaned over to grasp the net mesh and overhaul the slack, using the roll of the vessel and a perfected balance to lighten the task. Clad in a long oiled frock, Grenfell hauled with the rest of the crew, delighting in the skill and rhythm of this task. That it could be dangerous added to the thrill, for if a man slipped while leaning over he could easily go overboard, and in hampering frock and heavy leather sea-boots getting aboard again was not easy. In bad weather, with an over-ambitious skipper who would fish to the last possible moment, the dipping rail scooped up seas, and men had to hold on and save the net they had gathered with water swirling to their waists.

Their reward was in the size of the cod-end as it came to the surface, a ball of net-held, gleaming, white-bellied fish. A good haul brought shouts of pleasure, a poor one groans of disappointment, for the men were paid mainly with a share of the value of their vessel's catch. As the bulging cod-end was dragged alongside a man leaned over and passed a rope strop round the net and hooked on a tackle from the masthead. All

D

hands manned the capstan to lift the cod-end upward. It rose, pouring water, dropping a fish from its mesh, to swing inboard. A man ducked under it, tugged at the securing knot, and then leapt backward as fish poured down into the box-shaped fish-pounds. At once the net was examined for damage, and if any tears were found string-loaded netting-needles moved deftly and speedily to repair them. When the 'Admiral' signalled, the net was pushed outboard and the warp paid out. The beam and its net sank under the surface, sail was raised, and the smack moved ahead again, with the men already stooped over the squirming mass of fish, gutting them deftly for stowing.

To Grenfell it was an exciting game. The hunter in him, the challenge he loved, was stirred by this searching of the sea-bottom for its wealth and the skill and effort needed to work ship and trawl. That it could be dangerous, and hard toil, did not yet concern him. He was a young man being tested physically, and neither cold, wet, nor weariness bothered him. This was man's work, and he loved it, and his admiration for the fishermen increased daily. He was to find much that was tragic behind all this that was picturesque and stirring, but he never really disapproved of the danger in the work. He was still daring to an extreme—not so much fearless as seemingly blind to danger. Friends who had sailed with him on board his small yacht were often alarmed by his ship-handling and navigation, for he would seem to forget he was holding a tiller, or that he was heading his craft towards a shoal or reef. When nervous shipmates expostulated he would laugh at their fears, telling them cheerfully that God would look after them. His faith was now absolute and left no doubts in him, and he was more and more accepting as an irrefutable fact that he had much work to do for Christ, and that Christ would see that he survived long enough to achieve this. So he ignored danger and went gladly towards every challenge the sea offered.

When he reached the shore after his first voyage Grenfell wrote to his mother, telling of his adventures. He had been well tested. Storms and cold persisted all the voyage. The little Mission ship had lost and refound the fishing fleets half a dozen times, in gales and fog. Her rigging and masts had been thickened and stiffened with ice that had to be cleared away to keep the blocks and gear working and the vessel from becoming top-heavy. She had lain hove to while gales battered at her, and when it was dangerous to be on deck, those on board wearied by her incessant and violent movements.

Grenfell had loved every minute of his new experience. He had worked with the crew on every task, eager to test himself in this hazardous world and meeting every challenge to his manliness joyously. He had helped to haul in the net with the temperature below freezing and his hands so numb that he hardly felt the cord cutting into his flesh. He had gutted and stowed fish with heavy spray falling on his back and shoulders and water swirling round his legs and trying to take back the fish; he had wedged himself into his bunk, wet and weary, to snatch an hour's sleep before the next call. His hardened shipmates could only admire this young man who wanted to share their toil and who asked for no privileges.

He knew from the beginning that he had found the work he wanted to do and the men he wanted to serve. "They are splendid," he wrote to his mother, "free and frank. I shall love them too well to be anxious to leave them." There was so much for him to do. When the weather permitted, boats carried injured and sick men to the Mission ship. The storm-tossed ships flung men across a deck, a boom swung, and men's bones were crushed or broken. The chafe of an oilskin on neck or wrist rubbed the skin, causing salt-water sores that festered quickly on men who believed it would bring bad luck if they washed while at sea—even if the fresh-water supply ran to this luxury. Gutting fish on a slippery, jerking deck brought them to be treated for knife-cuts and hands poisoned by fish-bones. Grenfell cleaned and dressed the wounds while the Mission ship tossed and rolled, and he had to be held up while he worked.

Five men were drowned from the fishing fleets during that first voyage Grenfell made. The cost of fish in men's lives was high, and some two hundred were killed or drowned every year in the North Sea. After every gale there was news of men washed from their vessel's deck by the sea, killed by falling spars. Ferrying the boxed fish to the carriers that came to collect the catch took heavy toll, for the fishermen made what was often a hazardous task more dangerous by competing with one another to reach the carrier. Skippers trying to make a name for themselves, young men showing off their skill and strength, launched boats in bad weather, loaded them high with boxes of fish, and raced other boats to the carrier's sides. They got there, crashing alongside and shouting for some one to take their painter, forcing their boat among others already alongside in a reckless attempt to get their fish away. Men scrambled to the ship's deck, or leapt for her rail as the sea lifted their boat high, then hauled up their boxes, sliding them to the hatches without thought of anyone in the way. Their cargo discharged, they tossed empty boxes to their mates in the boats, laughing when some one got in the way and was knocked over. Then they pulled back to their smack, or to the lurking coper. People made trips in the carriers to see this exciting part of a fisherman's life; journalists wrote it up in sensational terms to thrill the landsman. But every year hundreds of men were injured, and many were drowned in the mad scramble.

Grenfell was not the man to criticize daring or to object to bold men taking risks. But he was saddened by the number of men who came on board to complain of "sore stomachs," pains in their chests, and limbs twisted with rheumatism. The hazards of this trade were not only in the injuries the fishermen suffered. Tuberculosis, rheumatic fevers, stomach troubles, killed men just as surely, if less quickly, as falling spars and upset boats. The dark, airless, and damp forecastles where the men slept, often without bunks, were germ-traps. They were seldom cleaned out, and stank of unwashed bodies and wet clothing. Men rarely undressed, but lay where they could and as they came from the deck. Rheumatism ate into their bones, they spat wherever they were and breathed in one another's diseases. Their food was mostly salt beef that stank as it was fished out of the brine-tubs, hard ship's biscuits, heavy, sickly-looking duff, and fish. It was cooked by grimy-handed, sniffling boys and eaten from dishes that were never washed, but wiped with a dirty rag after each meal. Most of the fishermen suffered from stomach ailments; sores and boils were common.

The young doctor was kept busy, either on board the Mission ship or when he rowed to the smacks. He was made happy by having so much to do, in tending the sick and hurt, in easing the fishermen's hard lot by entertaining them on board the clean, well-kept Mission vessel, handing out books and magazines, woollen helmets and mittens, mugs of strong tea. This, for the time, was the extent of his service to them, his practical Christianity. Soon he was to discover that there were causes as well as effects, and to become indignant as well as loving. But he knew now how he could live his Christianity more and more, in giving himself entirely to those men whom he admired so much. In December 1888, after a well-filled year, he joined the staff of the National Mission to Deep Sea Fishermen as a missionary doctor, at a salary of £300 a year.

Within a year of joining the Mission Grenfell was promoted to be its Superintendent. For some time the Mission's affairs had been worrying its supporters, and there was an investigation that led to reorganization. The founder and Managing Secretary, Mather, resigned, and the work he had carried on was divided among several officers. Grenfell was put in charge of the activities and property at Gorleston, with the ships and their crews. This meant that he had to live at Gorleston, and he found lodgings with a Mr William Cockrill, an architect who had built a handsome home just clear of the town and on a bluff overlooking the river Yare and the long Dutch pier forming one side of the entrance to the river and beyond to the North Sea. Grenfell was given a bedroom and a large sitting-room with French windows facing seaward. He brought his possessions from London and called in the help of his landlord's two young daughters to help him arrange his room. They held up a piece of blue baize that he tacked above the mantelpiece for displaying his sporting trophies—the medals, caps, and badges he had won at Rugby, boxing, and rowing. He also gave the children a fright by placing two stuffed black seals in corners of the room, and he intrigued them by lying on the floor in a sleeping-bag at night in preference to his bed. Another eccentricity that caused the natives of Gorleston to shake their heads in wonder was climbing down the steep bluff to the beach every morning he was on shore and leaping into the sea for a swim, in winter as well as summer. He built a small canvas canoe, which he christened *Tip-me-Not* and in which he launched himself off the beach in the roughest weather and paddled far out to sea.

His work now was partly on shore, but he missed no chance to sail with the Mission ships. He had been shy with the fishermen on his first voyage, feeling an intruder among them, but he was soon at ease. The men liked him. He made it so clear that he admired them, and his eagerness to learn their craft and to serve them had a boyish quality few could resist.

Of course, he tried to convert those who were not godly, but he never blamed the sinners among them, or threatened hell-fire. "The offence of the visible churches," he was to declare, "that tells most against them to-day is not worldliness or unfaithfulness; it is their inability to shake off their untenable position as judges of others ... the holding up of skirts of this 'I-am-holier-than-thou' attitude is repellent." He respected honest doubts, and gave no thought to what church a man attended, or if he attended none. It was living in Christ's example that mattered, as he was striving to do. It was serving all, as Grenfell himself tended the ailments and hurts of all who came to him, asking no one if he were Roman Catholic, Protestant, or atheist.

His sermons were yarns about how he had found this way of life and what joy it gave him. The sermons rambled, as good yarns can ramble, and his little parables were drawn from the lives his hearers lived. They could understand what he was telling them. He made Christ seem like one of themselves, referring to Him as though He were standing among them, or was a fellow they were likely to meet any day—a Christ Who would yarn as Grenfell yarned, Who would grin and pass a joke even as He preached His Gospel. It was an entirely new sort of preaching, and these roughly clad, often far from clean fishermen gathered round the young man to listen to what he had to say, as other fishermen had gathered round the living Christ nearly two thousand years before. Grenfell made them feel neither shameful nor apart, and they began to love this young man who had come among them. He became something of a legend in the North Sea, and the "Cheer-oh's" that greeted him as he bobbed across the water in his ridiculous little canoe had a special note few other visitors got.

As a Mission Superintendent Grenfell was both a success and cause of anxiety to his employers. His mind teemed with ideas for extending and improving the work for the fishermen's welfare and salvation, and he could not stop to consult any committee or find out if the Mission Council approved his latest plan. He learned that an old seamen's hall in Gorleston was available, and he immediately announced that the Mission would take it over and make it into a place where fishermen could go when they were on shore. The Mission Council published a letter in the local Press, repudiating Grenfell's announcement, but by then their energetic young Superintendent had gathered a number of trustees, and the Mission accepted the accomplished fact, and a club for fishermen was started, a new building proposed.

Grenfell's hatred of drink, roused when he saw what it had brought to the people in the East End of London, had increased when he saw the extent of drinking among the fishermen. These men came on shore after months at sea, seeking relief and change from their hard life. They drew their pay and surged into the public-houses, and the streets of fishing-ports, like those of the industrial towns of the period, were the scenes of human degradation as drunken men fought one another, or were flung out of the drinking-houses, to lie in the gutter until the police lifted them on to barrows and trundled them to gaol. Women were no less degraded by the loss of their men's pay; children roamed the streets, ragged and barefooted and hungry. Homes were neglected, and diseases encouraged by drink and what it caused men to do were passed on to wives and children. Grenfell never blamed the drinkers, but those who made money from selling drink. He fought them with all the energy and eloquence he possessed, organizing opposition to every new public-house, and trying to have all the drinking-places in Gorleston closed. Failing in this, he wanted to offer the fishermen a rival attraction in a place where they could come and play games, read, and hear the Gospel. The new sailors' home would do this.

His duties included deputation work, speaking in public to gather funds for the Mission. He travelled round the country addressing audiences in halls and churches, and holding 'drawing-rooms.' Listening to missionaries was a contemporary entertainment, and a good speaker could draw large audiences. It was a social duty for wealthy ladies to invite their friends to hear the latest missionary; and Grenfell was a romantic figure —a young man of impeccable background and breeding who went to sea with fishermen and who spoke in a way both exciting and touching. He always declared that he disliked having to 'yap,' as he called it, but this is questionable. Grenfell was a talker, a man who had to pour out what was in him. He must share this joyous thing he had found, this living Christianity, with every one he met. He may have found himself out of the world he preferred when he was being conducted round a drawing-room by some beaming parson or gushing hostess, but talk he must. He might not be a good orator, but he possessed a gift for dramatization. The seeking of fish was, to him, a challenge, a storm, the testing of his manhood. The men who toiled and risked their lives to bring home fish were heroes. He saw the drama of it all, and told it as a drama. He was part of it, spoke its language as he re-enacted it all. And it was all Christ's work. He charged his audience with his own passion, and those who heard him could only want to share his adventure. They shared it from their purses.

He was almost too successful as a speaker, for he was away from his work at Gorleston too much and for long periods. The Mission Council often did not know where he was, until they received the money he had gathered and learned that a new committee supporting their work had been formed in some town. He did not follow the programmes they arranged. He obeyed no rules, and was irritated by attempts to control him. The Council had to withdraw him from deputation work, for too much was being left to the skippers and workers at Gorleston. He was relieved of part of his duties, a ship's husband appointed to look after the Mission fleet and its maintenance. Grenfell took advantage of this lessening of his duties to cruise along the south and west coasts of Ireland and find out how the fishermen there could be helped. He surveyed part of the Irish coast, travelling by foot when he was on shore and lodging where he could, in peasants' bothies, content to roll his coat up for a pillow and lie beside the family cow or donkey. He found opposition from the priests, and had to restrain his evangelistic fervour and confine himself to medical and scientific work. He investigated the methods of fishing and kept records that he sent to the Marine Biological Society, with suggestions on how the Irish fisheries could be developed. He was already taking this scientific interest to the North Sea fisheries and using his trained mind to solve the problems of fish movement and food, sending specimens of sea fauna to learned societies and reading papers on these problems.

His activities extended in all directions. He started a brass band for the fishermen in Gorleston, the Duke of Edinburgh presenting the instruments. He preached in local churches, not bothering which denomination he spoke to. He organized sporting events for the local boys, teaching them to play soccer and matching them with teams of boys from public schools and from his own school, Mostyn House. He kept in touch with the boys of his old club in London, and had them down to stay with him, helping them in their careers by finding the right jobs. He entertained friends like Treves and Henry Richards, tramping over the countryside behind Gorleston with guns to bring back duck. In the summer he went as volunteer surgeon to the first of the public-school camps, where boys from rich and poor homes gathered under canvas. He wrote, seated at a desk between the French windows of his sitting-room and from where he could look out and watch the entrance to the river Yare, the fishing-craft enter and leave, the life along the waterfront, and, in storm, see the rockets and flares of ships in trouble on the long, treacherous sandbanks which extend off this part of the coast. He wrote mostly for the Mission magazine, *The Toilers of the Sea*, describing what was happening in the North Sea, recording the deeds performed by fishermen and the tragedies of ships lost.

He seemed never to rest, and, indeed, he was up and out of the house before daylight for his morning swim, then at his desk and writing furiously and untidily until breakfast. He gulped his food, not noticing what he ate, then was running down the steep street from his lodging to visit the Mission workshops, rigging-sheds, storeroom, and the ships themselves. He ate wherever he happened to be, talking incessantly to his hosts, asking the fishermen questions, learning of happenings at sea and on shore that he would write about or describe to audiences. He spoke at mission halls or church halls most evenings, the fishermen gathering round him after every meeting to talk to him. He knew every man's problems and wanted to help, in advice and from his pocket. If they were ill on shore he treated them, annoying the local doctors, who wrote to the Mission complaining that its Superintendent was practising as a doctor when he should not be doing so. Treves replied to this letter, pointing out that Grenfell was a qualified practitioner and could practise if he wished, but Treves also wrote to Grenfell, advising him not to do medical work outside the Mission ships.

There seemed not enough to contain this energetic young man. Then, in 1891, a new horizon appeared, and Grenfell was fired with a new vision and a new challenge.

5

The Greatest Challenge

IN December 1886 the Council of the National Mission to Deep Sea Fishermen had considered a letter from a Church of England clergyman, the Rev. Henry How, of St John's, Newfoundland. The letter proposed that an arrangement should be made "by which my communicants might be regarded as Honorary Agents of the Mission to Deep Sea Fishermen and do work among the cod fishermen working on the Newfoundland Banks similar to that being done by the Mission in British waters." The Council decided not to give this authority and wrote to the clergyman, explaining that the Mission was undenominational, and so could not ally itself with any one Church. The Mission would, however, the Council offered, give as much assistance as was in its power, without committing itself to any distinct Church of England principles.

This was one of many appeals that the Mission was to receive from Newfoundland in the years that followed. Each had to be met with a refusal. The Mission was expanding its work round the British coasts, and new and heavy demands were being ·

made on its often inadequate funds. It was still a young organization, suffering the growing pains of youth. It was in no position to launch out across the Atlantic Ocean.

Apart from these obstacles, Newfoundland itself was known only vaguely to the members of the Council. Few people, in England even, knew much about this island, England's oldest colony. It was known to some to possess off its shores a vast fishing-ground that had been yielding cod since the sixteenth century, and fishermen sailed from France and Portugal every year to share the harvest of its seas with fishermen from the United States, Canada, and Newfoundland. The Newfoundland fishery had been discovered in 1497 by the explorer John Cabot, leading an English expedition, and for over three hundred years English ships had made the annual voyage to the Banks. They no longer did so, and this reduced the mother country's interest. Newfoundland itself was reputed to be a poor and unprofitable place, its Governments said to be corrupt and always asking for help from England. England and France had bickered and fought over the island for centuries, but with the Treaty of Utrecht in 1713 France recognized British sovereignty and Britain granted French fishermen the sole fishing rights along almost half of the Newfoundland shoreline—rights, jealousy maintained, which were to handicap the development of the island for over a hundred years. England herself took little interest in or had little sympathy for the colonists in this or any other question, and Newfoundland was of value only as a base for the Royal Navy, "A great ship moored off the coast of America," and a source of prime seamen for the fleet. This was, near enough, the sum total of knowledge of even the informed Englishman, and the Mission Council were more concerned with people and problems they knew better and whom they understood.

In 1891 a member of the Mission Council, Mr Francis Hopwood, who was also an official of the Board of Trade, visited Canada on business for his Department. With this completed, he decided to call at St John's, the capital of Newfoundland, on his way home, and find out what he could about the fisheries and fishermen and meet the people who had written to the Mission. He stayed in St John's a week only, but in that week he discovered a great deal. Much of his information came from a clergyman, Newfoundland's historian, Dr Moses Harvey. Harvey introduced the Englishman to fishermen and merchants who added to Hopwood's knowledge. As with Mather in the North Sea ten years before, Hopwood was shocked by what he learned, and when he got home and attended a Council meeting he described what he had been told and called on the Mission to help the fishermen of Newfoundland. His disclosures shocked the Council no less than he had been shocked, but the members did not feel that they could undertake work in this distant place. They invited Hopwood to write a letter describing what he had learned and send it to the Mission magazine. Hopwood did so. He wrote a letter of some six thousand words that was both a disclosure of a great scandal and tragedy and an indictment.

Considering he had been in Newfoundland only a week, Hopwood wrote a most remarkable document. He began by describing the country and its coastal areas and its government. Newfoundland had been granted responsible government in 1855, and was administered by a Governor appointed by the Queen, an Executive Committee, a Legislative Council of fifteen, and a House of Assembly of thirty-six members. The Colony had a population of around 140,000, including some 5000 people who lived permanently on that part of the Canadian mainland, Labrador, lying north of Newfoundland and separated from it by the Strait of Belle Isle, which was part of the political whole. The people of Newfoundland itself, other than the Frenchmen who fished along the northern coast, the 'Treaty' shore, were of English, Scottish, and Irish descent. There had been a great influx of Irish during the famine and plague in Ireland during the forties, and in St John's Irish Catholics were in the proportion of two to one of all other denominations, one to two in the outlying settlements. About 1700 of the Labrador residents were Eskimos, living along the northern half of the coast. A few Indians remained, moving restlessly in their nomad life, and there were a number of half-breeds, of mixed white and Eskimo parentage. The remainder were white, mostly of Cornish or Devon ancestry, calling themselves 'Liveyeres,' the people who 'live here.'

The main industry of the Newfoundlanders and their Labrador brothers was fishing—fishing for cod. No other sort of fish was valued, except salmon, herring, and a small fish named caplin that was used for bait. Indeed, the word 'fish' was used to describe cod and nothing else. Sole, turbot, plaice, and halibut gathered in with the cod were thrown back into the sea as worthless or fed to the dogs. No Newfoundlander would eat these. The cod, when caught, were gutted, headed, and split, then salted and dried for sending abroad to Roman Catholic countries like Italy, Spain, and the South American countries. Seal-catching was an important activity, and some tentative attempts were being made to exploit the vast timber resources of the country and to find minerals. Cod was King, however, and the success or failure of the fisheries dictated the economy of the Colony.

The pleas that had come to the Mission to Deep Sea Fishermen had been for missionary work among the men working on the Newfoundland Banks. Some 350 vessels, carrying around 4400 men, fished on the Banks from April to the end of October every year. The Newfoundland, Canadian, and American boats were the famous and graceful 'bankers,' schooners of from 30 to 100 tons. The others were Portuguese, French, Breton, and other foreigners. The fishing was carried on from small flat-bottomed, open boats, 'dories,' and by hook and line, the parent ship being the home and headquarters of each small group of men. It was hard and dangerous work, and there was a high mortality rate both in craft and in men.

Hopwood decided that his Mission could do little to help these 'bankers.' The vessels worked separately and were scattered over a wide area, and the crews were away in their boats except in the worst of weather. Mission work in the British fisheries had been possible and practicable only because the boats worked in fleets.

But Hopwood discovered that not all Newfoundland's fish came from the Banks. Fishing was carried on round the coast of Newfoundland itself and far up the coast of Labrador. Every May or June, when the ice should have cleared from the coastal waters, as many as 30,000 people sailed from St John's to work the Labrador fisheries, being joined there by the 3300 Liveyeres who came from their winter quarters high up in the many inlets indenting the coast. The fishing was carried on from schooners or from the shore, either on the mainland itself or, more often, from any of the hundreds of islands that lie in a long archipelago along most of the 1000 miles of Labrador's eastern coast. For most of the season the schooners were merely floating headquarters, anchoring in the natural harbours among the islands while the crews fished and brought back their catches for cleaning and salting. Only towards the end of the season did the vessels move outward, following the fish and catching them in deep water.

Most of the fish were caught in traps. The trap, the invention of a famous Newfoundlander, Captain William Whiteley, was a net 60 fathoms round and 10 deep, shaped like a lidless box. It was moored strongly about two cables from the rocky shore, held to the surface by floats. Extending from this trap to the shore, a deep, wall-like net hung as an obstacle to the fish, guiding them towards the trap and an opening where they could enter but not escape. The fishermen came by boat every four or five hours and emptied the trap, carrying the fish back to where they would be gutted, cleaned, and salted ready for drying on the rocks or on platforms of small tree-trunks when the weather was right. Those working from the land dried their fish as they caught them; the men working from schooners stowed them 'green,' to be dried when the vessels reached Newfoundland again. When the fish were not plentiful enough to fill the traps they were caught by jigging weighted hooks from the boats, but this was a slow, wasteful method compared with trapping.

Many of the fishermen worked for 'planters,' who supplied the nets, boats, salt, and fed and housed their men and their families. One or two planters paid a wage, but most paid by shares of profits. The majority of the land-based fishermen, however, worked independently, trading in their catch to merchants who established posts where the fishing was going on and in certain places convenient for storerooms and ships. Large vessels came from Europe and elsewhere to load the dried fish for Europe and South America. Schoonermen either owned their own vessels and employed their crews or worked for owners in Newfoundland. The total value of all Newfoundland's fisheries was six to seven million dollars a year, the bulk of this coming from Labrador.

What had shocked Hopwood were the conditions under

which the fishermen and their families going north travelled
and lived while on the Labrador coast, and how they were rewarded for their work. The annual voyage northward, picturesque in its bustle, its hundreds of ships and thousands of people
cramming St John's waterfront, was a trial of endurance. The
fishermen and their families were crowded on board whichever
ship they found room in, taking their boats, nets, what food
they could afford, and even their domestic stock in hens and
goats. These possessions were dumped on the ships' decks, and
the owners camped beside or on them. Men, women, and children slept where there was room to stretch, in the fish-hold and
in the open, with no privacy whatever. They cooked their own
food. There were no proper sanitary facilities on board the
schooners, and there was little fresh water. What regulations
there were for limiting the number of passengers the vessels
could carry were winked at, and no real effort was made to
check the vessels' seaworthiness. Those who travelled by a mail-
steamer that called along the coast three or four times every
summer were little better off.

Each year this vast exodus took place, hundreds of schooners
passing out of St John's Harbour and heading north, joined by
other vessels from smaller harbours and from Belle Isle Strait.
Reaching Labrador, the fishermen and their families and possessions were landed at the places where they believed the fishing
would be good, and there they took possession of huts and sheds
they had built in previous years, or they set to and built themselves new ones. The huts were small and primitive, built with
what timber the fishermen could find or bring from the wooded
mainland, roofed and caulked with sod and moss. Most were
without windows; chimneys were holes in the roof. The floors
were the bare earth, and the furnishing was roughly knocked
together from bits of old timber. The beds, if any, were bunks
against the wall; the bedding was dried moss or deerskin. Water
was carried from the many ponds among the rocks, and there
were, of course, no sanitary arrangements whatever. The first
task the people had to do was to clear out the ice and snow
that had accumulated inside their huts during the winter.

While the women and children were busy preparing their
home the men were getting ready for the actual fishing. The
rough sheds where the fish would be headed, cleaned, and salted

were close beside the water, built where a platform of small
fir-tree trunks would extend from the open door to overhang
where the boats could bring the fish and the men could toss
their catch upward to the platform with long-handled forks.
These 'stages' were dismantled at the end of every season, or
they would have been carried away by the ice crushing on shore,
and now the fishermen had to rebuild them. The sheds were
cleared of snow and ice, patched where they had been damaged
by winter gales. The men could then carry their traps to where
they believed the fish would run, and the fishing that would
continue on to October began. In hundreds of tiny natural harbours, on rocks beside the channels between the islands, known
as 'tickles,' tiny settlements of fishermen and their families
were gathering. Schooners anchored while the crews worked
traps along the near-by shores. Many vessels continued northward, to sail beyond Hamilton Inlet, which was as far north
as the shore-based fishermen worked, and to where the population was almost entirely Eskimo. There these schoonermen
sought fish as far as Cape Chidley, at the entrance to Hudson
Bay. The whole coast and its islands, empty and desolate during
the winter, became, for four months every year, alive with striving, toiling people.

Only a very few of them had started the season clear of debt.
Hopwood had discovered that being in debt was the accepted
and common lot of almost every fisherman who sailed "down
north." Merchants in St John's, traders who located themselves
along the coast, advanced credit in fishing-gear, salt, and food,
and claimed all a man's fish. They also decided the price the
fisherman would get for his catch, and what he would have to
pay for the goods they supplied. The power these merchants and
traders wielded was complete and unopposable, for if they refused a man credit he and his family would starve. There was
no appeal against a merchant's or a trader's edict, no alternative
in work other than fishing. Fish bringing four dollars a quintal,
the measurement used and equal to a hundredweight of the
fish when dried, in the European market earned two dollars
and less for the fishermen. The merchants reckoned on a 200-
per cent. profit margin for the goods they sold. They stood to
lose heavily in those years when fishing was poor, or when men
were consistently unsuccessful in their fishing, but more often

E

they made themselves wealthy. On the hills behind St John's merchants built themselves large and handsome homes, and their wives carried on their social rounds in smart carriages. The effects of this 'truck' system on the actual producers was what horrified Hopwood. Few of the fishermen made enough to carry them through the idle and empty winter months.

Even more tragic and horrifying was the utter and complete lack of thought or effort for the fishermen's welfare, physical or spiritual, while they were in the north. When they sailed through the high, narrow entrance from St John's Harbour they passed into an abyss where they could die or rot for all anyone seemed to care. Only the fish they returned mattered. Along the whole of the Labrador coast there was not a single doctor, and the only medical service the 30,000 people could call on was when the mail-steamer made its brief halts at the larger settlements and a doctor paid by the Government to sail with the ship could give hasty attention to anyone who went on board. As the ship seldom waited at any place longer than an hour or two, this doctor could do little more than attend to a few and cursorily.

A few missionaries and clergymen travelled along the coast in summer as best they could, and by any boat they could find. In the northern half of the coast the Eskimos were better served by missionaries of the Moravian Church Mission, first established there at the end of the eighteenth century and carrying on noble work ever since. But the white population, the summer fisherfolk and the Liveyeres, could be born, mate, and die without ever seeing a clergyman or hearing a word of God's truth from a churchman. They could be injured, sicken, and die without a trained hand of nurse or doctor, and many did die who could have been saved by skilled treatment.

This was the bones of the story Hopwood had to tell, and he wrote it eloquently and with passion in the letter that was printed in *The Toilers of the Sea*. In the letter Hopwood offered to subscribe £100 from his own pocket towards any work done by the Mission for these distant people. He and the Mission Council must have been surprised by the effect of his letter. Seldom has anything printed in the magazine of a charitable organization received such attention. Within a fortnight of its publication comments and extracts were being printed in news-

papers in the United States and Canada, as well as in Great
Britain. The *Canadian Gazette* declared that Hopwood's article
"should command the earnest attention of the Newfoundland
Government," and called on public men to "remedy some of
the evils as far as possible." *Truth*, in England, "deplored the
Newfoundland Government's neglect of the workers in its chief
industry," and the London *Daily Chronicle* repeated Hopwood's words: "Hunger and want caused an exodus from Newfoundland to Labrador, where people lived in a state of squalid
promiscuity that is sickening to hear about." This newspaper
"felt that the Imperial Government should restore and keep
order in these squalid fishing settlements," and that there should
be an investigation to "test the validity of Hopwood's indictment." The newspapers which commented demanded that
something should be done for the Labrador fishermen and their
families.

Early in 1892 the interest and pity that had been aroused by
Hopwood's disclosures increased with the news that 40 out of
200 fishermen working from Trinity Bay, in Eastern Newfoundland, had been lost. They had gone out to fish while the
ice was still in the Bay, and been caught by a blizzard. Boats
were crushed, and men were stranded on the ice to freeze to
death. Boats were driven far out to sea, to be found with their
crews frozen to death. The Lord Mayor of London opened a
fund for the families of these unfortunate men, and Queen
Victoria contributed and sent messages of sympathy. Requests
came into the Mission for something to be done to help these
fellow-Britons across the sea, and the Mission Council met to
discuss the matter. It was decided to send a hospital ship that
year, 1892, on an 'exploratory' voyage. The Mission's young
Superintendent volunteered to sail with the vessel.

The ship chosen for this new venture was the *Albert*, one of
two smacks built for the Mission in Fellowes' Yard at Gorleston
in 1889. She was said to be the finest smack ever launched on
the river Yare, being built entirely of oak and teak, and, with a
length of 110 feet, was larger than most fishing-vessels. She was,
of course, a sailing-vessel, ketch-rigged, and she had been built
and equipped as a hospital ship. Below decks partitions could
be slid aside so that 100 people could be seated for services. This
sturdy and handsome little vessel was sent back to her builders

to be sheathed and for her bows to be reinforced with thick beams for working among ice. A 40-foot yard for carrying a square sail was fitted to her mainmast. Stores for five months were put on board, with many bales of used clothing, magazines, and books that would be distributed to the people in Labrador. Grenfell, delighted to be setting out on this new adventure, wrote to *The Toilers* to tell how the living-quarters were getting smaller and smaller as more and more bales arrived for stowing, and that he had overheard a fisherman say, "She is very much by the head." His companion replied, "That's because she has so much reading in her... and it ain't light reading."

Articles were signed on June 10, 1892, at Yarmouth. The Agreement was for a voyage from "Yarmouth to St John's, Newfoundland, and thence on a cruising voyage on the Newfoundland and Labrador coasts, with liberty to call at any port or ports within the latitudes of 40 degrees north and 60 degrees north, the voyage to finally terminate in the United Kingdom and not to exceed two years." The mate and crew of seven were all fishermen from Gorleston, and Grenfell signed the Articles as ship's surgeon. He had taken and passed the Board of Trade Examination for a Yacht Master's Certificate on June 1; but, though he always liked to describe himself as a "Master Mariner," his Certificate authorized him only to "Take command of your own yacht *Vagabond*," the small yawl he sailed with Treves. A properly and fully qualified master was engaged for the *Albert*, Captain John Trezisse of Penzance, "A man greatly recommended by many of our Christian friends," and an experienced officer who had visited the coast of Labrador in merchant vessels. The mate, Joseph White, and the bosun, Robert Hewer, had both been skippers in command of Mission ships, and one at least of the crew had served in square-rigged vessels. Altogether officers and crew numbered nine, the same complement the *Albert* carried when working in the North Sea.

She was towed clear of the river Yare by a tug on June 12. Three Mission ships moored in the river dipped their colours in salute, fishermen and relatives of the crew lined the quays, and more watched from the long Dutch pier, waving and calling, "God speed." Captain Aldrich, R.N., a local resident and supporter of the Mission, had his yacht dressed from stem to stern with flags and fired off a salute of nine guns as the *Albert* passed. Her crew answered each salute with cheers, Grenfell waving his cap and aiming his camera. When they were clear of the river compasses were corrected and their error listed; then, while the vessel was held by the tug, Grenfell entertained friends and officials who had come this far to luncheon. When it was over and the visitors had gone on board the tug the *Albert*'s sails were raised, and she headed southward towards the Channel.

She made two stops before setting a course across the Atlantic. She stopped off Lulworth Cove to take on board an ex-naval sailing-cutter that Grenfell was borrowing from his Boys' Brigade camp, then sailed west, meeting head-winds and fog that lasted two days and delayed her. She reached the Irish coast and ran into Crookhaven, where the vessel was beached so that a search could be made for a suspected leak. The *Albert* had been making thirty inches of water a day, and Captain Trezisse was worried. Nothing could be found, and the leak, if any, must have closed itself, for the ship made no more water on the voyage. At Crookhaven people remembered Grenfell, and many came on board for medical treatment, paying him with milk and eggs—and a fox's tail. The *Albert* left Crookhaven on July 4, to find strong winds and bad weather that were to continue for the first thousand miles, but the *Albert* proved herself a fine sailer and, despite the poor weather, averaged around 130 miles a day. Calms delayed her towards the end of the crossing, but by the evening of Friday, July 22, she was nearing St John's, and her sails were trimmed for her to lie to until daylight.

Grenfell enjoyed this new experience of ocean sailing, but he and Captain Trezisse did not get along very well. Trezisse, Grenfell told his mother in a letter he wrote from St John's, was "too canny" for her son's liking. The shipmaster was a professional sailor who would consider his task to be getting his ship safely across the Atlantic. He would not be interested in making a record passage, while Grenfell always wanted to test himself and his ship. This young fellow with his pretensions to being a sailor would irritate the Cornishman, and his gaiety and pranks—Grenfell spent much of his time teaching his black retriever to fetch and carry—would seem to turn the ship into a playground. Trezisse was a solemn-faced, bearded man with deep religious convictions who would not understand Grenfell's sense of humour nor his love of skylarking. Religion was a sober affair to the sailor.

Grenfell's letters leave the impression that he was liable to step out of his place on board the *Albert*. He was ship's surgeon, but he liked to help with the ship's work, and he was practising his navigation and comparing his results with the shipmaster's. He was not always impressed by the other's navigation, and believed that he could have done it better himself. Grenfell was to become a seaman in the future, but his experience until now had been far from extensive. It is easy to understand how a hard-bitten old sailor like Trezisse would be annoyed at times by his over-gay, talkative, impulsive surgeon, who seemed not to appreciate the importance of a ship's captain.

To the crew Grenfell was "the Doctor," and if the master did not appreciate him, they did. The carpenter was also a cornet-player, and Grenfell loved to gather the men together and, with the cornet going, sing his beloved Sankey hymns as the *Albert* sailed along. He worked with the men, covering himself in blue and red paint. All hands were determined to bring their vessel into St John's in perfect condition, and Grenfell ceased teaching his dog to 'die for the Queen' and 'speak for his dinner,' while he practised his hand with a paintbrush and holystone. The *Albert* was to earn high praise for her seamanlike appearance and spick-and-span condition when she entered St John's, the crew smart in their serge trousers, blue guernseys with the name of their Mission on the chest, and wearing round sailor caps.

Grenfell and his companions found St John's a burned ruin. They had seen smoke and flames from far out at sea, and had learned from a passing sailing-vessel that a great fire was raging in the capital. As the Mission ship lay off the port that night the Englishmen could watch the flames and smell the pungent smoke that was being blown towards them. With the dawn the flames were less, but the smoke was thick above the high land. It was a dramatic sight, and the drama was heightened when a huge iceberg floating near the *Albert* turned slowly over and, with a vast booming and crashing, broke up and squeezed a large wave towards the vessel. Obligingly a whale then broke surface near the *Albert*. With the daylight a tug came from the entrance to the harbour and closed the Mission ship. A pilot came on board, and soon the small vessel was being towed through the narrow, cliff-walled entrance into the long and hill-surrounded harbour. Two men-of-war anchored there dipped their colours in salute, and the *Albert*'s ensign dropped in reply. A boat came from the shore, bringing Dr Moses Harvey, to greet this doctor who, Hopwood had written to say, "is not only a medical man but a scientist," and who had come across an ocean to help the fishermen of Newfoundland and Labrador.

Grenfell's first task was to give what aid he could to the stricken people of St John's. Now that the *Albert* was inside the high land that had screened the town from seaward the devastation lay exposed on the steep slopes where St John's is situated. The fire, started by a carelessly thrown match in a farm barn above the town and driven by a fresh north-west wind, had consumed the town. Most of the buildings were wooden, but even the solid stone and brick of the Anglican cathedral and public buildings had been gutted and destroyed. Chimneys, the only stone part of the wooden houses, stood erect among the smouldering black ruins of what had been the homes of over 11,000 persons. More than 2000 buildings had been destroyed, and when Grenfell went on shore people were searching through the ruins for what might have survived of their possessions. The authorities had forbidden the sale of all liquor, and police and volunteers patrolled those places left untouched to prevent looting. Fortunately, there had been few casualties, and Grenfell's medical skill was not required. He was able, however, to supply the town's two doctors with instruments and medical supplies and to clothe some of the unfortunate people from the bales of second-hand clothing on board the *Albert*.

Grenfell stayed with Dr Harvey, whose house was beyond where the fire had started. Despite their desperate condition and the problems that had to be faced in feeding and housing the homeless, the merchants and officials of St John's gave what help and advice they could to the young Englishman. The *Albert* was brought to a jetty and opened to visitors, to be admired by the seamen who came on board, her accommodation for the sick praised by all. No charge was made for anything done for the strangers, and an experienced pilot, a cheer-

ful, yarn-spinning Irishman, Captain Fitzgerald, whom Grenfell took to at once, was engaged and paid for by the Newfoundland Government. The Governor, Sir Terence O'Brien, was
away from the Colony, in London, but the Premier, Sir William Whiteway, and the members of his Government showed
by the help they gave that they appreciated Grenfell's coming
and were grateful to the Mission to Deep Sea Fishermen who
had sent him. Grenfell was entertained as an important visitor,
shown the country behind the town as far as the primitive roads
would allow, and was able to exercise his skill as a fisherman
and test a new rod his brother Algernon had given him in some
of the 'ponds' that are a feature of inland Newfoundland.

The departure of the *Albert* was delayed by fog and adverse
winds, but she got away at last on August 2. She was towed
clear of the harbour, and, with the tow-rope dropped and sails
filled, slanted outward to get clear of the land. She ran into fog
almost at once, and this continued, with short breaks, until the
following Saturday. No land was sighted in this week's sailing,
but on the Saturday "an effect of the sinking sun revealed to
us some twenty miles to leeward the bold headland and hills of
Cape Bauld." Cape Bauld is the most north-easterly point of
Newfoundland, and from there the *Albert* was headed northward to cross Belle Isle Strait. Fog hid the sheer cliffs of Belle
Isle itself, but it cleared on the Sunday, and Grenfell got his
first sight of Labrador.

He could only be thrilled by what he saw. The sea was calm
that day, the sun bright and warm, the sky a pale-blue background for slowly drifting white clouds. Ahead of the *Albert*,
beyond the inshore waters where islands raised themselves like
a passing fleet, the high Labrador mainland showed, dark
and remote, extending until it faded into the summer haze.
Nearer, islands, rounded and treeless, made a scattered bastion,
their sides cut down in sheer cliff or broken in tumbled boul-
ders. There was colour apart from the sun-breathing sea, pale-
yellow and sombre blue moss cloaking the summit of each
island, trailing as an untidy garment into seaward valleys and
over cliff-edges, each isle petticoated with a fringe of white as
the Atlantic swell surged and broke against the rocks. "God,"
it was said, "made the world in five days, Labrador on the
sixth, and on the seventh he threw stones at it." A desolate,

empty land, writers described it, but there was a beauty in its seeming desolation to the young Englishman who stood on the *Albert*'s deck as Captain Fitzgerald conned the vessel cautiously towards these islands. There was challenge as well as great beauty in the icebergs Grenfell could now see as the fog cleared. Here, at the place where the *Albert* made her first Labrador landfall, the sea bottom rises from a depth of more than a hundred fathoms to fifty or so fathoms. Icebergs, drifted by the Labrador current from where they had been calved from Greenland's glaciers, blown inshore by the easterly winds, grounded and were held. They towered high, shaped by wind and melted by the sun into fantastic and beautiful shapes. Noble, graceful arches were carved out by the beating sea, caves hollowed. Inside these rainbows formed and colours danced against the palest blues and dark-blue streaks of hard 'glass' ice of the berg itself. The lofty surfaces glistened, ridged and corrugated by the water streaming downward as the sun's heat ate into the softer ice. Now and then there was a deep, warlike rumble as a berg broke apart or was toppled by the water dissolving its underwater bulk. Loud crashes followed the rumbling, and there was sad grandeur in the slow tilting and collapse of the giants. The water growled and swelled to the impact, and waves, sheened by the sunlight, came swelling towards the small Mission ship. This was drama indeed, and Grenfell gazed in wonder and admiration.

6

The Urgent Call

WILFRED GRENFELL's first visit to the coast of Labrador lasted a little over two months. In this time the *Albert* sailed as far north as Hopedale, over 1100 miles northward from St John's, Newfoundland, and on her return passage she cruised into Belle Isle Strait and visited along the northern coast of Newfoundland itself for two weeks. Altogether, on this first visit, the Mission ship sailed over 3000 miles, and, in addition, Grenfell sailed the Boys' Brigade's cutter, or went by traders' launches, to settlements which the *Albert* could not reach. He visited 50 settlements, saw and treated 900 patients, distributed the clothing, books, and magazines the ship had brought from England, and, with Captain Trezisse, conducted dozens of religious services either on shore or on board the *Albert*.

From where the pilot had picked a landfall at Domino Run, a hundred miles from Belle Isle, the *Albert* moved northward, close by or inside the islands off the coast. She dared not move during darkness, for the whole coast was inadequately charted, and there were neither lighthouses, buoys, nor marks to aid the navigator. Labrador coastal waters are never entirely free of ice, either in scattered pans or icebergs, and for a moving ship to strike either of these could be fatal. Much of the inshore water was unknown, and even experienced pilots like Captain Fitzgerald dared not venture too far among the islands. Even to-day the charts are far from complete, and it is only now that the Canadian Government is starting the gigantic task of surveying these waters thoroughly. In 1892 what charts existed gave little more than the information from Captain James Cook's voyage of exploration in 1770. Schooners navigated by men who had worked the Labrador coast all their lives were still caught and lost on some unknown shoal or underwater rock. So the *Albert* sailed northward with caution, anchoring each night, in havens where the fishing-schooners gathered or settlements were established.

Here, in these treeless, glacier-rounded islands, few of them higher than 250 feet, Grenfell found a place and people to stir the romanticist and the adventurer in him. Labrador lies in almost the same latitudes as Great Britain, but, where the climate of the British Isles is tempered by the warmth of the Gulf Stream curving from the Atlantic, Labrador's climate is sub-Arctic. The Labrador current that comes from the Arctic and moves southward to flow over the Great Banks and begin its merging with the north-going Gulf Stream influences the climate. The water's cold breath meeting the warmer air from the Gulf Stream or from the sun-heated land mass breeds the additional hazard of fog. Labrador summer days can be fresh and invigorating, even hot; then a change of wind will bring the raw bite of a winter's day in England or smother the islands with dense fog. It is a climate where few days are alike, and where winds can spring up suddenly and rush with violence between the islands and into the long, loch-like tickles, to tear schooners from their anchors and cast boats away.

The islands have a dramatic quality that appealed to Grenfell at once. Lifted peaks of underwater ledges running outward from the mainland, they are seldom of any great height, and are often within a stone's throw of each other. The channels between them are shallow, and thrust up rocky snares for the unwary. The rock itself ranges through gneisses, schists,

marbles, limestones, and granite, twisted by great earth disturb-
ances of the past, rubbed smooth and rounded by ancient glacier
movement, cracked and split by frost, until on one cliff-face
alone the interested viewer can see a dozen colours, from the
gleaming white of a poor marble to the solid black of a volcanic
out-thrust. The surfaces gleam or glow to the ever-changing
light, their patterns twisting into and round each other. There
is cruelty in some of it, a harsh majesty where a cliff rises sheer
from the water, a surprising warmth in the reds and browns.

The struggle for existence and survival of the growing things
has its own drama. Few trees can resist the cold of the winter
and the stormy winds from the Atlantic. On the mainland, in
the long, fjord-like inlets, the country is thickly wooded with
spruce, firs, and less hardy timber, but along the coast and on
the islands life has to crouch low for survival. Most of the
growth is moss and small, hardy plant-life. The mosses cover the
rounded hills with a deep carpet of extraordinary beauty in
rich, low-toned colours; the flowers of the tiny plants seem
to sparkle against this moss, as stars against a night sky, and
with the late summer the flowers become berries of brilliant
reds and purple that carpet large patches and pour around the
darker mosses. In every hollow of those hills ponds have
formed, gathering into their peaty-brown depths pale-coloured
weed and green water-plants. It is a lesson in the tenacity of
life.

The country's and the sea's quality is in their challenge, and
to a man like Wilfred Grenfell Labrador was a place to stir and
exhilarate. A place to conquer and understand. As the *Albert*
sailed northward he was helping a passenger, Mr Adolf Neilson,
the Fishery Experimental Officer for the Newfoundland Government, to note the movements of currents and the temperatures of the deeper waters. He sketched landmarks and made
drawings and plans of the channels through which the ship
passed. To discover that the charts were inadequate was, for
Grenfell, to start making charts. To be told that a channel was
not followed because it might contain hidden dangers in shoal
or reef was to sail into those channels and locate the dangers.
He and Trezisse could not agree on this, for the careful shipmaster would take no risks with his command. Grenfell could
only make notes of where the *Albert* did pass, and promise him-

self a more daring voyage when he was not restrained by over-cautious companions.

He found the people he had come to serve, and discovered that all Hopwood had said and written was true. This was a land where the lives of human beings were as harsh as the country itself. Grenfell had seen poverty enough in the East End of London and among the fisherfolk at Gorleston and on the West Coast of Ireland, but it had never made such impact on him as did what he found in Labrador. In cities and large communities the destitute were the defeated, the weaklings, existing and concealed in their own places and part of the accepted pattern of the industrialized community. Grenfell's mission had been to encourage these beaten people to a new, Christian way of life, to be one of the many who brought them charity. He believed their lives could be brighter in following Christ. He had taken this message to them.

Lately he had been realizing that this was not enough, that a Christian should concern himself with the material welfare of his people no less than with their spiritual being. He had begun to criticize trawler-owners, commenting on their large profits and seeing a reason for poverty other than weakliness, or even the drink he blamed for so much. What he thought Grenfell said, and he could be a disconcerting guest of those who profited from the toil and hardships of others.

Now, in Labrador, he found such poverty as he had not seen, even in the London slums, and his indignation as well as his pity was roused. That people worked Grenfell accepted, and he was a strenuous worker himself. That men challenged the waters to bring home food for a world was their task and their nobility. But that they should do so and yet live in destitution and in fear for their families horrified him. The fishermen in the North Sea and in Ireland who found and caught fish did at least earn enough to maintain themselves and their families, even if not rewarded as they deserved.

Here there was no such guarantee. Men might load their boats to the gunwale every four hours, their wives and children might work long hours, cleaning, salting, and drying the catches, but a dozen or so other men gathered round a table in St John's would dictate their reward and see to it that the profits came to themselves. Grenfell was to be told by the merchants and traders that they preferred to have fishermen, particularly the younger men, in debt, for that was a way to hold them in their service. They set their prices to achieve this. It was a form of bondage that only a few ever won free of, and which gave the fishermen the scantiest of livings. Grenfell learned that the most the people could expect after five months' hard toil in the North was to lessen their debts and return to their settlements with enough food to last them over the winter. A few barrels of flour, some molasses, tea, cheap fat, and what fish they could dry and keep for themselves would be their winter diet. Where there was game and a man owned a gun caribou meat might be added. Even in the prosperous years the fishermen expected little more than this.

It was when he found himself among the permanent inhabitants of this coast that Grenfell discovered the full degradation people could suffer. These Liveyeres, with good English and Scottish names like Blake, Broomfield, Goudie, and Mac-Donald, people who still spoke the dialects of their ancestors, were indeed a forgotten people. They lived on the mainland during the winter, moving to the islands and along the coast for the summer fishing. They had spread themselves widely to share the game, and their ramshackle, primitive huts, stilted to a level on the steep hillside and rocks, were no better than the Newfoundlanders' temporary homes. The Liveyeres trapped in the winter, and shot what game they could to augment the flour and molasses and tea that were their main diet. Their poverty was appalling, and many of them had lost all initiative and ceased to make a struggle against the difficulties of life in this hard land. The Newfoundlanders could leave the coast and get what charity or help there was for them in the larger communities of their island. The Liveyeres had to take what they received for their fish and pelts and hope to exist through another Arctic winter.

Grenfell was horrified by what he found among these people. He saw men going out to fish in crude, unseaworthy boats built by themselves, short of fishing-gear and unable to get credit for more. Women came to the *Albert* with their bodies scarcely covered with garments made out of old flour-sacks; children went barefooted and almost naked, crawling on the vermin-ridden floors of the huts and in the open in torn and dirty vests.

The men wore old patched garments that gave little protection. They were often cruelly exploited by itinerant traders from New England and Canada who cruised the coast, and Grenfell heard of one man who received tobacco worth 75 cents in Newfoundland for a fox-skin that would fetch 35 to 40 dollars in the outside market. Some of the traders established along the coast asserted seigneurial power over the people, even forbidding marriages and dictating a man's movements. Many of the Liveyeres lived worse than the Eskimos and Indians, and had never adapted themselves to the coast. They had ceased to make much effort, and took what relief the Government might occasionally give them—a barrel of flour and a little molasses to maintain a family for a whole winter. Grenfell realized that much of their destitution came from their own resignation and lack of effort, but his heart was torn by what he found. When he returned to St John's he wrote home:

> How could any human being with a heart of flesh, after seeing such sights, enjoy a Christmas Dinner in old England, as we hope to, with our minds haunted by these hungry pale faces of people of our own race and blood. . . . Pray God this voyage of the *Albert* will be repeated again and again.

He had found a desperate need for his medical skill not less than for his gifts in clothing. Many of the Liveyeres had never seen a doctor before, and he was asked, "Be ye a real doctor?" as though he had come from a fairy-tale. Ailments were brought to him as though the sufferer expected to see a miracle performed, and he treated sores and pains that people had had for months, even years, and become resigned to their suffering. Whole families were riddled with tuberculosis and still worked. Men hauled their traps in the coldest weather when they should have been in a hospital. Children were twisted with rickets, men spat out blood from their lungs, women bore their children and were infected by the midwife's dirty hands. The only attention any ever had was from superstitious old women with reputations as healers. Grenfell heard of some remarkable 'cures.' One old woman treated the *grippe* that broke out and ravaged the coast regularly with nine lice swallowed every third day for nine days. A favourite cure for abscesses was a mixture of white paint and herbs mixed into a poultice. The tooth of a dying deer worn round the neck was accounted a cure for fits, and liniment was drunk as treatment for chest diseases. Charms were worn by many, and time after time Grenfell was asked to "charm" away a pain. He grinned and waved his hand and said, "Meenie Mini Mo," then got to work properly.

He found that many of the fishermen would not come to him for treatment, or, if they did, they wanted only something to ease a "bad head" or a "bad stomach." They would have no treatment that meant lying down or stopping work. They had come north to fish, and fish they must, or they would starve through the winter. To be sent back to a hospital in St John's was economic disaster; for the schooner skipper with ailments or injuries aboard, sailing home with an empty vessel was ruination. They must complete the season, sick or well, suffering what they must, as long as they could move around their vessels' decks. Fishermen told Grenfell that they were not sure that a doctor on the coast was a good thing, for in this hunt for a living weaklings had no value, and death removed a responsibility from others who were in no position to carry a burden.

Grenfell gave and did what he could on this first visit. At each stop the *Albert* made, as soon as the anchor was down he was on shore or off to the anchored schooners, a quick-moving muscular young man dressed in the rig of a fisherman, or in a well-worn tweed suit, demanding of whoever met him to be taken to the sick and the poor. His coming had been announced by boats passing north. People awaited his arrival without belief that he was actually coming, for they could not understand why anyone should come from England to help them. Outsiders did not do such things for those on the Labrador. When passing fishermen called and said they had actually seen this ship and her doctor they were discussed half in wonder. A missionary at a settlement in Belle Isle Strait who was to meet Grenfell described the people's interest and curiosity:

> All through the summer we had heard about it; many vessels, either trading or fishing, had visited our harbour, and the friendly crews had aroused our curiosity by their recitals of the work being done by the Mission ship and its crew. "Them are good men, whom ever they be," said one, while another expatiated, with all a sailor's delight to sailors equally delighted, upon the size and rig and sailing powers of the vessel, until we were all hoping she

would pay us a visit. The probability of this latter question was very freely discussed among our fishermen, who, now the season was well-nigh over and no more fish to be caught, were to be found daily sitting about in small groups, smoking and talking with that peculiar gravity which belong to the Liveyeres of the coast.... Would she come here? Many shook their heads. "No." ..."But why?" Then followed an argument on the pros and cons in fisherman fashion, with sundry allusions to the weather, the rough harbours, strong tides and the lateness of the season....

But she came, and the missionary, Mr John Sidey, who was to become one of Grenfell's most loyal admirers, described her coming:

A strange-looking vessel was slowly making her way round the point. Two flags were flying, and, as she dropped anchor, we were able to read the insignia of the Mission plainly.... We decided to go on board. Boats filled with fishermen were already on the way out. We were just ready for a start when a sharp knock came on the door and on opening it we were greeted with "I am George Stoney, and this is Doctor Grenfell." Not much time did the worthy doctor give us for fraternal chat. He was soon asking us about the sick and the needy, and, with a promptness that was calculated to teach us a lesson, the three of us were out visiting the poorest of the families.

This was the scene to be repeated at every place Grenfell visited. He was on shore and seeking those he could help, examining the ailing, cleaning wounds, and mending hurts. He ordered the half-clothed women and children on board the *Albert* to be given clothes. He handed out books and magazines and religious tracts, and he drummed up a service on the ship's deck, or in a trader's storeroom, to tell these people of his wonderful Christ, Who had sent him here to serve them. He roused no emotional revivalist excitement, but in clear, direct speech gave the people who crammed the *Albert*'s deck or the trader's stores some of his own brightness and hopefulness. He showed them that they were not a forgotten people, but God's, and his own, family. His love for all of them glowed through his eyes and charged his voice.

He left behind him people who admired and were already adoring him, half wondering in their gratitude. This was so new in their lives—that some one thought of them, and that

F

people across an ocean had sent him for their sake. Word sped ahead faster, and the *Albert* was surrounded by boats from schooners and the shore the moment she anchored. Grenfell greeted the visitors cheerfully with a grin and handshake, this young man who would abuse them for their dirt as well as clothe their children. He would joke with a man, and when that man spat on the *Albert*'s deck, as he had been used to spitting on his own deck, Grenfell reached over and whipped off the man's cap, bent, and wiped the spit off the deck, and then handed back the cap, to lecture the culprit on the evils of spitting. Those who suffered the often sharp bite of his tongue could only grin and admire. This young fellow was a man. He could sail a boat with the best of them, swim across their icy harbour for the fun of it, square up in a friendly boxing match, and outshoot their smartest gun. They took him to their hearts, and he became "the Doctor" to them as he had become "the Doctor" in the North Sea. It was a title of affection.

By the time the *Albert* was sailing back to St John's Grenfell knew that he had found the place where he could live his Christianity fully, the challenge that his vigorous and adventurous character needed. He already loved this land of "fog, dog, and cod," and could never see it as the bleak, empty place so many visitors had said it was. To the young Englishman the land and the sea were an exciting panorama of colour and life, an eternal and magnificent adventure. He had watched from the *Albert*'s deck icebergs in magnificent procession, the leaping colours of the Northern Lights, mirages where schooners and great icebergs hung upside-down in the sky and the world was seeped in the palest tints; he had moved among the dark islands and through channels with names that were the poetry of the simple men who had named them; Smoky Run, Cutthroat Island, Iron-bound Island, Tub Island, Battle Harbour, Paradise, Dear Man's Rock. The scientist in him had been stirred by the pattern of the cliffs the ship sailed past, and his daring spirit excited by the winding, unknown channels of the long archipelago. The hunter in him was delighted with the game to be found in ducks, geese, partridge, and other targets for his gun, the magnificent trout- and salmon-fishing in the rivers and ponds. And he met people to love and to admire, and to serve. At Hopedale he had visited the missions set up by the

Moravian Church, meeting missionaries and their families who would remain away from civilization all their lives to serve the Eskimos of this northern end of Labrador, and his heart ached to do for the white fishermen what the Moravians had been doing for the Eskimos for over a hundred years. He was stirred as he had never been before, and he was determined that he would return and bring these forgotten people the message of Christ and a better life. The young man had no thought that he was making a sacrifice of his own ambitions and worldly progress. This was life as he would wish to live it.

The *Albert* had to fight a storm before she reached St John's, but she did so gallantly, and once again she entered the steep-walled, narrow entrance to the harbour, to find the town being rebuilt, and to a better plan than before. The streets were wider, extending along the hill and up steeply from the waterfront to form squares where houses were rising. Most of the houses were still of timber, and Grenfell thought this a mistake; but he admired the spirit of these people who had so quickly rebuilt their town and their burned-out fortunes.

St John's already knew of the work done by the young Englishman and the crew of the *Albert* for the fishermen along the Labrador coast. Most of the schooners were home again, and their crews were full of stories of this remarkable young English doctor. The *Albert*'s ropes were taken by men Grenfell had treated hundreds of miles to the northward, men who already greeted him as an old friend. He was met by the Colony's notables and invited to stay with the Governor, now back from England. The town's newspapers interviewed him and printed high praise of the work he had done, and he was invited to meet a committee of merchants and politicians, to tell them how they could help this work among their people to be continued. He told them, without mincing words, and if any of the merchants disliked his directness they said nothing. Some of them had long since realized that something should be done for the fishermen, and now this straight-speaking young man showed them how much was needed and how they could help. The Rev. Dr Harvey worded a resolution, thanking the Mission to Deep Sea Fishermen and their servants, Dr Grenfell and the officers and crew of the *Albert*, for the work they had done this year, and stating:

This meeting also desires to express the hope that the Directors of the Mission may see their way to continue the work thus begun, and should they do so they may be assured of the warmest support and co-operation of all classes of this community.

A Committee was formed to organize this support.

Grenfell wrote to Treves in England, explaining that "there is always a risk of mishaps in transatlantic passages," and he would wish the Mission to know what the Newfoundlanders were prepared to do. He had been told that the Government would erect two hospitals, at places and on sites chosen by the Mission, furnish them according to plans submitted by the Mission Hospital Committee, and make a grant for their maintenance. A merchant, Mr Baine Grieve, had offered a large house on one of the islands as a hospital. Others had promised 50 to 100 dollars apiece and a second house with service and board for a doctor at Smoky Run, at the mouth of Hamilton Inlet.

From their experience during this first voyage both Grenfell and Captain Trezisse realized that, excellent ship though she was, the *Albert* was not suitable for work on this coast. Her deep draught stopped her reaching many of the fishing settlements, and she was limited as a purely sailing-vessel. She had almost been lost when one of the fierce gales that spring up unexpectedly in those waters caused her anchor to drag and she was pounded badly against the rocks. Grenfell wanted a steamer, a vessel not relying on the changeable and often dangerous wind. He asked the Mission Council to find him such a vessel. He asked for nurses for the new hospitals, for women patients would be admitted. Two doctors would be needed for the hospitals. Grenfell would be cruising in whichever vessel was there. Already his plans were ambitious, his mind soaring to a vision of this coast being served for the healing of its people's bodies, the salvation of their souls.

With this letter dispatched, Grenfell continued to publicize the great need of the Labrador fishermen among the people of St John's. He preached at several churches, accepting invitations from every denomination, and at each service the churches were crowded. His sermons and talks were praised for their simplicity and sincerity, and the young man was admired for his friendliness. Wherever he went the fishermen and their families gathered round to tell him of their gratitude and to shake his hand. The *Albert* was visited daily by people who came to admire her seamanlike condition, her neat little hospital, and the ship herself. She sailed for England on November 8, to the farewells and God-speed's of a crowd gathered on the wharf, Grenfell standing on her after-deck to wave and call a promise that he would return.

7

Impudent Voyage

THE *Albert* had a comfortable and fast run home, making the crossing in twelve and a half days, against the eighteen days taken on the outward passage. She was delayed only once, when Grenfell dived overboard in mid-Atlantic to recover the last ball he possessed, which had gone over the side in a game of cricket he was playing with the crew. What Captain Trezisse thought, or said to his ship's doctor, is not recorded, but pranks like this would infuriate any shipmaster, especially when his ship is bowling along sweetly. Some sympathy can be spared for Trezisse. A story is still told on the Labrador coast of Grenfell's asking the shipmaster to stop at what seemed a likely place for duck, and when Trezisse refused to delay the ship for this reason Grenfell, from the deck, shot and brought down a bird, then leapt overboard to recover it. The *Albert* had to be hove to while the venturesome doctor swam back and climbed on board, the duck triumphantly in his grasp. This sort of humour and high spirits is seldom appreciated at sea, and there must have been times when Captain Trezisse did not share the fishermen's admiration for Grenfell.

On arrival at Yarmouth, where the crew of the *Albert* were welcomed home as heroes, Grenfell went to London to make his report to the Mission Council. He was thanked and congratulated for what he had achieved, then informed that his duties as Superintendent would be not quite the same as they had been. For some time, before Grenfell left for Labrador, the Council had been getting increasingly worried by their energetic and enterprising young Superintendent's long and frequent absences from Gorleston. If he had an idea—and he had these suddenly and often—and this involved going somewhere, he took himself off, carried out the idea, and then informed the Council. They could never be sure where he was or what he was up to, and there had been complaints that the work at Gorleston had been neglected by his absences. While Grenfell was in Labrador a deputation investigated this complaint. The Mission now owned and ran eleven ships, besides a great deal of property in stores and workshops and a Mission Room, and its activities had extended to the south and west coasts and to Ireland. Whoever superintended all this had to be where he could be found and must work to some sort of rules.

At a Council meeting in August that year new conditions were laid down for Grenfell. He was to remain as Superintendent, but to be in London. A local superintendent was appointed to look after the shore activities at Gorleston, with the ship's husband to supervise the maintenance of the ships. Grenfell's chief duties were to be

> the superintendence of the Medical, Mission, and fishing work at sea. He would report to the Secretary for the information of the Council on all matters relating to the general efficiency of the fleet at sea, appointments of skippers, etc., but he would make no appointments or changes without the direct authority of the Council, nor would he interfere with the ship's husband.

This was a clipping of Grenfell's too easily spread wings and autocratic methods. He probably did not mind being relieved of the administrative work, and it is equally probable that this work went on more smoothly without him. Grenfell's gifts were not suited to routine work at a desk and the checking of lists of ships' stores.

The Council's plan, to keep Grenfell under their eye in

London, was not very effective. Just before Christmas he and Treves took a new Mission ship to sea for her trials, and during January and February Grenfell was on board other vessels working in the North Sea. He had returned to England full of new ideas, and was urging skippers of trawlers to use oil to quieten the sea while ferrying their fish to the carriers, and had started classes in First Aid for trawlers' crews, teaching them to "caulk a leaking body and scarf a leg," as he put it. He found time to write a long report on Labrador fishing for a learned society, and he was addressing meetings for the Mission. His new office saw little of him, though he was in London to spend Christmas with his mother, a proud little lady who was now convinced that her second son was destined to do great work for the Lord, and whose pride in him was immense.

In February 1893 the Mission to Deep Sea Fishermen decided to continue and to extend the work for the Labrador fishermen. The Council had received a letter from the Committee set up in St John's under the chairmanship of the Governor, Sir Terence O'Brien, asking that the *Albert* be sent out again and that two hospitals given by Newfoundland merchants be maintained by the Mission. At first the Council were uncertain how to reply. The *Albert*'s first voyage had cost over £2000, and some of the Council members thought that extending the Mission's work to Labrador would restrict their activities in British waters. Grenfell argued strongly for the continuance of the overseas work, and he and Treves prepared an estimate of the cost of this work. The Council decided to take the risk and to make a special appeal for funds for the new venture. Grenfell and Captain Trezisse set out to conduct meetings all over England.

Grenfell had a wonderful story to tell now, and he made the most of it. His manner and appearance on a platform, speaking without gestures, his not impressive figure dressed in well-worn tweeds, his clear skin and calm, grey-blue eyes, a very picture of the best type of young Englishman, accentuated the drama he spoke of, the horrors he described, the exploitation of a people by the 'truck' system, the hazards and harshness of life on the Labrador coast. He was not falsifying the picture when he chose to describe the worst he had seen. To Grenfell it was for the sickly and the poorest that the money he wanted was to be spent. If at times his pictures were larger than life, that was how he saw and how he felt. His talks made a great impression and drew large audiences, and his tour was something of a triumph. He introduced a special plea for equipment for the two hospitals, and sympathetic people formed local committees to maintain beds named after their towns.

His other special plea, for money to buy a steam-launch, was less successful. He wanted such a vessel desperately, and tried hard to find the money to buy her, but the Mission Council could not see their way to give such a large sum. It seemed as though the work on the Labrador coast would be restricted to what could be done with the *Albert* and the two new hospitals. One of these hospitals was to be at Battle Harbour, an island just north of Belle Isle Strait, and the other at Indian Harbour, an island off the entrance to Hamilton Inlet and 200 miles north of Battle Harbour. Treves found a doctor, Eliot Curwen, M.B., B.A., and two nursing sisters, Miss Cecilia Williams, whom Treves described as "possessing no nervous system," and Miss Ada Carwardine, who was to have the distinction of starting a long record of marriages between doctors and nurses of the Grenfell Mission. Grenfell found the second doctor needed for the hospitals. He never looked far for helpers, and did not hesitate to tell his friends where their Christian duty lay. He enlisted his old friend of the East End boys' club, Dr A. O. Bobardt, of Melbourne, Australia, and King's College Hospital, London.

The first half of that year, 1893, was a busy time for Wilfred Grenfell. He was addressing meetings almost every night for weeks on end. The *Albert* had returned to her work in the North Sea, but was now withdrawn and sent to Gorleston for a refit and for loading. Grenfell gathered in many tons of medical stores, clothing, and books from sympathizers, and kept on pleading for a steam-launch. All these activities kept him away from his duties in London, and he wrote to tell the Council that he was too busy to attend to the practical work of the Mission. The Council, feeling themselves being carried out of their depths by this whirlwind of a servant, and finding themselves involved in expenses they had not approved, laid out yet another set of rules for their Superintendent, forbidding him, among other instructions, to pledge the Mission's credit without their permission. Grenfell had little money sense, and was liable to order a thing to be done and the bill to be sent to the Mission. When anyone expostulated he dismissed their protests with an assurance that this was Christ's work, and Christ would see that the money came in. He spoke as though Christ had assured him of this personally, and his complete faith disarmed his greatest critics. There could be no arguing with a man who referred you to the Deity.

Still, he had not got his launch, and time was getting short. The *Albert* was stored and ready for sailing, Captain Trezisse again in command. She sailed from Gorleston early in May, to make a tour of seaports along the south coast of England to publicize her work and gather funds. She was towed out of the river Yare, the fishermen's brass band playing on her deck, her sister ships dressed in flags, signal guns being fired, and crowds on shore watching and cheering. Once clear, the band and visitors climbed on board the tug, and the *Albert* was off again. Grenfell and his two doctor friends were on board. The nurses were to cross to St John's on board an Allen Line steamer.

The ship called at some half-dozen ports along the South Coast, the doctors holding tea-parties on board and attracting a great deal of attention and admiration. Grenfell had to leave the ship, to attend the Mission's Annual Meeting at Exeter Hall, London, where he spoke enthusiastically of the work to be done in Labrador and, once again, pleaded for a steam-launch. He returned on board the *Albert* at Exeter, to sail with her round Land's End and to Swansea. There sympathizers purchased a small boat for the ship, and a message came from London, telling Grenfell that the money needed for a launch had been donated. He had already located a craft, a 45-foot steam-launch lying at Chester. He left the *Albert* and went north, to buy the launch for £250 and to write jubilantly to the Council, saying that the craft had cost £600 to build and had done little service. He used his rapidly developing powers of persuasion again, and the Allen Steamship Line agreed to carry the new boat to St John's for £50 instead of the usual charge of £120. The launch was named *Cloyd*, but Grenfell suggested new names for her: *Herald of Mercy*, *Princess May*, *Lady O'Brien*, or *Rescue*. The Council decided on *Princess May*, and wrote to Her Royal Highness, later Queen Mary, wife of King George V, asking for permission to name the launch after her. This favour was granted, Her Royal Highness expressing great interest in the Mission's work.

The *Albert* ended her coastal cruise at Bristol, and sailed from there, giving Grenfell the opportunity of pointing out that she would be leaving from the same port that Cabot sailed from on the voyage when he discovered Newfoundland. Grenfell himself was not on board the *Albert* when she left Bristol. He was at Liverpool, arranging for the launch to be shipped. He crossed to Ireland and rejoined the Mission ship at Queenstown. She left there early in June, clearing Fastnet on the 7th of that month. On the third day out she encountered a gale and had to heave to, but the wind came fair, and she logged an excellent nine knots. Her passengers occupied themselves with games and religious services when they were not working. Bobardt, an accomplished musician, organized a ship's band with instruments on board, while Grenfell read medical books three hours a day and practised his navigation. He learned something new, for Captain Trezisse followed a Great Circle course that made the distance shorter than on her previous voyage. This Great Circle course also took the *Albert* farther north than before and among a large number of icebergs. Fog came, to make the icebergs a menace, and Trezisse had to heave to for forty-eight hours. Despite some fast sailing it was not until June 26 that the *Albert* entered St John's Harbour.

A tremendous welcome awaited the voyagers. During the winter the Mission's work on the Labrador coast had been a favourite topic of conversation in the Colony, and already the fishermen looked on Grenfell as their special protector and champion. Letters had come from the few missionaries on the coast, praising the Englishman, and newspapers, Canadian and Newfoundland, had described the first voyage as an "Angel's Visit." The *Albert*'s return was hailed as the "Silver Lining of the Year," and the Mission's willingness to extend the medical service earned the people's gratitude. As a colony of Great Britain Newfoundland had been neglected shamefully, and now it seemed that the people of the mother country remembered their fellow-Britons after all. This smiling young doctor whom the fishermen praised to the skies brought a new hope for those who had believed themselves forgotten. When the *Albert* was towed through the narrows and berthed alongside the people of St John's gathered at the jetty and welcomed the crew as old friends. Dr Harvey was there to greet Grenfell; the Governor sent to invite him to stay at Government House. Invitations to conduct services came from every church; the Committee set up to help the Mission work in the North announced that it had collected 1500 dollars and that the two hospitals were being prepared. The house at Battle Harbour was ready for its installations, and a prefabricated building was already on its way north to Indian Harbour by the mail-steamer.

The Allen Line steamer carrying the new launch and the two nurses arrived, and the nurses were considered much more approvingly than the launch. They were the first fully qualified nurses to visit St John's, and the townspeople asked Grenfell to let them stay in the town. The launch was looked on less favourably by those boat-wise Newfoundlanders. They could see little to admire in this craft. She had been built for river work, and seemed a frail thing to venture among the ice and face the gales of a coast such as the Labrador. She was 45 feet long, but her beam was only 8 feet, and she would roll like a log. Her deck was within 2 feet of the water, most of it occupied by a long cabin-top, with a slender mast forward and a small enclosed shelter for the wheelsman. She could carry a small sail, but would rely almost entirely on a tiny 9-horse-power steam-engine. Below decks there was little space. Grenfell's cabin, which would also be hospital and passenger accommodation, was 8 feet by 4 feet, his bed the hard cushions of a side-bench. Altogether the *Princess May* was no sort of craft for the open Atlantic and one of the most dangerous coasts in the world. When Grenfell announced that he intended to steam her to Labrador, with himself as captain, an engineer, and a crew of one, taking Bobardt as a companion, experienced seamen in the port tried to dissuade him. This toy of a boat would never make such a voyage.

The launch had lost her funnel while being shipped, and her propeller shaft was bent. These defects were made good at St John's, and on July 6 the launch was christened. The town made this an occasion to show their admiration for Grenfell. The wharves danced with coloured flags, ships in the harbour dressed overall, as a large crowd gathered to watch Lady

O'Brien break a bottle of water over the stem and to hear the Governor make a speech praising Grenfell and thanking the Mission to Deep Sea Fishermen for sending him. The *Albert* had waited for this ceremony, but now, on the same day, she sailed, carrying the two nurses and Dr Curwen. The next morning, at five o'clock, Grenfell steered the *Princess May* out of the harbour for the voyage north.

The voyage of the *Princess May* that year can be reckoned something of an epic of the sea, or an epic of sheer impertinence. Grenfell was not an experienced seaman. He had sailed small yachts in well-marked and well-charted waters during the summer months, and he had helped fishermen to manage their vessels; but this was no qualification for taking a small and far from able river launch hundreds of miles along a coast he did not know, a coast inadequately charted, and with no navigational aids. Grenfell had not even bothered to check his compass or to give his engines a proper trial before sailing. The *Princess May* was hardly clear of the land before the engine began to give trouble, and the engineer had to adjust and repair with the launch rolling heavily to the Atlantic swell. A course was set, and when a large cliff appeared ahead Grenfell discovered that his compass had an error of two whole points. At first he blamed this on the compass binnacle being screwed down with iron nails, but even when these were removed the error was still there. The compass was then taken well forward of the steering position, and it seems, from Grenfell's own story of this voyage, that he had little idea of how to work out his compass error and allow for this when laying his courses. On one leg of the journey along the Newfoundland coast Bobardt, with no sea experience, was at the wheel all day, and steered a course that was two points away from what it should have been. Only a meeting with a fishing-boat told the voyagers where they were. It seems to have been an entirely unseamanlike and happy-go-lucky adventure, and it is not surprising that when the *Princess May* met bad weather, to roll heavily and take water on board, gear left lying unsecured on deck went overboard.

But Grenfell was happy. At last he was Captain of his own ship and with no sober-faced Trezisse to check his actions. He worked the *Princess May* northward, taking risks that would have made a professional sailor die of fright. He threaded the launch between islands and a fearful collection of submerged rocks, trusting to his own quick reactions and his sure belief that God had work for this vessel and her crew and would see that they reached their goal. He went through fog and pushed against strong winds and heavy seas, sheltering where he could every night and treating the sick who came when they heard that the famous Dr Grenfell was in their harbour. Attempting to cross Belle Isle Strait in bad weather, the launch was driven back to the shelter of the land, but Grenfell waited in the lee of a stranded iceberg until the wind eased and then crossed. Ice in bergs and scattered pans was encountered when the Labrador coast was reached, and had to be avoided, but late one evening Grenfell steered the *Princess May* into the narrow tickle between two islands that is Battle Harbour and made fast alongside the *Albert*. What Captain Trezisse thought when Grenfell described his passage-making is not known, but he must have decided that God kept a long deck-watch when this young man was afloat.

The day following his arrival Grenfell inspected the hospital, the first hospital on the Labrador coast. It was a two-storey wooden building built close against the rocky face of a small cliff, overlooking the tickle and the traders' warehouses. The crew of the *Albert* were already carrying up beds and equipment, and the two nurses and Dr Curwen were arranging the wards. Grenfell left Bobardt at Battle Harbour to help there and to take over the hospital, and sailed for Belle Isle Strait and a tour of the southern coast of Labrador. His crew had been, until now, the engineer and the steward for this new hospital. He left the steward on shore and went out with only his engineer. He was to continue this foolhardy practice on much of his long cruise that summer, though he used what passengers he carried, a Roman Catholic Bishop and a Methodist preacher among them, as deck-hands and stokers. Grenfell followed the south coast of Labrador as far as the boundary with Canadian territory, then returned to Battle Harbour. He did not stay long, for he meant to see much of this coast now that he had the launch. He went north, winding among the islands and along the mainland. He could take the power-driven craft where a sailing-vessel would have been managed with difficulty, and he explored every place that attracted his eye or challenged his curiosity. He put the *Princess May* on shoals and rocks several times, but the Lord was with him indeed, and he got her afloat again each time.

He had a wonderful voyage. With no sailor's disapproving eye to check him, he did what fancy or inclination urged. He drove the launch into bays and inlets, where he found a Labrador entirely different from the harsh and bare coast. He followed deep-walled inlets to where noble rivers poured and the hills were covered thickly in spruce- and larch-trees, where salmon came eagerly to the fly he cast and his gun brought down duck, grouse, partridge, and other game. He learned quickly to endure the attacks of hordes of stinging black flies and mosquitoes, accepting this torment and revelling in the excellent sport the country provided, the discovery of flowers and plants that made the place a naturalist's treasure-house. This, indeed, was no barren land, and Grenfell was thrilled and delighted.

He visited the harbour of Cartwright, in Sandwich Bay, where the only real attempt to settle this country had ever been made. At the end of the eighteenth century a colourful Englishman, Major Cartwright, had discovered the bay that he named after a noble kinsman, Lord Sandwich, and the beautiful and sheltered, almost entirely enclosed haven he named after himself. He brought 400 Devon and Cornish people from England, to catch fish and trap for fur that he shipped to England. Cartwright's settlement lasted for sixteen years, its master living in state and asserting royal authority over his people. During Britain's war with the United States in the first years of the nineteenth century his ships were captured by American privateers, and though Cartwright was later recompensed for this loss, he returned to England with most of his settlers. The settlement, when Grenfell visited it, was now only a few huts and a Hudson's Bay Company post, but he was delighted to hear the story of this other Englishman who had seen what he was seeing and who had proved that this country could support its people. Cartwright had been far from Grenfell in godliness, but he was a man after the missionary's own heart in many other ways.

Grenfell went from Cartwright to Indian Harbour, feeling

and finding a way among the dangerous and uncharted reefs and shoals in Sandwich Bay, winding outward by channels where no other vessel had ever sailed. For a man who had so little experience in navigation it was a remarkable performance. He reached Indian Harbour, to find the new hospital erected close to the shore and under a high, sheer-sided, rocky bluff that, viewed from the right angle, showed what looked like an Indian profile. This was a favourite gathering-place for the schooners going north, and dozens of the graceful vessels were anchored round the *Albert* when Grenfell steamed in with the *Princess May*. He found Dr Curwen and Sister Williams hard at work, treating the men who came from the schooners and trying to get the hospital ready for service. It was clear that this last would not be accomplished before the summer ended, so Grenfell arranged for Nurse Williams to go south to Battle Harbour, where her help was badly needed, and for Curwen to go on board the *Albert* and do what he could farther north.

Grenfell himself headed for Rigolet, at the entrance to Hamilton Inlet, the inlet extending a hundred miles inland and ending in magnificent rivers and waterfalls. Grenfell could explore only a little way into this noble waterway, but he promised himself a longer stay another year. But even at Rigolet the growth was rich enough, the country covered with spruce and larch, the climate so mild that Grenfell could picnic on the grass and gather flowers with the Hudson's Bay post manager's two small daughters. From here northward the inhabitants were almost all pure Eskimo. Grenfell treated some of these cheerful if unsanitary people, then continued his voyage north to Hopedale, where he was to meet up with the *Albert* again.

The coast north of Hamilton Inlet was then little known, except to the fishermen, who sailed their schooners almost to Hudson Bay. What charts Grenfell carried were unreliable and incomplete, and there was danger every mile in the hundreds of islands and rocks extending out from the coast. At one place the *Princess May* got entangled with a series of reefs, and, with the sun's going down, strong winds came from the north, to make her situation precarious. The rising seas broke and exploded over the reefs and unseen dangers, and the little steam-launch rolled and plunged with a movement that

tested even Grenfell's muscular body. He used the breaking
seas and water boiling over the rocks as warnings of danger
and managed to reach the lee of an island. Even there the craft
was not safe, and it would have meant keeping the launch
dodging into the seas all night if Eskimos had not appeared
and come out in their skin boats to help Grenfell and his
solitary companion to work the *Princess May* inside a narrow
gut between the rocks where she could lie in safety. Grenfell
had visited this island in the previous year, and he was recognized and welcomed and taken to a tent where the sick were
brought to him. He amputated a man's frostbitten toe and
treated others, then held a service in the tent. The Eskimos,
converted by the Moravians, listened as best they could to the
white man's language, but enjoyed the hymns more. They
loved music, and the Moravians had taught many of their race
to play instruments.

The *Albert* was at Hopedale when the *Princess May* steamed
into the haven, Curwen already busy with the sick and the
hurt from over a hundred fishing-schooners at anchor there.
Grenfell could exchange his hard bench cushion for a bunk.
He visited the schooners and the Moravian missionaries, and
held services on shore. With so many fishermen in the harbour,
all wanting to hear and to meet the young English doctor, the
biggest room in the settlement was crammed, and Captain
Trezisse had to hold an overflow service. Grenfell was at his best
with such an audience as these weathered, roughly clad fishermen. As with the fishermen of the North Sea, he spoke their
language, his own naïvety matched their simplicity, and, if he
was not their equal in seaman's skill, he had that quality, the
utter lack of all pretence and the humility, that the sea gives
to men. His sincerity was in every word he spoke; his complete
belief and trust in God was an aura he moved in. His jokes were
an intimacy giving brotherliness. He could cry with them with
a frank emotionalism as easily and naturally as he laughed with
them. To these often hard men he seemed a very saint. He gave
them something they had not had in their toiling lives, a full-
ness in his friendship, a growth as men in his open admiration.

They worried over his daring. When he said he was going
farther north they warned him of the dangers along the coast
and instructed him on how to go. A Moravian, a Dane, joined

him as pilot, and he steamed the *Princess May* out of Hopedale and northward again, the second steam-driven vessel ever to go so far north. They went as far north as Okkak, 160 miles from Hopedale, with Grenfell mounted on a ladder he had borrowed and lashed to the launch's mast, conning the launch among the rocks and reefs of this dangerous and entirely uncharted coast. Time after time disaster was avoided only by Grenfell's keen eye and quick reflexes. He steered into channels, only to find that they ended in solid cliff, and had to turn the launch and seek another way. But he was thrilled by what he saw. Here the coast and cliffs rose thousands of feet sheer from the sea, and the land beyond lifted in giant peaks. Magnificent fjords cut deeply inland, and Grenfell would have dearly liked to explore each one. He promised himself that one day he would, but now he must restrain himself. It was already late September, and the sea was taking on that oily appearance that is a warning of its freezing. Reluctantly—for this land attracted him tremendously—Grenfell turned south and made for Hopedale. He had seen wonderful things, to call him back for their own sake as well as for the work to be done for the people of this land.

The launch reached Hopedale, to find the *Albert* still there and Trezisse heading an inquiry into a tragedy that showed how close to savagery these christianized Eskimos still were. Four women had been found dead in a hut on one of the islands, and Curwen had diagnosed death from hemlock poisoning. Two men were arrested, and would be taken south for trial. This grim task completed, the *Albert* sailed. Most of the schooners were already on their way south, and winter was being announced in the snow spreading over the hills and ice growing to the rocks inshore. Grenfell followed, taking a route among the islands and visiting the Liveyeres, now hauling up their boats and preparing their traps for the winter. As he moved from miserable home to miserable home Grenfell compiled a census and wrote a report of what he found—the food families had to see them through the next eight months, their physical condition, and their needs. It made a grim document, for few had more than the bare necessities, and many did not possess even these. And no help could come to the sick or destitute throughout the frozen winter. They might die in their miserable huts, and the bodies would have to lie unburied until the ground softened in the summer. The Indians moved south now, and the Eskimos had learned how to maintain themselves on the ice, but these Liveyeres, with some exceptions, seemed to have lost all their resolution. They took what they were given and somehow kept alive. Grenfell gave what clothing he had on board the launch and resolved that one day the Mission should have doctors on the coast in winter as well as in summer.

He met the *Albert* at Indian Harbour, where the hospital building had been erected but not equipped. The stores were put into the buildings, and a Liveyere promised to keep an eye on them during the winter. The two vessels moved south, to meet again at Battle Harbour. Here great work had been done by Dr Bobardt and the nurses. The hospital had been full all summer, patients even having to be bedded in near-by huts. Some of the worst cases had been sent to St John's by the mail-steamer; the others must now be returned to their homes while the sea was still open.

The hospital was closed, and Curwen, Bobardt, and the nurses went on board the *Albert*. Grenfell with one helper remained with the launch, sailing three hours before the hospital ship left, and making a short run to Forteau Bay, at the entrance to Belle Isle Strait. The *Princess May* lay there while a gale raged in the Strait, and when the weather eased, though it still blew hard, Grenfell steamed the twenty-five miles to the Newfoundland shore. He had arranged to meet the *Albert* in St Anthony Harbour, a magnificent, hill-surrounded, and almost completely enclosed haven twenty miles south of Cape Bauld. The *Princess May* had to fight into a hard wind and heavy seas to reach this place, and when she arrived the *Albert* was not there. She had met the gale Grenfell had evaded by anchoring in Forteau Bay, and Captain Trezisse had decided that Grenfell could not have crossed the Strait in such weather. While entering a harbour near Hopedale the *Albert* had run aground and been badly pounded on the rocks. She was hauled clear by a Captain Moses Bartlett, father of the famous Arctic seaman Bob Bartlett, and sixty of his men, but her keel was damaged. Now, in the gale she fought in Belle Isle Strait, the hospital ship lost her jib-boom and some of her sails, and Trezisse decided that the sooner she was in dockyard hands the better. He kept her clear of the land and reached St John's.

Grenfell waited several days for the *Albert* to arrive, for she carried his supply of coal for the launch's boiler. When she did not appear he piled the launch's deck with billets of wood, and a schooner captain augmented this with several sacks of coal slack. Grenfell continued his voyage south, holding close inshore, encountering more bad weather. While he was making across White Bay against a heavy sea, and with the launch rolling and pitching violently, his compass was flung out of its box and went overboard. Grenfell had to steer by what land he saw and recognized from his northward journey. He entered the harbour at Toulinguet, on the southern side of Notre Dame Bay, to find the mail-steamer there and her captain carrying written authority from the Governor to search for the *Princess May*. She had been reported lost, and it was believed she had foundered in the gale that damaged the *Albert*. Fortunately, Grenfell was able to send a telegram from Toulinguet, announcing that he was safe, but it came too late to prevent the news of his being missing reaching England. He was already sufficiently well known for the London newspapers to publish this, and there was much sorrow that such a man had been lost. One person did not believe he was. Henry Richards, Grenfell's helper with the boys' camps, carried the message to Mrs Grenfell and asked if he could do anything. "Do anything?" she said. "What do you mean?" "Is there anything I can do to help?" the young man explained. "I need no help," she told him. "I have help in my God. Wilfred has not gone."

By then her son was moving towards St John's and over a smoother sea, his crew of one augmented by a Salvation Army Captain who helped to pay for his passage by playing his violin to Grenfell as the launch went ahead. To show that he was very much alive—and despite the *Princess May*'s now badly leaking boiler tubes and a propeller shaft bent during one of her several groundings—Grenfell called for a full head of steam and raced three steamers through the narrows, leading the steamers triumphantly into the harbour and ending what is probably one of the most impudent voyages ever made. Grenfell had steamed and steered this frail ex-river craft over 3000 miles, along one of the most hazardous coasts in the world, a coast with no lights

to help the mariner and poorly surveyed where it had been surveyed at all. With comparatively little experience he had found
his way into dozens of lonely settlements and explored channels
where only a few fishermen, if anyone, had penetrated before.
His craft had been dented and damaged repeatedly, his engine
tested far beyond what it was made for. Wilfred Grenfell was
proud of being able to call himself a Master Mariner. He must
have known himself fully one when he made the *Princess May*
fast alongside the *Albert* in St John's Harbour.

8

Trials and Triumphs

GRENFELL did not return to England with the *Albert* that year. He saw her off, Dr Curwen and the two nurses on board, then he and Bobardt, after a stay of a week or so in St John's, sailed on board a passenger steamer for Halifax, Nova Scotia. The Mission Council in London learned of this only when Grenfell wrote, saying that he had been advised to visit Canada, and proposed to do so at his own expense. He hoped to interest Canadians in the Mission work, and he intended to petition the Canadian Government for a grant of 5000 dollars to build a third hospital on that part of the southern Labrador coast at the inner end of Belle Isle Strait that was Canadian territory. He had been told by Sir Terence O'Brien that the people on this 'French shore' were now convinced of Grenfell's 'goodness,' and would gladly pay for the maintenance of a hospital if one were put on their coast.

Before he left St John's Grenfell made a report of the

summer's work to the committee of townsmen who were supporting him. He was able to quote some impressive figures: 2493 out-patients had been treated by the three doctors, and 37 cases, including 28 major operations, had been received at Battle Harbour and on board the *Albert*. Seventeen of these major operations had been performed under chloroform, 11 without chloroform, and there had been 269 minor operations carried out. Many of these operations had been performed on board schooners and in the settlers' huts on kitchen tables and with friends holding the patient down while the doctors worked. A large quantity of clothing, books, and magazines had been distributed. Services had been held everywhere the ships had called, and regularly at Battle Harbour.

Having described some of these cases and the desperate condition of many of the people along the coast, quoting one case of a man refusing charity and killing his three children before committing suicide, rather than face a winter of starvation, Grenfell spoke "emphatically" of what should be done. He called for a survey of the coast, saying, "It is a national disgrace that while all our ships can be gathered for a sham fight, not even a gunboat or launch can be sent down here for surveying." Vessels were being lost every year because the coast was uncharted. He asked for whatever laws there were for inspecting schooners and carrying passengers to be applied. A schooner, the *Rose*, had gone north this very year with 62 souls on board, men, women, and children. While moving through dense fog the vessel struck a large pan of ice, and her bows were crushed. She filled and sank in eight minutes. A few men managed to get on to the ice with ropes, and tried to hold the schooner alongside, but because of the panic these ropes were not secured on board, and the *Rose* drifted away from the pan. Boats were thrown into the water, but few people reached them before the schooner sank. Men, women, and children were struggling in the freezing water to keep afloat among the wreckage. After a hard fight by men who managed to reach two of the boats 50 people survived, many, who had been asleep in the hold when the vessel struck, almost naked. Twelve people were drowned— 8 men, 2 boys, and 2 young women. The survivors would surely have died also if another schooner had not arrived on the scene. The law, Grenfell declared, should forbid schooners to carry so many passengers, and proper accommodation should be provided for those they did carry. The vessels themselves should be more strictly surveyed, for many that went north were old and far from seaworthy. Grenfell was particularly critical of girls being employed on board schooners. They were carried as cooks and to help with cleaning fish, and, unless they were sailing with relatives, were in moral danger. One girl was to tell Grenfell that "If the crew are decent men we are all right, but if they aren't there is nothing we can do about it." Already Grenfell had encountered tragic cases of ruined girls, and had been told that once a girl went on board a schooner her good name was gone.

Grenfell attacked his old enemy strong drink and those who sold it. Labrador was legally dry, but some of the traders, relying on the complete absence of law officers, sold the stuff. Liveyeres set up stills, and the Eskimos made some vile concoctions for themselves that schoonermen bought. Grenfell had already declared war on this trade, and now he asked that law officers be sent to the coast during the fishing season. One magistrate was stationed at Cartwright, but he was known to be a drunkard and of little value.

The first signs of the opposition Grenfell was to endure were already appearing, and Grenfell recognized its presence. He wrote to his mother from St John's, sending her a copy of his report and telling her:

> They received it very well, and offered more than I had asked. Only touched on medical work, and if I had said a word about religion the whole pack would have been at one another's throats in a twinkling. The truth is that there exists a bitter struggle between Church and Methodism . . . the Church is dead . . . appears to have no life, no soul, and mad to be seeking the bread that perishes. Methodism is alive, earnest, spiritual—seeking the conversion of the souls of the people and putting up with any sacrifice for it. Making inroads into the Church and Catholicism. The Bishop dare not say anything against us, but he is not with us, and told a great friend of mine here that our preaching the Gospel and people being converted was pulling down the work of the Church.

When he presented his petition to the Canadian Government Grenfell was to find that this opposition could be active and effective. The proposal to place a hospital on the French shore was opposed by the Roman Catholic Bishop, who disliked non-sectarian, Protestant evangelists working among a people mainly of French extraction and Roman Catholics, and by the doctor who travelled on the mail-steamer, Commander Wakefield, who accused Grenfell of "pauperizing" the fishermen and Liveyeres.

This opposition was not yet in the open, and Grenfell still had the support of the merchants and the Newfoundland Government.

On December 1 that year Grenfell and Bobardt set out for Halifax. On arrival they presented their credentials to the Prime Minister of Nova Scotia, the Hon. William Fielding. He heard their story sympathetically and introduced them to many influential people. The two young men canvassed the churches, and a first meeting was arranged at the Orpheus Hall on December 8, with the Commander of the North American forces, General Sir Alexander Montgomery-Moore, in the chair, and an Anglican Bishop and the Prime Minister on the platform.

Grenfell's disclosures of the plight of the Labrador fishermen made a deep impression on those who heard him. The meeting was not very well attended, and Grenfell was unexpectedly nervous. He stammered badly when he started speaking, but as he went on he lost his nervousness and spoke in what the newspapers reported as "a conversational way, so that he was immediately liked and impressed people." The scantiness of his audience was made up for by the newspapers' reports the next day. The *Halifax Herald* said that "no more interesting public meeting has taken place in Halifax for many a long day," and covered the meeting with many columns of Grenfell's speech. A letter published in the *Acadian Recorder* supplemented this paper's long report:

> Listening to the deeply touching address by Dr Grenfell at Orpheus Hall last night, I could not help wishing that thousands, instead of the small audience present, could have had their hearts stirred by the simple story of the noble and sorely needed work among deep-sea fishermen of Labrador.

Other meetings followed, and churches and societies offered their help. A committee was formed, the first American mainland body, "to assist the work of Dr Grenfell." It was a personal triumph for Grenfell. He wrote happily to his mother, sending her some furs he had bought in Labrador, to tell her of this success in Canada. He was going on to Montreal, and hoped to interest Sir Donald Smith, once a Hudson's Bay post manager at Hamilton Inlet and now a very wealthy man, the future Lord Strathcona, and the last Resident Governor of the Hudson's Bay Company in Canada. Smith had just given a million dollars to Montreal Hospital, and Grenfell hoped to share in such generosity. He told his mother that he liked the Canadians' matter-of-fact directness and the way he could walk into the office of any official or businessman and say, "I am Doctor Grenfell; I want you to work up a meeting for me," and the reply would be, " I will" or "I won't." To a man as direct as Grenfell this was the correct way to reply.

The young Englishman's name was already known in Montreal when he reached there, and he found people interested in his mission. He met Sir Donald Smith, and the two men talked long and happily about the Labrador. Smith's wife was an Indian from Hamilton Inlet, and he was sincerely concerned about the people on the coast. He presided at a meeting in Montreal where Grenfell told his story. Other influential people came in, among them Sir William Dawson, founder of McGill University. The churches offered their aid. Again a committee was formed "to assist the work of Dr Grenfell," and 1300 dollars were collected and another 1000 promised annually. Sir Donald Smith provided the two young men with first-class tickets on the Canadian Pacific Railways, and they set out to cross the continent and continue their campaign as far as Vancouver Island, on the West Coast. They were welcomed everywhere, Grenfell continuing to impress with his friendliness, his direct way of speaking, and his sincerity. He interrupted his journey to stop off at a small town called after a relative, Pascoe Grenfell, one of the many Grenfells who have left their names on the world's maps.

His tour a success, Grenfell wanted to achieve another ambition; he wanted to sail with the sealing fleet out of Newfoundland in the spring. Every year dozens of sealing-vessels sailed from St John's, bound for Belle Isle Strait to gather what was one of Newfoundland's most important harvests, the seals then breeding on the ice. This was the Newfoundlanders' first opportunity in the year to earn money, and men travelled long distances, hundreds of miles across the ice or round the coasts of Conception and Trinity Bays, to secure a berth. They could, if they found seals, earn up to 100 dollars on a month's voyage, and this was an important start to their summer earnings.

Grenfell wanted to share this experience. He wanted to see how the sealers lived and if mission work could be extended to them, and he also wanted the new adventure of hunting seals. He wrote asking the Council to permit him to join the fleet this year, but permission was refused. He was Superintendent of the Mission at home as well as in Newfoundland, and he was needed in England. Disappointed but accepting, he returned to England in late February.

There was much for him to do when he arrived home, and the Mission Council, while grateful for the support he had gathered in Canada, were worried by their Superintendent's long absence and by his somewhat cavalier manner of going off on the Canadian journey without first consulting them. This Labrador business was being taken out of their hands, and they could not fail to note that the Canadian committees were being formed "to assist the work of Dr Grenfell." That it was the National Mission to Deep Sea Fishermen which had sent him to Labrador, and which was carrying the financial burden, seemed to have been forgotten. It was, however, difficult to blame Grenfell. His visit to Canada had been effective. Sir Donald Smith had written to offer 1800 dollars to purchase another steamer, and a suitable vessel had been found in Canada. Another Canadian, Dr Roddicke of Montreal, telegraphed the Council, "Ask Grenfell to procure a suitable handsome boat fitted complete fifty pounds or so," and the committees in Canada were proving their interest and sincerity by collecting medical stores and money. That they were doing this "for Dr Grenfell" soured the gifts a little.

Meantime Grenfell had returned to the North Sea. He found much to put right, for not all the Mission-ship skippers and crews were the ardent Christians they should have been, and Grenfell made out a long report, suggesting changes. He set a high standard, and, though he had all the tolerance in the world for sinners and declared that the "Gospel of pills and poultices knows no creed," he would not tolerate backsliding among those who professed to carry Christ's message to others.

The Mission could chalk up one important victory this year: the copers were gone, except for a few who dared imprisonment. All the countries concerned, with the exception of France, had now ratified the pact against the grog-ships, and their notorious career was at an end. Only France was to "carry the stigma of alone refusing to share this great triumph for good," though France's objection was that it would be British gunboats that would police the North Sea.

Grenfell's work at home, at sea, and in the lecture-hall prevented him sailing with the *Albert* when she left Yarmouth on May 24. She was not going to St John's this year, nor would she work as a hospital ship. Trezisse had reported her as too heavy and deep-drafted for sailing among the islands and on the unmarked Labrador coast, and she was too valuable a ship to lose. She would carry supplies to Indian Harbour and Battle Harbour, and then return to England. She would also carry the two nurses who had visited the Labrador the previous year, and two doctors. Dr Curwen had now gone as a missionary to Peking; and Bobardt had written a pathetic letter to Grenfell, resigning from the Mission and saying that he was hesitating between joining the Navy and studying as a surgeon. But, he wrote, "My conscience is troubling me, and I feel I am betraying my Christianity and not following in the footsteps of my Redeemer, Jesus Christ." Two new doctors were sailing with the *Albert*, Dr Fred Willway, loaned to the Mission by the London Missionary Society, an outstanding personality and a fine seaman, and Dr J. K. Bennetts. Willway and Nurse Williams were to go to Indian Harbour and open the hospital, Bennetts and Nurse Carwardine would go to Battle Harbour.

The *Albert* visited coastal towns again, making her final departure from Swansea. Grenfell went there to see her off. Then, with a missionary with engineering experience, Dr Wakefield, an athletic, forthright man, he travelled to Liverpool to pick up the boat being paid for by the Canadian doctor, Roddicke. Named *Euralia MacKinnon*, she was a 16-feet, half-decked sailing-boat carrying a large dipping lugsail, and was to be used at Battle Harbour. Having seen her loaded on to a steamer, Grenfell and Wakefield sailed from Liverpool on board the s.s. *Monica* on June 12. They arrived at St John's on the 24th, and on the following day, at a meeting of the committee of local people supporting the Mission work, Grenfell learned that the *Princess May* would require a great deal of repair before she could be used again. He had tested her beyond her endurance on the long voyage of the previous year. Her hull was dented, her decks needed caulking, all her boiler tubes would have to be replaced and a new propeller shaft made and fitted. Job Bros, a prominent merchant company, offered the use of their dock free, but even so the repairs would cost 1500 dollars. It was decided to go ahead and get the launch ready this year.

Meantime Grenfell would take a crew to the Gulf of St Lawrence, where the new ship, now to be named *Sir Donald*, after its donor, was being fitted for Mission work. Dr Wakefield would act as engineer, and a pilot, Captain Harvey, would share the command with Grenfell. With a crew of Newfoundlanders Grenfell crossed to Canada, to find that work on the new vessel had been delayed, and he had to wait until late August before setting out. This was a disappointment, for Grenfell had made wonderful plans for the year, now that he would have two new steam-vessels working on the coast, and two hospitals. The new vessel was a great improvement on the *Princess May*, being 75 feet long with a beam of 14 feet. Her hull was teak, and she was entirely enclosed below decks. She was well powered, having an engine of 35 indicated horse-power. Grenfell was delighted with her, and only regretted the delay.

The ice this year had stayed on the coast longer than usual, and the *Sir Donald* was held up as she tried to pass through Belle Isle Strait. She was delayed several times, and though Grenfell could help the people on the south coast, he wanted to get north with his new ship. It was September before the Strait was cleared and the *Sir Donald* headed for Battle Harbour. The sea was still full of ice, and the hills had not rid themselves of the winter's snow. It was with relief that Grenfell sighted the group of rounded summits of the islands containing Battle Harbour. He had his little ship dressed overall with signal flags, and with Captain Harvey he went forward to the bows to con the *Sir Donald* among the rocks and small islands at the western end of the channel between Battle Island and near-by Great Caribou Island. The vessel approached from the north-west, with the bulk of Battle Island hiding her from the settlement and hospital. She reached the point where Grenfell and the pilot believed her to have a clear channel ahead, and Grenfell called for full speed to make a triumphant and impressive entry. The little steamer surged ahead, a wave curving from her stem and her flags whipping to the breeze. The entrance to the tickle was in sight when she struck. The deck lifted under her crew's feet, and there was a terrible grinding amidships. She stopped, to lurch to the swell coming in, and ground ominously. Her engines were put astern, but she remained fast. The crews of two schooners watched the tragedy, but dared not take their vessels into the shallow water to help. Grenfell ordered the boat out, and he and Wakefield rowed ashore for help. They had to scramble up the steep hill, and run across its mossy, pond-dotted summit, then descend by a steep path to the cluster of wooden buildings and wharves that was the settlement. The *Albert* was alongside a wharf, and Grenfell went on board, humiliated and heartbroken, to tell his story. The trader Baine Grieve had steam raised in his launch, and it went out and towed the *Sir Donald* off the reef she had struck and brought her into harbour. A worried and guilt-tormented Grenfell learned that his new ship was badly damaged. Her sternpost had been wrenched to one side, so that her rudder was useless, her propellor shaft had snapped and the propeller was lost. She was making only a little water, but her usefulness was gone. So were his wonderful plans for the year.

It was a tragedy for Grenfell; and now he learned that the *Princess May* would not be ready for work this year. The *Albert* could not stay. Trezisse's orders were to return to England, and he wanted his vessel away from this coast. She had already received more abuse than was good for her. The passage across the Atlantic had lasted twenty-eight days, the ship beaten by storm after storm. When she reached Labrador waters the *Albert* was held off the coast by the exceptionally thick ice of this year, and had had to cruise back and forth, seeking a way through the barrier, for days. Captain Trezisse had not left the deck for almost a week, and had shown himself a magnificent seaman. The nurses had been hard tested, first by the rough time they suffered as the small vessel was tossed and swamped by heavy seas, and then while hemmed in by the ice. Both had been seasick most of the voyage. Sister Williams had needed to "possess no nervous system," for she had been very ill. She had been taken from the stuffy cabin and sat on a chair on deck, the chair lashed to an anchor to prevent it being flung overboard by the ship's violent rolling. She had sat and watched the pans grind and crash against each other, rearing up over their neighbours, to fall and be shattered with a sound like a giant's roar, threatening the ship's safety as they closed against her sides. It had been a fearsome experience for two young women unused to the sea and to such places as this. Now, with the ice still thick off the coast, Trezisse did not want his ship to suffer more. He would tow the *Sir Donald* to St John's and then leave for England.

Grenfell would be without a craft, except for the sailing-boat *Euralia MacKinnon*. She had been dropped at Battle Harbour by the mail-steamer, but Dr Bennetts, inexperienced in sailing, had had to row the boat to visit other islands. Baine Grieve's manager offered to put his launch at the doctor's disposal, and Grenfell waited only until the mail-steamer, *Windsor Lake*, returned north, and then had the sailing-boat slung on board and went north with her. He was determined to do something. He remained on board the mail-steamer as far as Rigolet, seeing Willway when the ship stopped at Indian Harbour and learning that there had been a near-tragedy here also. The hospital building had caught fire, and part of it was damaged. The fire had been extinguished, but it had been a narrow escape.

The Wilsons housed Grenfell at Rigolet for several days, and he treated those who came to him. He picnicked with the trader's children and went hunting with their father, and then sailed the *Euralia MacKinnon* back to Indian Harbour, a distance of fifty miles, landing on islands and sleeping on the ground each night. He called on those Liveyeres working from the islands, learning that the fishing this year was very poor. With the ice staying so long on the coast the fish had not come in, and there were grim faces among the Liveyeres as they contemplated a winter without the food and supplies they should have earned. There would be much hunger along the coast in the next ten months.

Grenfell was heartened to find how well the work at Indian

Harbour had progressed. Willway was showing himself an energetic and enterprising missionary. He had painted the wards himself, and with Nurse Williams had got the hospital working. Already patients were in the beds, and men were coming for treatment from the dozens of schooners that called. Nurse Williams looked tired and ill, and was still feeling the effects of her voyage from England, but she was carrying on nobly. Grenfell and Willway talked over the plight of the Liveyeres, and Willway suggested that he stay on the coast over the winter and do what he could to make up for the failure this year. Grenfell had hoped to be the first doctor to winter on the Labrador, but he knew he could not stay this year. He agreed that Willway should stay, working from Battle Harbour.

Grenfell did not remain long at Indian Harbour. Captain Moses Bartlett arrived with his schooner, *Victor*, and Grenfell had the *Euralia MacKinnon* lifted on board the schooner and sailed with her as far as Gready Islands, 75 miles south of Indian Harbour. From there he sailed, either by himself or with a Liveyere as crew, the remaining miles to Battle, to do what he could in the few weeks remaining of the summer. It was then in the last days of September, and soon the winter would clamp down on land and sea. Grenfell moved southward, treating those who needed his skill, holding services wherever he went, and showing Biblical pictures with a magic lantern he carried. He could carry little in the small boat, but he gave out what clothing he had managed to bring, and he was heartened to find the people grateful even for his coming. He was welcomed at one place by a stout, cheerful woman on whom he had operated the previous year. He had expected to hear she had died, but now she greeted him as her saviour and sat him down to a feast of boiled cod. Her gratitude was some consolation for the disappointments of this year. He could be further heartened when he reached Battle Harbour and found that, despite their handicaps, the three doctors and two nurses working at Indian Harbour and Battle Harbour had achieved an amazing amount. They had, between them, treated 1306 patients, and this year the proportion of serious cases had been higher than in 1893. The work had been far from a failure. Grenfell could return to St John's with this proof of the Mission's usefulness, to ask for money for the repair of the *Sir Donald* and to outline plans for the following year. Willway would stay at Battle Harbour, and when the sea froze over he would set out with dog team and komatik to visit along the coast.

Grenfell reached St John's to learn that disaster had hit the Colony again. The banks had failed. There seems to have been no real need for the Newfoundland banks to suspend payment, but one did, the Commercial Bank, and a run on the other two caused them to close their doors. Banknotes became worthless. Businessmen, not recovered from the losses by fire two years previously, went bankrupt. Destitution was imminent, and there was panic and rioting in the town. A new Government, lately elected, resigned, and the Governor was pleading for help from London. On top of the poor fishing year this new disaster was terrifying. With their own troubles so great, Grenfell could expect little help from the Newfoundlanders. He sailed for England, arriving home in December.

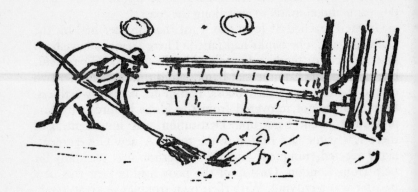

9

The Finding of Pomiuk

GRENFELL's first task when he returned to England was a melancholy one; he had to go to Gorleston to see the damage done by a gale in the North Sea. This had been one of the worst storms ever known in that restless grey sea, and many trawlers had foundered with heavy loss of life. Mission ships had been damaged, but all had returned to port. Grenfell watched the battered survivors of the gale enter the river, snapped masts replaced by jury rig carrying the remnants of torn sails, bulwarks crushed, and flags at half-mast to announce another man or men lost. The Mission workers had to carry to the wives and families news of the loss of their loved ones, and give what help they could to those now without a breadwinner. This was the 'price of fish' indeed, and Grenfell spoke passionately of the cost of the nation's food in men's lives when he addressed a large public meeting held by the Mission at Queen's Hall in London. He came to this meeting from his bed, for he had been ill after catching a cold when in the North Sea on board a Mission ship in January.

He travelled round England a great deal this spring, lecturing on the Mission's work and appealing for funds. He spoke more and more about the work being done in Labrador, showing pictures of life there on his magic lantern, and dressing a missionary skipper in Eskimo skin clothing as an added novelty. His lectures were now very popular, for he could make his stories into thrilling adventures, and his platform manner was improving with practice. He was still liable to jump from subject to subject, but he held the attention. He was known now as "the Labrador Doctor," and his reputation increased when his first book, *Vikings of To-day*, was published this same year. The book was little more than a survey of Labrador life and a report on the Mission's work there, but Grenfell made it readable, and the critics praised it for its vigorous prose and the nobility of its story. All the profits from the book were given to the Mission funds. The Council, still apprehensive of their Superintendent's sometimes disconcerting frankness, insisted on seeing the chapters before they authorized its publication. But for the time Grenfell was offending no one.

He sailed for St John's on May 1, 1895, eager to be back on his 'beloved' Labrador. He reached the Colony, to find that the Newfoundlanders had tackled their problems with vigour. The British Government would not undertake to finance the Colony, but did allot a sum of money for relief work and sent a commissioner, Sir Herbert Murray, to St John's, to administer this aid. Sir William Whiteway, whose Government had been replaced just before the bank smash, had been recalled, and was working hard to restore the country's economy. Canada had been asked for help, and Canadian banks had set up branches in St John's. There was talk of confederation with the Dominion, but this was not to come yet.

There was a new spirit in the Colony, and determination to restore its prosperity. The Colonial Secretary, Sir Robert Bond, had pledged his private fortune to save the Commercial Bank. Economies were being made, and one of these affected the Mission to Deep Sea Fishermen. The doctor sailing on board the Labrador mail-ship was to be withdrawn, and the Mission was to have sole charge of all medical work on the coast. Four thousand pounds was still owed by the Newfoundland Committee on the equipment for the two hospitals, and the new

Government offered to pay this sum if the Mission would undertake to run the hospitals. The Mission Council agreed, though their own finances were then low. Grenfell was delighted. The money would come—this was Christ's work—and the Mission would have sole charge of the coast. Sir Herbert Murray asked Grenfell if the Mission doctors would distribute relief along the coast; and Grenfell himself was to arrange for supplies of salt to be given to those fishermen whose traders and merchants had been bankrupted and gone out of business in the bank smash.

Despite their many troubles the St John's Committee had not forgotten their promises to Grenfell; and he found, on his arrival, that the *Sir Donald* and *Princess May* had been repaired and were almost ready for sea. The outlook for the year was bright. Two steam-vessels would be at work, the hospitals equipped and ready. Large stores of medical supplies, drugs, instruments, clothing, and furniture had been bought in England with money collected by the energetic committees in Canada, and the Allen Line transported this free of charge. The Hudson's Bay Company had given and shipped iron fittings for the hospitals with other gifts; Job Bros gave and brought out coal. The company who had repaired the two steam-vessels cut their price by 30 per cent. as a further aid. The bank disaster had brought the people of the Colony together as they had never been before, and the Mission was sharing in the new spirit.

With a crew of two Grenfell left St John's on the *Sir Donald* on June 18. He found ice and fog all along the coast, and the grim aftermath of the terrible winter. The poor fishing of the previous year and the failure of so many merchants who might have carried the fishermen over the long months had brought near-starvation to the coast, and Grenfell found destitution and illness from lack of food everywhere he went. He found, also, a wonderful optimism; for news had spread of the aid that was coming, the fishing-gear to be supplied from the British funds, boats repaired and new ones financed from the same source, and the Government doles of food. And this year, already, the fishing was good. Caplin had come in hordes, piling themselves on the beaches as they came inshore to spawn. Grenfell found the people grateful for his coming and for the heartening news he brought. He was given presents—the only payment the people could make—in live lobsters and a goat that he tethered forward on deck.

Grenfell arrived in St Anthony Harbour on June 23, anchoring just inside the narrow entrance to the long, loch-like haven he was to know so well in the future. He had made friends with the seventeen families who lived there, their houses close to the water and their stages thrusting above the rocky shores. A trader's long jetty extended out into the haven from the western shore, and there was a Methodist church on one side of the harbour and a thin-spired Anglican church on the opposite shore, the families living on that side where their church was. Behind the buildings hills rose steeply, covered in pointing spruce and the paler birch and with excellent grassland on the lower slopes. Now, in the early summer, the snow had gone, and the country was softening to the colours of growing things. The spruce on the hills showed dark green above the brighter tone of the grassy slopes beneath. The low vegetation was in bloom, flowers lifting themselves to the sunlight. It was a lovely scene, the long natural harbour edged with black rock and holding at anchor a dozen black-painted schooners. Grenfell watched his anchor chain stiffen, then sag, as the anchor gripped and the small vessel swung to the wind. A boat put out from the near-by point, and Grenfell waved to his friend Reuben Sims, a trapper and fisherman, whose house and stage were on the point nearest to where the *Sir Donald* was anchored. Sims came on board, to be joined by many others who had seen the vessel arrive, her two huge blue flags flying. Soon Grenfell was examining men, women, and children, bandaging cuts, pressing out pus, and lecturing them all on cleanliness and diet. He sent some of them on shore to pick dandelions and bring them to him as payment, explaining that the plant could be cooked and provide an excellent vegetable and prevent scurvy. Then he gathered his visitors on deck and led the singing of a hymn before he prayed with them and gave a short sermon. This over, he went on shore to visit the sick there.

He waited at St Anthony until the mail-steamer arrived from St John's, bringing the two nurses who would complete their journey to Battle Harbour on board the *Sir Donald*. With the nurses' luggage piled on deck beside the tanks containing the lobsters, the goat, sacks of dandelions, and extra fuel, he steered out of the harbour, rounded the dark bulk of Cape St Anthony, and passed along the coast to Cape Bauld. The weather was excellent, and the steamer made a good and fast passage to Battle Harbour. The hospital was ready for opening, gleaming with polish and with many improvements that Dr Willway had carried out while he was held there at the beginning of the winter. Grenfell waited only to land the nurses and talk to his friends, then headed south again to cruise along the Strait. He had much to do, and he had some wonderful ideas for the welfare of his people. They were now 'his' people.

His great scheme, this year, was to start a co-operative. When he was lecturing at Manchester, in England, he had met a schoolmaster named Paton, a keen co-operator, who had been greatly interested in the economics of Labrador fishing. He had explained to Grenfell how the evils of the truck system could be evaded by the fishermen setting up co-operative stores and managing their own affairs. Grenfell was fascinated by the suggestion. This, he felt, was the Christian way, and he was to write:

> Co-operation needs love for the other fellow, and love is the greatest force in the world. That is why, if the world were peopled by unselfish and wise folk and a co-operation of hearts were achieved, co-operative systems would always be best.

He had asked Paton how to start a co-operative, and had written down in a notebook all he learned. Now he was on his way to instruct the Labrador fishermen on how to keep for themselves the profits of their labour. They need no longer be the victims of a vile system, nor accept a price for their fish set by agreement among the merchants. Grenfell blamed most of the tragedies of sickness, destitution, and crime that happened on the Labrador coast on the credit system. He had listed the causes of poverty and hardship in one of his reports to the Mission, naming the credit system first, then the isolation of the people and lack of education that made them easy victims of greedy traders. Long exploitation had made the people careless, even dishonest. Men who contracted to give all the fish they caught to the traders who supplied them with stores and gear sold fish to passing trading schooners from Nova Scotia, who did not give credit, but who were far from scrupulous in taking what was legally the property of other traders. The goods offered by the Nova Scotians were not subject to the heavy import tax laid on Newfoundland goods, and so were cheaper, and the schooner traders were always willing to pass over a stone jar of cheap liquor. To the fishermen, so heavily in debt that they knew they could never get those extra little luxuries from their own trader, the temptation to be dishonest was great. What was even worse, some Liveyere women sold themselves to the men on the schooners in exchange for food for their families; and schooner-owners, rather than return to Newfoundland and sell their vessels and gear after a bad year's fishing, wrecked them for the insurance money. Grenfell blamed all this on the credit system. A co-operative, Grenfell was now convinced, was the way to freedom and prosperity for the fishermen.

He brought his suggestion first to the people of Red Bay, on the southern Labrador shore. This had been one of the most poverty-stricken places Grenfell had visited, and he wanted to prove that his scheme would work there. He steamed into this lovely corner, the settlement a scattered collection of huts and fish-stages corded together by steep, winding footpaths on the lower slope of a high, grassy hill. It was a place Grenfell believed could be prosperous, for the high hills overlooking the enclosed bay and the settlement were covered with trees that could be cut for timber, and grass on the lower slopes would support sheep and cattle. It was a picturesque corner, the rocks a deep, rich red in places and waterfalls twisting from the heights like silver against the dark hills. Here, in this sheltered bay, a great new movement would begin. Grenfell spoke to an intelligent young fisherman named William Pike, one of the few Liveyeres who could read and write, explaining how the co-operative would operate, and suggested that Pike find twenty or so heads of families who would invest a few dollars in shares to begin the venture. He told Pike that he, Grenfell, would get a grant from Sir Herbert Murray to buy a schooner that would be owned by the co-operative and would carry their fish to St John's and bring back the supplies purchased with the payment for the fish. Grenfell had asked one or two traders whether they would object to a co-operative being started, and had been assured that anything that would teach the fishermen to work on a cash basis would benefit them as well. Grenfell was not sure of this goodwill, and advised Pike not to let the trader at Red Bay know what was being proposed. The Englishman guessed that his project would lose him many of the friends he had made among merchants and traders; but he was prepared to be unpopular if he could free the fishermen and their families from their bondage.

He left Pike to make the first advances to the men of Red Bay and continued his voyage to the west, going as far as Harrington, inside the Canadian border, and then crossing the Strait to Flower's Cove, a larger settlement on the Newfoundland shore. On his return to Red Bay he learned from Pike that the fishermen were not over-eager to share in a co-operative. Few had even the small number of dollars that would buy shares, and many of the men were frankly apprehensive of antagonizing their traders. They had lived so long under domination that they exaggerated the traders' power. Grenfell told Pike to continue his efforts to convince his neighbours, then sailed on, working out plans for overcoming the fishermen's fears and for putting his great scheme into operation.

He reached Battle Harbour, to find a new missionary, Dr Robinson, come out from England, and Dr Willway just preparing to take the *Princess May*, brought from St John's by a skipper and crew, to St Anthony to bring back the husband of a woman who was in the hospital and dying. Willway had a wonderful report to make to Grenfell. He had covered 1200 miles by dog team and komatik during the winter, travelling along the southern shore and as far north as Hopedale. He described a Labrador Grenfell had not yet seen, a land and sea covered in snow and ice and with its people withdrawn from the coast and located along the inlets where they could get wood for fuel and set out their trap-lines. Willway had visited hundreds of families, finding great poverty after the poor fishing year and much sickness. There had been an outbreak of typhoid among the Eskimos in the north, and almost a hundred people had died there. But Willway was enthusiastic about his winter's work, of the trials and excitements of travelling behind a dog team. He was now convinced, after what he had found, that there should be a doctor on the coast every winter and that the people should not be deserted each autumn.

Grenfell listened to his colleague and was humanly envious. He wrote to his mother, saying that he might resign from the Mission to Deep Sea Fishermen and give himself entirely to work on the Labrador coast.

With *Sir Donald*'s deck, and what space was available below deck, crammed with foodstuffs and bales of clothing, Grenfell went north. As he passed along the coast, treating the sick, holding services, sketching the coastline, and filling in a large book with a record of the people's condition, he distributed barrels of flour and other food, and clothing to those he found needed this help most. There was still great hardship among the Liveyeres, but the fishing continued to be good. Salmon had come in well, and the cod had followed. There were great hopes that this would be a good year. Grenfell reached Indian Harbour, to find the hospital open and Nurse Williams in charge until Willway returned. Assured that all was well, Grenfell moved on, calling on his friends at Rigolet and exploring high up into Hamilton Inlet, then making for Hopedale. He found over a hundred schooners there, some of them rich with foods they had taken from the cargo of a ship wrecked on Belle Isle and lying there for the picking. After holding his usual surgery and conducting some services on shore Grenfell went on, still northward, ambitious to go beyond the point to which he had taken the *Princess May*. He found and treated the aftermath of the typhoid epidemic, trying to teach the Eskimos the need for cleanliness and some sort of sanitation, and to get the sick to lie down in their tents and not go outside.

This year Grenfell reached as far north as Nachvak Inlet, a long fjord more than a hundred miles farther north than he had taken the *Princess May*. This was magnificent land, with mountains rising to over 4000 feet and the coastline a lofty buttress of sheer rock. As Grenfell steamed through the narrow entrance, between lofty headlands, into the mile-wide Nachvak Inlet his ship seemed very small between the towering mountains and over the smooth, sheltered water. A rock stood against the sky in the shape of a naked man, and waterfalls bounded and twisted downward, to drop and explode against the cliffledges. This was indeed a scene to rouse and challenge a man. Grenfell drove the *Sir Donald* deep into the inlet, until he sighted the Eskimo village of Nachvak and the trim building, with its Union Jack flying, that was the Hudson's Bay post here. The manager, George Ford, was waiting to welcome the stranger, for he knew that this must be the famous Dr Grenfell whose name was blessed along the coast and who was praised by the schoonermen who visited the settlement. Ford was glad the young Englishman had arrived, for he had a story to tell him.

He took Grenfell to his house and showed him a letter. It was addressed to an Eskimo boy named Pomiuk, and Ford explained that it had been forwarded by his company, with a request that he locate the boy and read the letter to him. Ford knew enough of the story to describe to his visitor what had happened. Pomiuk was the child of a man who had been murdered some years before, and, as is the manner of the Eskimo people, the widow and her children had been adopted by another man, Kupah, and his wife. The widow had gone off with a new husband, taking all her children except Pomiuk.

In 1890 a white man had come north seeking Eskimos, who were to be one of the attractions at the World Fair in Chicago. Kupah was one of the people who were tempted by the promises of rich rewards for going to America, and he took Pomiuk, then a child of eight, with him. The Eskimos were shown in an 'Eskimo Village' at the Fair, and attracted a great deal of attention with their skill in handling dog-whips. The visitors tossed coins to them, and the Eskimos flicked these towards themselves with their deerskin lashes, gathering in what was to them a fortune.

Pomiuk had been especially popular, the promoters giving him the title of "Prince." He was then a mere child, but was expert with a whip, and had a particularly happy nature and laughing face, which brought many to the 'Eskimo Village.' Among them was a minister, the Rev. Charles C. Carpenter, from Boston, and Carpenter was particularly interested. Forty years before he had been a young missionary on the south coast of Labrador, and, though he had never worked among the Eskimos, he had a sentimental affection for anyone coming from the country. He visited the Eskimos every day of his ten-day stay in Chicago, and was attracted by the cheerful fortitude of the boy, Pomiuk, who had broken his thigh in some frolic and was now able only to sit outside one of the huts where the

Eskimos were lodged and watch his friends flick coins with the whips. The minister and the boy could converse only in the few words of English Pomiuk knew and the even fewer Eskimo words Carpenter had learned. But they became greatly attached to each other, and the boy always gave a special welcome to the kindly American. When Carpenter's stay in Chicago was ending he came to say *Auksheni* ("Good-bye") to his small friend and promised to send him a photograph of himself.

He did so, with a letter containing a few words in Eskimo. By then the Fair was ended, and the Eskimos had been taken by the promoters of their show as far as Newfoundland and dumped there, to find their own way back, over 2000 miles, to Northern Labrador. Carpenter's letter was sent to Bonne Bay, on the west coast of Newfoundland, where the Eskimos had been left, and in time a reply came from Pomiuk written by some kindly settler and telling the minister, "I got my health pretty well. When I get home I will write you." The boy remembered his elderly friend and did write again that year, from Nachvak. Carpenter told the story of his friendship with the boy in a religious weekly, the *Congregationalist*, for which the minister conducted a children's page under the name of "Mr Martin." In the next few years Carpenter tried several times to locate the boy, and finally he asked the Hudson's Bay Company if they could help. The company offered to forward a letter through their agent at Nachvak, and it was this letter that George Ford now showed to Grenfell. Grenfell, fascinated by the story, asked Ford if he had found the boy, and was told that he had not, but that he had heard of a boy lying sick and reported to be dying in a tent some miles up the inlet. This might be Pomiuk. Grenfell was sure it was, and suggested they find out.

They found the tent after a search that lasted two days and involved some hard climbing along the rocky and boulder-strewn shore. Grenfell described later what was to be a most important moment for the Englishman:

> It seemed almost like looking for a needle in a haystack to search for a tiny tent no bigger than one of the boulders that lay in thousands at the feet of those stupendous cliffs. . . . We climbed a high promontory and searched the shores of the inlet carefully

with our glasses. There it was, sure enough, nestling in near the mouth of a mighty torrent that was rushing headlong down the cliff. Soon we were peeping into the little *tubik* and found Kupah's wife and a young boy of about eleven years, covered with an old reindeer skin . . . his long black hair cut in a straight frieze across his forehead, his face drawn with pain, and his large hazel eyes fixed wonderingly on us strangers.

This was Pomiuk, and Grenfell examined the pitiful body, to find the boy filthy and with dreadful wounds suppurating on his thigh. The broken bones had never been set properly, nor had there been any after-treatment. Infection had spread and become terrible sores that were sapping the boy's strength, and Grenfell said he must take Pomiuk away from this tent and carry him south for treatment. Ford explained this to Kupah, who had arrived at the tent, and the Eskimo shrugged his shoulders to say he did not mind. The boy was a handicap to people who must travel for their food, though Kupah had done all he could.

Carefully and tenderly Pomiuk was carried to the Hudson's Bay post and on board the *Sir Donald*. There Grenfell stripped and washed him, an experience that terrified the boy, for this was the first time in his life he had been thoroughly cleaned. Grenfell treated the terrible wounds, and then laid the boy on a polar-bear skin he had bought. He gave him food, the raw walrus meat he knew Eskimos loved, and the boy lost his fears and lay contentedly, his large eyes watching Grenfell. When the *Sir Donald* was headed south Pomiuk was on board, his fears gone and becoming more and more cheerful. Grenfell began to teach him English and to count, using cartridges as tokens. Only during the daily cleansing of his wounds did Pomiuk complain, and Grenfell stopped this by chalking the days of the week on a cupboard door, and marking up a 'G' for 'good' when Pomiuk did not cry and a 'B' for 'bad' when he did. Soon the boy was proud of his list of 'G's.' Grenfell discovered that his passenger had never had any religious instruction, and on the way south he stopped at Hopedale while the boy was told about Christ and baptized by a Moravian missionary, being given the baptismal name of Gabriel Pomiuk. He was tremendously proud of this new name and insisted on being called by it. The stories of Christ delighted him, and he learned some hymns from Grenfell that he sang happily as he lay on his bearskin in the cabin or on deck. He was given a concertina by the Moravians, and, loving music, like most of his people, he learned to play very quickly. By the time the *Sir Donald* reached Indian Harbour and the boy was placed in hospital he was a laughing, happy child and Grenfell's devoted admirer. His wounds were still serious, but Grenfell intended to leave the boy under hospital care all that winter, in the hope that the wounds would clean and heal.

When stripping the boy of his filthy and verminous skin garments Grenfell found a deerskin bag hung by a cord round his neck. He opened this, to discover the Rev. Charles Carpenter's first letter and his photograph. When questioned Pomiuk said, "Yes, me know him—me even love him," and Grenfell was sure the minister would like to have news of his small friend. He wrote from Indian Harbour in September that year, telling Carpenter how he had found the boy, and ending the letter: "We shall keep him until next year, when, God willing, I shall take him back to the North. From your letter I judge you may care to pray for a blessing on this little outcast."

Carpenter replied at once. He asked how much it would cost to maintain Pomiuk for a year, then put the whole story in his 'Corner' in the children's page of the *Congregationalist*: "Let us remember this poor boy on the bleak Arctic shore. He belongs to us; let us take care of him," the minister wrote, and the response was immediate and generous. Pomiuk had found many friends now. When Carpenter wrote next he took up a suggestion Grenfell had made in a second letter, that he extend the Canadian lectures he proposed to give that winter to take in the United States. Carpenter invited him to Boston. The Eskimo boy had come to decide Grenfell's whole future. When the Englishman came to Boston in February the story of Pomiuk was already well known, and Carpenter had prepared a ground that needed only Grenfell's attractive personality and sincerity to sow a harvest that would be the richest of all. With the well-liked minister as his sponsor, Grenfell met influential people and won the support of the churches. A young lady, Miss Emma White, who was librarian to the Congregational Church headquarters in Boston, volunteered to serve as secretary to a committee Carpenter formed for the support of Grenfell's work. She helped to arrange meetings for the Englishman, and at one of these a Boston banker, Arthur F. Estabrook, was so impressed by the young man that he offered to supply and finance an office and to join the committee.

By the time he left Boston Grenfell had made many supporters and friends. Carpenter's two young daughters were his devoted admirers. They had expected an elderly, grey-bearded missionary to arrive, and found themselves being greeted by a good-looking young man—he was then thirty-one—who laughed and joked with them and seemed no older than they were. He discovered that one of the sisters collected crests, and immediately cut out dozens from his correspondence, to make the girl the envy of all her schoolmates. Grenfell was the biggest adventure that had happened to the sisters in all their short lives, and they were to be his friends for life.

10

Recall to England

GRENFELL did not go to England that winter. It was November before he had left the coast of Labrador, and there had been danger of the *Sir Donald* being caught by the ice. Late in October, while Grenfell was at Battle Harbour, he had received a message from Nurse Williams at Indian Harbour, telling him that Pomiuk had taken a turn for the worse and she was worried. Despite the lateness of the season Grenfell steamed the *Sir Donald* the two hundred miles to Indian Harbour, and after treating the boy carried him another fifty miles to Rigolet. Dr Robinson was to remain on the coast throughout that winter, and the Hudson's Bay Company Manager at Rigolet had offered him a house as headquarters. Pomiuk would stay there and be well cared for. He had improved under Grenfell's treatment, and was once again a cheerful and happy boy, practising his concertina-playing and learning to draw and write.

By the time Grenfell was back in Battle Harbour the snow was thick on the land and ice forming along the shore. All the fishing-schooners had gone south, carrying those fishermen and their families and possessions not taken by the mail-steamer. The Liveyeres were shifting to their winter quarters deeper into the coastal inlets, cutting and stacking logs, mending their dog-harness, and seeing to their traps. It was time to leave the coast. Nurse Carwardine was to keep the hospital at Battle Harbour open through the winter; and now, swathed in a thick shawl and with many petticoats under her skirt and wearing sealskin boots, she came to the wooden wharf to say good-bye. Willway and Nurse Williams were going to Newfoundland with Grenfell on the *Sir Donald*, on their way to England. With a farewell toot on the steam-whistle, a waving of caps to the figure on the jetty, the first Mission nurse to winter on the Labrador coast, Grenfell steered the small steamer out of the tickle, to swing southward and head for St Anthony. Willway and Nurse Williams were dropped there, to take the mail-steamer to St John's, and Grenfell cruised along the New-foundland coast after them.

He did not stay long in St John's, but crossed by passenger ship to Halifax, where he lectured and told the story of little Pomiuk. He went on to Montreal for meetings there, then to Toronto, where yet another supporting committee was being formed. Late in December he was back in Montreal, staying there until he went south to make his first visit to the United States. His successful campaign in Boston completed, he accepted an invitation to New York, where he made his usual good impression and was promised support.

Meantime Grenfell's relations with the Mission to Deep Sea Fishermen were being subjected to some strain. In December, while in Montreal, he had written to a member of the Mission Council, Mr W. F. A. Archibald, outlining plans for his work the following year. He wished to remain on this side of the Atlantic, and to sail with the sealing fleet in the spring. After-wards he would go straight to Labrador, taking the *Sir Donald*. Willway, who was returning, would have the *Princess May*. The London Missionary Society had wanted Willway back, but Grenfell had written asking that he be released by the Society and allowed to join the fishermen's Mission, as he was so eminently suited to the work and loved it. Willway was allowed to transfer, and now Grenfell proposed that both he and Willway remain on the coast all through the next winter.

Grenfell wrote lengthily and earnestly, using all his considerable gifts of persuasion and skill in argument to try to convince
the Council of the importance of this work. The letter was discussed at a Council meeting in January. The members were
more worried than ever, for Grenfell was badly needed in England, and his wanderings in America and Canada seemed to
be having results over which they had no control. It was decided "That Dr Grenfell be requested to return home after
the seal fisheries are over, and if possible in time for the Annual
Meeting, in order that the Council might make arrangements
with him for the future conduct of his work in England."
Treves, concerned at the way his protégé was behaving, wrote
privately, to say, "You have established the Mission in Labrador
and done the pioneer work, but the North Sea is suffering.
Things are not going so well at Gorleston, and as a matter of
duty you ought to return." The word 'duty' was underlined.
Grenfell could only agree to return; but first he would achieve
his ambition to sail on board a sealing-vessel.

He joined a 400-ton vessel, the *Greenland*, on March 30 that
year, 1896, one of 300 men crammed on board the small, sturdy,
black-painted vessel that sailed with the rest of the sealing fleet
between the still snow-covered heights walling the entrance to
St John's Harbour, and headed north for Belle Isle Strait. Grenfell, in knee-boots, thick guernsey suit, and fur cap, was in his
element, happy to be part of this entirely masculine company
and bound for a new adventure. He moved among the sealers,
listening to their yarns of other voyages and storing these tales
away for use on platforms and in print. The sealers liked him.
Even though he did corner them now and then and try to
convert them, he could laugh and joke and share their boisterous play. He was no finicky Englishman, but ate what sealers
ate and slept as hard on his straw mattress, asking no privileges.
The men crowded into the empty holds, squatting on their
'donkeys' breakfasts,' the straw mattresses they had brought for
beds, to hear him preach. He had to climb to a top rung of the
hold ladder to give his sermons, an arm inside a rung to support
himself against the ship's rolling, or the jolting she got as she
was pushed among the ice. The sealers took his straight speaking and approved him, and made the ship tremble with the
power of their lungs as they sang the hymns he led.

I

The ship reached the Strait. The sea did not freeze solid here, but vast fields of ice formed and drifted back and forth to wind and tide; and it was on this ice that the seals bred every year. The ship pushed into the ice, her master standing in a large basket lashed to the masthead, conning her. He could look down on a pattern of gleaming ice veined with green water leads, and he worked his ship into the leads and followed them as far as he could. Small pans of ice were ridden over, to break and roll away from the ship's soon-scarred sides. When no leads appeared the ship was driven into what appeared to be the weakest ice, her forefoot mounting the pan and her weight splitting it so that she could push deeper into the field. Time after time she was held, and this could be dangerous. If the wind rose and pressed the ice upon the ship she could be crushed; and two of the ships in the fleet Grenfell sailed with were to be caught that voyage, their crews escaping over the ice to other ships.

From his lofty perch the master looked for seals. When he sighted a large enough colony of the distant dark specks he hailed the deck. The men scrambled over the side, each carrying a club or pole to kill the seals, a length of rope to drag the skins back to the ship, and a small canvas bag containing a mixture of oatmeal and sugar that they would moisten with water from the ice surface and have as their next meal. On the ice the sealers made a competition of their task, for they were paid by results. They strung out, a long column of dark figures, the more active getting ahead, choosing what seemed to be the easiest route among the broken, piled ice that had been wind-carved to grotesque shapes of animals, figures, arches, and tall pillars where the light, broken into its elements, tinted the shapes or a cloud darkened them to sombre blues. The men kept in pairs, for in places the surface was thin, or narrow leads opened suddenly under the racing feet. If anyone fell into the water he would be lost if a helping hand was not near.

Grenfell was well in the van of the hurrying men, his mate having a hard time in keeping up with the agile and athletic Englishman. This was a game he delighted in, a challenge he answered with joy. He believed that the seals did not suffer and died instantly—and, indeed, they did die easily. When the men came among them they seemed stupefied, and the hunters could rush from seal to seal, striking each a single blow on the snout that dispatched it. The young seals, the soft-furred whitecoats, were killed first, for their coats were the most valuable, and would fetch as much as ten shillings each in the market. With these young ones killed, the older seals were attacked, only a few of them showing fight.

Her hold filled with the 23,000 pelts her 300 sealers had dispatched, skinned, and dragged back to the ship, a cargo worth 43,000 dollars, the *Greenland* headed for St John's. The men had been crowded out of the hold by the pelts, and now had to lay their straw mattresses anywhere they could find space—on the deck or on the extra coal piled there. But they were content. They had made their first money of the year, and when fishing started they would have something with which to buy gear and supplies. They congratulated their new chum, for Grenfell had brought back 91 skins, above the average for the ship. The men made a whip round and presented him with 37 dollars to add to what he had earned as a seal-hunter and which would help the Mission funds. He said good-bye to the rough, unshaven, unwashed, but jubilant company at St John's, they to hasten home with their earnings, or to go to the public-houses and get rid of the money quickly before seeking another voyage, and Grenfell to take a horse-cab and be carried up the steep streets to Government House, where he was to stay, carrying with him a gift for the Governor, a half-dozen of that special Newfoundland delicacy—seal flippers.

On May 1 Grenfell was in London and facing his critics on the Mission Council. He gave his report of the last year's work and told of his success in Canada and the United States. He explained why he had remained so long in America, saying that "the problem was now assuming such large proportions that I felt the Society at home should not be called upon to finance it." He was thanked and congratulated, but the Council were concerned at his long absences. The work in England was being neglected. He was asked bluntly if he wished to remain as Superintendent and with the Mission, and he said that he did. But he also wished to develop the work in Labrador. He read from letters he had received from Newfoundland merchants and officials, praising the Mission for what had been done for the fishermen. This work, he went on, was now so much identified with his own name that it would do much harm if he withdrew. This was one of the things the Council disliked; it was becoming far too much 'Dr Grenfell's work.' The meeting decided to appoint a sub-committee to decide what would be done, and a week later Grenfell was informed that he must spend most of his time in England. He would be permitted to return to Labrador this summer, but must be home by December, and he was to undertake to instruct Dr Willway, now appointed Assistant Superintendent and to be in charge in Labrador, on the work there. After that year Grenfell would go to Labrador "only occasionally and with the sanction of the Council."

He accepted the Council's decision. It was a heavy blow, for he had grown to love Labrador, and he knew he could do much for its people—more than anyone else could, for the fishermen admired and respected him, and he had earned a warm affection few others would get. Willway was an outstanding man and a sincere Christian; but so was Grenfell, with an extra quality of naïvety, a simplicity and directness, that brought him nearer the character of seamen. The fishermen's attitude to him was both paternal and filial, for his sailor's aspirations enabled them to advise and instruct him, and yet he could speak and comfort them like a father. He was "the Doctor," and they could take their troubles to him as they took their hurts. With him they never felt uncouth or deficient, for he accepted them as they were, sat with them at their tables, ate their kind of food, and joined in their conversations as naturally as their own mates. They were the people he loved, and, even as he knew many of them tricked him to secure a garment or some benefit, he understood why they did so and blamed what had conditioned them to such trickery. He gave them what he had to give, the Word of God, his doctor's skill, or a pair of trousers. With his Christianity went a vast and uncritical humanitarianism. He knew, as the Council took these people from him, that he would be missed, and he knew he would miss them.

He went to Parkgate, where his mother was now living, and she comforted him. He would still be carrying out God's work and be serving His people. Only the form of his work would be changed, and this was a sacrifice he must accept with Christian fortitude. He took this comfort and sailed for St John's on what might be his last visit there. Willway accompanied him, and on the way across Grenfell instructed his successor on what was to be done. He had many plans for the future of the Mission in Labrador, including a new hospital at Harrington, on the south coast. A deputation of fishermen had travelled 200 miles to ask Grenfell to place a hospital on this part of the coast, and a wealthy young Englishman who had cruised with him on the *Sir Donald* had offered to design and pay for a building to be erected there. With the Canadian Government's rejection of Grenfell's petition, the Montreal Committee had offered to maintain this third hospital. There were other plans. The Mission had been giving away the second-hand clothes, but now Grenfell wanted these to be earned. He had no desire to 'pauperize' the people, as he was now being accused of doing, and had schemes for road-building and timber-cutting, with the workers being paid with clothes and food. He explained these and other schemes to Willway on the voyage across.

There was concern, and some relief, among the Mission's supporters in St John's when it was learned that Grenfell would not be returning to Labrador after that year. Some of the merchants had heard of his plan for co-operatives and disliked it intensely. That the Mission set up hospitals and relieved sickness, that it held religious meetings and even gave some charity, was a benefit they shared in having the fishermen healthier and more honest; but for Grenfell to start competing with them in business was far from what they wanted. Also, he had been somewhat too outspoken in his criticism of traders and their methods. Perhaps it was best that this over-energetic and too enterprising Englishman stayed in England. His schemes were not always beneficial for the merchants, and he had been seeing the fishermen's side of the question rather too much. Missionaries should not intrude into business or politics.

Grenfell realized that he was not now altogether approved, but he cared little. He had no admiration for much that went on in St John's, and had told his mother that Newfoundland politics were riddled with corruption and that the merchants did not want the people freed from the credit system, nor even educated. Much that should be changed was not, because the politicians wanted votes more than reforms. The scandal of girls on board the schooners continued, because no politician would antagonize the schooner-owners and lose their votes by proposing a law to stop girls being employed on these fishing-vessels. Sir Terence O'Brien had told Grenfell that the whole Newfoundland Government was a disgrace, and that what was needed was a peppery old soldier from the British Army who would put the Colonials in their place. Grenfell wished Sir Terence himself were a bit more energetic and tough with the politicians.

Meantime he himself was prepared to oppose anyone for the good of the people. His Christianity had gone far beyond mere preaching, and had become a militant campaign for the people's stomachs as well as their spiritual salvation. When he had taken the *Sir Donald* away from St John's and carried a new missionary, Dr Apsland, to Battle Harbour he headed for Red Bay to find out what the people there had decided about a co-operative store. He found them in good heart and prepared to share in the venture. A good year's fishing, and their larders stocked with flour from a ship that had been wrecked on their coast, had heartened them and given them new courage. They were still apprehensive, however, about the local traders' re-actions, and asked that their names should not be written in the society's books. Some did not have the money to take up shares, but Grenfell offered to take up some himself, and these would be passed to whoever wanted them when they had money. Sir Herbert Murray, now replacing Sir Terence O'Brien as Gover-nor of Newfoundland, was helping. He was giving 500 dollars towards the buying of the first lot of stores, and Dr Robinson, sailing with Grenfell and on his way home after a winter's work in which he had travelled over 2000 miles by dog team and sledge and treated nearly 400 sick people, would purchase the goods in St John's. Three merchants there had agreed to pay cash for the co-operative's fish.

Grenfell gathered the Red Bay fishermen together in a fish-store and explained the rules of the new society. Its members would be the heads of the families and they would appoint a storekeeper. Goods would be sold for cash, and no credit or charity would be given. The goods would be sold at cost price, plus freightage—the ambitious plan to have their own schooner would have to be postponed—and plus 5 per cent. for the store-keeper and another 5 per cent. to cover any loss and to build up a reserve. Because of the accusations already being made that Grenfell was scheming to make a profit for the Mission and for himself he had a record of the whole proceedings taken down in shorthand by a young man, Justice Cramer Roberts, whom he had brought out at his own expense as his secretary. Grenfell also read out what he had to say from the notes taken from Paton in Manchester a year before, and shaped into a lecture on elementary economics—a "Five-dollar Capitalist Economy," Grenfell called it.

William Pike was appointed storekeeper of the new co-operative, and Grenfell mischievously chalked the name "Red Bay Co-operative Society" on the building where the society had been born. He was delighted, and already saw the whole life of the coast changed by a string of co-operative societies. That he would be criticized and would lose many friends by starting this competition with the traders and merchants he knew, but he was concerned with the people and not their masters. He took the *Sir Donald* along the whole of the south coast, then back to Battle Harbour, where the new doctor, Apsland, was eyeing Nurse Carwardine with interest. This young woman had done wonderful work during the winter, and Grenfell was told of her goodness by many. This was another advance, and from now on and for many years Battle Harbour Hospital would not close its doors. One day other hospitals would be open during the winter and doctors would travel along the coast, as Robinson had done so magnificently this last winter.

Grenfell moved northward, making his calls, and saddened only in knowing that this might be his last voyage along the coast. His affection for the land was great, each rounded island top, each lifting bare headland, now an old friend, and the hazards of their waters were a stimulant he would miss. There was so much that delighted him in this place: the majestic procession of icebergs whose shape and colour were never the same and each a story of lonely voyaging. He had been inspired to give the beauty he found here to others, and had written:

> A most glorious red light covers the sky as I write, tingeing the fleecy clouds, lighting the rippling sea, and even colouring the tips of the gaunt icebergs. In places the red is succeeded by a deep purple, and again the tint changes and everything is golden-edged.

And around him were the swooping gulls, the duck skittering a track across the water surface as they fled from his little ship. There was nothing empty or desolate in the Labrador for Wilfred Grenfell, and each moment brought a new discovery, a new adventure.

He was thrilled each time he passed into one of the hill- and rock-formed harbours where settlements had been built. There was a similarity but never a sameness, for the grey, weathered huts and fish-stages, the little wharves made from spruce poles, had fitted themselves to the rocky shores and slopes with a new character for each place. As he approached and blew his steam-whistle as a greeting the husky dogs, staked well apart between the huts, set up a howling, wolf-like challenge, leaping to their chains with excitement. Men straightened themselves in their boats, or from spreading the split fish on the rocks, men and women came from the gutting-sheds and houses to watch the Mission ship, its huge blue flag flying, coming in. When he came alongside he was greeted with handshakes that were the touch of his brothers; women smiled their pleasure, and the ragged-clothed children watched shyly this man whose eyes were so gentle and kindly. It was a home-coming. Even the clouds of mosquitoes and the stinging black flies that could raise a lump within the minute were a torment that had their own place in his emotions for this country. Now he might never see either land or people again, and his heart was sad as he steered the *Sir Donald* away from each rocky shore, each group of watchers.

He found Dr Willway busy at Indian Harbour. Pomiuk had been taken to Battle Harbour, and Willway believed his leg would have to be amputated. Now this energetic doctor was laying the foundations of a mission hall he meant to build against the hospital for the use of the fishermen whose schooners gathered by the hundred off the island. Grenfell took the *Sir Donald* to Hamilton Inlet and piled her deck high with timber, to carry back for the new building. Then he went north, to help where an epidemic of scarlet fever was raging, and then go on to visit his friends the Moravian missionaries and the Eskimos along the northern coast. He had meant to explore this part of the coast and make charts. Now he would never be able to do this. He could only go home and urge others to do what he so much wanted to do himself.

He was back in Battle Harbour in November, staying until the last minute he dared and then sailing south in bitterly freezing weather. The liquid in his compass froze as he went south, and he was caught and held for a time in an icefield off the Newfoundland coast. But he reached St John's, and from there, still reluctant to sever himself from his work for the people of Labrador, he sent a telegram to London, asking if he would be permitted to visit Canada and promising to be back in England by February. "I am of the opinion that a visit from me would be of advantage in every way," he said. The Council decided that he could go. The Mission had just been honoured by Queen Victoria, who had granted it the privilege of naming itself the Royal National Mission to Deep Sea Fishermen, and it was considered a favourable moment for advancing the Mission's cause in the Colony. But Grenfell must be in England by March 1.

Before Grenfell left St John's he addressed a large meeting held in his honour. Sir Herbert Murray was in the chair, and made some blunt comments. The Newfoundlanders were not keeping their promises to the Mission, and had never cleared the debt of 4000 dollars owing for the hospital equipment. They had promised to supply drugs and had not done so. From the Mission records, one fisherman in every thirteen sailing north had benefited from the doctors' and nurses' work, and so the Mission should be supported and helped by all. Grenfell then gave a talk describing the year's work. At the end of his talk he said that this would be his last visit to Newfoundland, and he asked that his successor be given the Colony's support.

He sailed for Canada in the last days of the year, accompanied by Dr Apsland, who was going on to Montreal to study for a degree. The two men arrived in Halifax on January 1, in time to take part in a social convention. On this day the gentlemen of the town wore their best clothes and either walked or rode from house to house, leaving cards or staying to take tea or cocoa with their friends, an obligation that Grenfell, who detested the social round, found somewhat a bore. He would sooner have been gathering funds for the Mission. He did hold a meeting in Halifax, and then went on to Montreal to discuss with the committee there the new hospital at Harrington. His next call was in Toronto, where he thanked a Miss Greenshields, who had written to the Mission offering £500 for the purchasing of another steamer. The Canadians were being very generous with their help now, and a shipowner guaranteed 250 dollars towards running the new vessel, and helped to find a small tug that could be converted for Mission work. At each of his meetings Grenfell told the story of little Pomiuk, and soon toys and other gifts were pouring in for the boy. Besides their gifts in money and goods the Canadians wished to share the work, and the first Canadian volunteer, a Miss Evans, of Montreal, arranged with Grenfell to go to Labrador the following year.

Grenfell went on to Boston, where he found that the Rev. Charles Carpenter and Emma White had arranged a great many meetings for him. Grenfell wrote home to say that he was having a "perfect whirl of activity" and that the Americans were being very generous. With an office in Boston, the support was now continuous and active, Carpenter keeping the enthusiasm going through his talks and writings. By now the Englishman was a well-known figure in the New England city, and in this state he was to find a second home. On this visit to Boston Grenfell was to get a special thrill, for the American evangelist D. L. Moody was conducting a campaign in the city, and Carpenter arranged for the two men to meet. Grenfell called on Moody at his hotel, and told the stout, bearded, and now elderly evangelist how it had been at his meeting that he had been inspired to live his Christianity. Moody asked the younger man what he had done about this, and Grenfell described his life and work since he had made his resolution. Moody inspected his visitor critically, then said, "Come with me and tell people what you have done"; and the two men went out together, and Grenfell spoke of his work to Moody's congregation. They never met again, though Moody's son was to become Grenfell's friend and supporter, and visit him in Newfoundland.

Grenfell spoke at Harvard University, then at Yale, and at those places he was immediately a success. The young men of the United States, no less than their like in England, had been stirred by Moody, and now responded to this Englishman with enthusiasm and admiration, many coming to him after his talks to ask how they could help. He told them to gather money for the work and to come to Labrador and serve with him. Much was to come from these first talks at American universities.

Grenfell ended his stay in the United States at New York. There he found that the supporters made during his previous visit had increased, and that they were willing to organize themselves into a committee to help his work. He had an introduction to a wealthy banker, Mr Eugene Delano, and he called and asked this gentleman if he would act as treasurer and take charge of all moneys raised in the city. Delano and his son William, a young man newly married, who was to play an important part in the growth of the Grenfell Mission in America, agreed to help. Grenfell, well satisfied with his success, and grateful to the Americans and Canadians, sailed for England, his work on the Labrador, as far as he knew, ended.

11

Return to Labrador

GRENFELL spent the next two and a half years working for the Mission in England. If he missed Labrador and regretted not being able to continue his work there, he did not let this interfere with his efforts to serve the fishermen of Great Britain. He sailed with them in the North Sea, on the Irish coast, and to Iceland, seeking to extend the Mission's activities to every place where British fishermen were to be found.

The industry was changing again. Steam was replacing sail no less than in other navies, steel replacing wood. The handier otter-trawl displaced the clumsier beam-trawl and made it possible to use bigger nets. The new trawlers did not stay at sea so long, for they brought home their own fish, and ports like Grimsby, handy to the fishing-grounds, grew to importance. The day of the huge fleets of smacks and their attendant carriers was almost gone, and those owners who did not adopt the new ways were soon to be out of business. Grenfell, in those last years of the century, was to look down from his room in the Cockrill home and see the first of that sad armada of fishing-smacks that were to line the banks of the Yare and lie there until their timbers rotted. The great fishing company of Hewett, over a hundred years old, the pioneer of fleeting and the use of ice for preserving the fish, the owner of hundreds of vessels sailing as the Short Blue Fleet, and whose Principal, Mr Samuel Hewett, had first invited missionaries to the North Sea and had supported the Mission to Deep Sea Fishermen since its beginning, was only one of many companies that were to suffer, and even to disappear, because they would not conform to the new methods. Hewett's was to recover and rebuild itself under younger members of the family; but with the company's decline in 1899 its vessels disappeared from Gorleston, and the town felt the loss acutely.

The new ships and methods brought new problems for the Mission workers. Their activities had been possible only because the smacks worked in fleets and hundreds of men were gathered in one place. Trawling under sail had stopped when the winds were too light to drag the trawl over the sea bottom, and there were times when the craft lay idle and the men could row to the Mission ships, either because they were sincerely religious or needed tobacco or were bored, and the missionaries could visit round the fleet. Other opportunities to serve the fishermen came when the carriers arrived, and the smacks hung off while their fish were being ferried. The need for the Mission services, apart from the evangelistic work, was greater when vessels stayed at sea for months on end, and the harsh conditions on board the smacks brought so much illness and so many accidents.

The crews of the new ships were not so much in need of the missionaries' help. Their living conditions were better, and the ships stayed at sea only for a week or two. Accidents were not so frequent as with small sailing-vessels and clumsier gear, and men could reach medical services on shore. The ships worked separately and fished continuously, in every sort of weather short of a full gale. They carried two trawls, so that if one were ripped or torn away by an obstruction on the sea bottom the other could be streamed at once. There were no longer times when dozens of trawlers lay idle and the Mission ship's deck was crowded with fishermen. The Mission ships still used sail, and could not overtake or keep up with the steam-driven vessels, and the fishermen did not seek out the Mission ships as they had in the past. From the moment the new ships reached the fishing-grounds the crews had little time for visitors, missionaries or others. The trawl was raised every three or four hours, emptied into the pounds, and re-streamed at once. The men bent over the mass of fish, slitting, gutting, and passing to the mate, who stowed the catch in the hold. By the time the pounds were cleared and washed out it was almost time to haul again. Sleep was snatched by the hour. There was no let-up. Steam trawling was making money for the fisherman as well as for the owners, and it was possible for a skipper who found fish and who kept working to make as much as eight pounds a week.

Grenfell found a new and regrettable spirit among the fishermen. He could reach them only by boarding the trawlers and staying overnight, hoping to catch some of the crew in their few spare moments. He carried his canvas canoe on the Mission ship and paddled to the trawlers, to be lifted on board with his craft. He was still a popular and admired visitor, the men grateful for the medical treatment he gave them, but the response to his evangelistic talks became less and less. The older men, to whom religion was a real force in their lives, and who welcomed a godly hour, were fewer. The new ships needed younger, more aggressive skippers. Grenfell addressed a special message to those skippers who did profess Christianity:

> To all who read these lines I would say, God has given you a new and important opportunity and responsibility. . . . The sailing Mission ship cannot reach the steam-trawlers. Band yourselves together to be missionaries yourselves; you can reach them when we cannot. You can bring them to the Mission ships when we can't fetch them and they don't feel inclined to come. You can live on a steam-trawler and be a true Christian.

Fewer and fewer hearkened to him.

The Mission had to adapt itself to the new conditions. Grenfell recognized this early, and soon after he returned from America he wrote to *The Toilers*: "Obviously the most important problem the Mission has to solve in the near future is How shall we adapt ourselves to the exigencies of steam trawling?" He answered the question by suggesting that new attractions in games and entertainment be offered by the Mission ships. "The men must be tackled from the outside to get inside," he said. The Mission ships would have to be steamers, trawlers fitted as hospital ships but able to fish and maintain themselves. But more and more the Mission work must be carried out on shore. It was there that the dangers to men's decency, and a threat to the Christian way of life, now lay. In those new ports, their docks filled with hooting, jostling steam-trawlers, clog-clattering fish-markets, and the rumble and banging of salt-smelling fish-trains, temptation was being offered in the gleaming glass-and-mahogany public-houses that were being built at every street-corner. Gaudy attractions in theatres and dance-halls came to take the fishermen's money, and the only answer to this could be counter-attraction. The Mission must move on shore.

A new and splendid mission hall was being built at Gorleston, and now Grenfell visited other fishing-ports trying to get support for halls. He got them opened at Grimsby, Aberdeen, Fleetwood, Milford Haven, and other ports. There fishermen could find Christian men and women and friendly, decent company. Food was served at low prices, and stalls were set up on the quaysides where fishermen could buy a plate of potatoes, vegetables, and meat for a few coppers. Men who might have been tempted into public-houses could go to these halls and stalls. This service was even extended abroad. The old Mission ship *Thomas Grey* was moored in Ostend Harbour as a place where fishermen could call, and a Mission room was opened at IJmuiden, in Holland. There was still work to be done at sea— still the remains of the fleets of smacks to serve, an occasional 'pirate' coper risking imprisonment to be reported to the guard-ship; men were still hurt or were ill; but each year this work afloat became less and the work on shore more and more important.

As he worked energetically to help adapt the Mission work to the new conditions Grenfell also spoke at meetings throughout the country, seeking funds and championing the fishermen in their troubles. He was becoming outspoken in his criticism of the trawler-owners, blaming them for much that was unchristian in the more mechanized industry. He was particularly bitter against the new steam-trawlers fishing on Sundays, and compared this with a Labrador fisherman who, rather than put his boat out on the Sabbath, let his valuable trap and his year's earnings be torn away and lost. This man had seen an iceberg drifting towards his net and could have saved it, but it was Sunday and he was the settlement's preacher and must set the example. He stood by the hall door, welcoming the congregation while his net was destroyed. To Grenfell this was true Christianity. He himself had never moved ship on a Sunday.

The trawler-owners' insistence on their '10 per cent.' was introducing a new greed for money among the fishermen and a brutal rivalry. If a skipper failed to bring in fish for a voyage or two he was quickly replaced; and now a man's misfortune or bad luck was watched with eagerness by others hoping to get his berth. The men Grenfell had so admired for their simple nobility and brotherliness were being tainted and tempted by the new materialism, and, though he realized that the better wages of the industry were giving fishermen and their families a higher standard of living, Grenfell was saddened by the lack of Christian charity that was changing their characters for the worse.

He was concerned with the lot of the older fishermen, those displaced in the quicker pace, and demanded old-age pensions. "I visited last week," he wrote in *The Toilers*,

> that haven of condemned hulks, the workhouse. It makes one's heart ache to think of those poor fellows . . . so many aged fishermen, after a life of peril and hardships, of hair-breadth escapes in gales and collisions, of privations and hours of toil unknown to landsmen . . . nothing looms ahead of many but the cheerless workhouse. If there is a class of men on earth who deserves of our seafaring nation a better fate, who are they? When will old-age pensions come in? Sailors, soldiers, servants of firms, all look forward to a pension, however small; but these men of the sea, often heroes of as noble and unselfish actions as ever called forth our praise and gratitude, go quietly downward as they get older. From skipper to mate, mate to deckhand, deckhand to cook, until their little homes are broken up and the poor fellows reappear stamped with the badge of poverty, the despised inmates of the workhouse.

As he worked for and with the British fishermen Grenfell did not forget their brothers across an ocean. In every talk he gave he spoke about the Mission's work in Labrador. He had many grim tales to tell. The missionaries there were achieving a great deal, certainly, but conditions on the Labrador were no less brutal than they had been. Willway's reports were of continued destitution, sickness from undernourishment, and apathy. The doctors travelled thousands of miles every year, by boat in the summer and by sledge in the winter, encountering as part of their mission the hardships and dangers of the coast. The nurses lived and worked heroically, staying long months by themselves and undertaking journeys to the sick over snow and ice and in temperatures far below zero. But neither doctors nor nurses could reach every sick person, and Grenfell described to his audiences many grim tragedies. A man whose wounded foot had developed gangrene got his two young daughters to attempt amputation of the limb with an ordinary knife, and only the fortunate arrival of a Mission doctor saved his life. The doctors, coming upon a lonely hut or a settlement, found whole families helpless with pneumonia, too weak to keep fires going or to find game. Epidemics swept along the coast, and many died before word reached the hospitals and help could reach the sick.

There were tales of other tragedies. Forty-five sealers were frozen to death when the ice they were on was driven to sea by a sudden gale and their ship was unable to reach them because of the ice barrier. Other ships strove heroically to break through this barrier, while the marooned men tried to keep themselves alive by rubbing one another's faces, the older men clearing the ice from the faces of the boys who were with them. They burned their poles to get warmth, but when the ships did reach the drifting pans it was too late. Two young girls on the coast had been attacked and killed by hunger-maddened huskies, one child half eaten before the dogs were shot. These stories shocked Grenfell's audiences, and he made them vivid with his dramatist's gift of narrative and his passionate concern for the victims. He made many weep as he described the death of little Pomiuk, and read aloud a letter the Eskimo boy had written to him, describing his Christmas at Battle Harbour Hospital:

> Me got a nice time at Xmas, sweets and a cake. Lot of little girls and boys got a tea. It makes them laugh to look at Xmas big tree. Sister got Tommy and me jack in box. I opened box. I very

K

frightened and make people laugh very much. I make paper chains very long for sister, also candles in lanterns, very pretty .... I want a letter by and bye, please. Me like to see you next year. Im sorry you stop home. . . . *Aukshenai*, Dr Grenfell, very much, Gabriel Pomiuk.

Not long after he wrote this Pomiuk died.

But among the tales of hardship and tragedy there were many bright spots. The Mission work was increasing and its activities were expanding. A Canadian, Dr Grierson, was now working on the northern coast of Newfoundland, and each summer Willway travelled far north with a new ship, the ex-tug *Julia Sheridan*, while another doctor took the *Princess May* along the southern coast of Labrador. The numbers of patients treated annually exceeded 2000, and with this medical help the doctors were carrying on evangelistic work and giving out clothing. Willway had been appointed by the Newfoundland Government to distribute aid, though he declared that this was not the solution to the people's problems. Some form of employment should be given to them, road-making, tree-felling, so that they could maintain their self-respect. He insisted on men cutting timber for fuel for his steamer in return for the clothing he gave out.

The Red Bay Co-operative Society was prospering, and Grenfell could tell his audiences how the people in this Labrador settlement were benefiting. A young student from Harvard University had gone to Red Bay to instruct the storekeeper in book-keeping and the organization of his store. The student wrote to Grenfell to say that the co-operative was now paying a 5 per cent. dividend, and by managing its own affairs Red Bay had been saved from destitution following a bad year along the coast. No one starved in the settlement now. Grenfell was jubilant, and urged that other co-operatives be started along the coast. He only wished he were there to supply the incentive.

Meantime he could help by finding money for the Mission's work, and in particular for the building of a proper hospital ship for the coast. Willway and his assistants were working with the sorely tried *Princess May* and the 45-foot *Julia Sheridan*, but neither of these was large enough for the expanding efforts and the greater calls being made on the doctors' services. The *Sir Donald* had continued to be unlucky, adding to a long list of misfortunes by being carried out of her winter harbour by the ice, to be found far out at sea by sealers who claimed salvage. When Willway tried to steam her to Battle Harbour to be used as an annexe to the hospital there her boiler manhole-cover blew off, and she had to be towed back to St John's, where she now lay a hulk and offered for sale.

Grenfell set himself the task of raising £3000 for a real hospital ship for Labrador. He proposed a special fund for this purpose, and, though the Council disliked their Superintendent's many 'special' funds for the Labrador Mission, which they believed lessened the contributions to their general funds, they allowed this one. Lord Strathcona, now living in England and taking an interest in the Mission's affairs, gave the first £500, and Grenfell worked energetically to find the remainder. At the Mission's General Meeting in 1898 he made a special effort. He had been told not to speak about Labrador, as Dr Willway was home and in the hall and would handle this subject, but Grenfell was determined to have his say. He began his speech by saying, "I was told not to say a word about Labrador, but I am going to transgress"; then made his appeal. Willway spoke next, somewhat wryly. "Dr Grenfell," he said, "is not only a good speaker, he is also a good beggar." He disclosed the fact that Grenfell already had £1500 pounds towards the new ship; but pointed out that, even if the total sum were collected, the steamer could not and should not be built until there was enough money to maintain her. She would cost nearly a thousand pounds a year to run. "My position," Willway explained, "is that of a safety-valve. Unless we keep a grip on Dr Grenfell he is likely to run away with us, and now we have to give him scope and now heave him in." Willway did not want the new ship built until there was money to run her. Grenfell was not worried by such a problem. The Lord would provide. That night, before the meeting ended, a member of the audience offered to give £100 if others would give the same amount and the total amount was raised by a certain date. The sum was raised; and the keel of the new ship was laid down at a shipyard in Dartmouth. Grenfell had 'run away' with it again. His next ambition was to sail the new hospital ship across the Atlantic.

Grenfell was not to achieve this ambition. In the summer of 1899 Dr Willway wrote to the Mission Council to say that his wife's health had broken down under the strain of sharing his labours and that he would have to bring her to England. He suggested that Grenfell bring out the new ship and relieve him. Grenfell was then in the North Sea, introducing a number of boys from public schools to life among the fishermen. He had spoken at many schools, urging the boys to the Christian way of life and to work for their fellowmen, inspiring many who were to take up missionary work. His new idea, to give both a lesson and an adventure, was only one of his efforts to interest the young.

This experiment over and successful, Grenfell cleared up his affairs in England. The new steamer, launched in June and named *Strathcona*, now being rigged and fitted out by the Mission's own staff at Yarmouth, was yet far from ready, so he took passage on board an ore-carrying steamer bound for Tilt Cove, on the eastern coast of Newfoundland. As the ship was not registered to carry passengers, Grenfell signed the Articles as ship's doctor at a shilling a month and 'worked' his way across. A friend, a Scot named Beattie, whom Grenfell had induced to work for the Mission as a volunteer, accompanied him, signing on as purser for the voyage.

Beattie was amazed by the welcome he shared when the two men landed at Tilt Cove. This was more than the usual generous hospitality of Newfoundlanders, for the people of Tilt Cove had not forgotten "the Doctor." Four years before he had sailed into this harbour with the *Sir Donald*, to find the people in desperate situation, half starved and ill-clothed and with many sick, after a year's bad fishing. Grenfell had been able to ease their condition from the clothing and food in his vessel, and to help the sick. The settlement was in better condition now, the men being employed in a copper mine that had been opened in the district, and they wanted to show their gratitude. The two visitors were loaded with gifts for the Mission and made much of. Grenfell was able to help again, for the resident doctor maintained by the mine-owners was away for a week, and Grenfell took over his duties. Then, with the *Julia Sheridan* arrived to pick them up, and her deck loaded with gifts of coal and vegetables, Grenfell and Beattie sailed for Labrador.

In late September, after having called on old friends and attended the sick at several places along the Newfoundland coast, Grenfell arrived at Battle Harbour. It had been almost three years since he left this Labrador 'capital,' and now the fishermen and their families who lived or who had come to fish from there showed how delighted they were that he was back. In his three years' absence his name had become a legend; stories of his coming to the coast were already part of Labrador history. To celebrate his return flags had been slung along the fronts of the traders' stores and on the hospital, and as the *Julia Sheridan* steamed into the tickle and headed for the wooden jetty men fired off their guns and gathered to greet their benefactor. Dr Apsland and his wife, who had been Sister Carwardine, were there to greet him and to escort him to the hospital between lines of smiling fishermen and their families. Grenfell was delighted to be back, and his eyes were moist with emotion as he looked at the familiar scenes or saw a face he recognized. This Labrador stirred and satisfied him as no other place did. Those treeless hills where spurs of dark rock thrust from the coloured moss, the rugged shore that the restless Atlantic swell edged with white, the roughly built shacks, their timber bleached grey by the weather, had a beauty for him that no softer or higher-coloured landscape could have. This, the place and its people, was home, and he would never wish to leave again.

He moved in royal progress up the steep path to the hospital, stopping to grasp a hand, ruffle a child's hair, and to remember some one he had treated years before. The hospital delighted him, "bringing a lump to the throat," for it gleamed with polish and shone with the new paint Dr Apsland had been applying. Seven years ago it had been an empty building, and now it was a well-equipped haven for the sick. The doctors and their helpers had installed a bathroom, built on a convalescence room, and made other improvements, nurses as well as doctors learning to be carpenters and house-painters among the dozen other tasks they undertook. As he passed through the ward, seeing every bed occupied, Grenfell was deeply moved. Lives were being saved that would have been lost, limbs that would have been twisted and useless without medical skill made good, and health restored to hundreds who would have been left to the dangerous ministrations of some old, foully dirty 'healer' if the missionaries had not sacrificed the comforts of civilization

to serve these people for Christ's sake. Grenfell had only gratitude in his heart for those who had continued and expanded the
work he had started.

He stayed at Battle Harbour only a few days, and then sailed
north as far as Rigolet to do what work he could in the short
weeks left of this season. Everywhere he stopped people gathered
to welcome him, to listen to him preach and seek his help. He
found the Liveyeres in little better condition than they had been
years before. There was still much poverty, the children were
still poorly clothed and barefooted, many showing in scrofula
and tubercular bones and coughs the effect of their poor diet,
the 'dry' food that was mainly flour. The Mission doctors and
nurses had done much in the last years, but there was still much
to do. As he passed north, then turned south again, Grenfell's
mind teemed with the ideas he would put into practice now he
was back.

Meantime he helped those he could, his pity making him
tolerant in getting payment for what he gave. The accusations
made in St John's that the Mission was 'pauperizing' the
people had increased. Traders complained that the clothing,
reconditioned guns, and other goods the Mission was permitted
to bring in free of duty were being used to compete with them.
Grenfell had no wish to pauperize the people, nor deprive the
merchants of trade, but he could not sail past people in the condition so many were in, particularly on this voyage of home-
coming. He gave to those who needed, and he avoided some of
his critics by organizing sports among the Eskimos and Indians
in the north and presenting prizes of clothing for shooting and
races, delighting the winners by handing them scarlet army
tunics, 'pink' hunting-coats, and other novel garments. He
could at least give his medical skill without fear of criticism,
and he treated over 300 patients during his cruise to the north
and along Belle Isle Strait, bringing the total for the Mission
workers that year to almost 3000 patients.

Early in November Grenfell laid the *Julia Sheridan* up for
the winter at St Anthony, in North-west Newfoundland. He
had intended to go to Canada and the United States after his
cruise, but instead responded to an appeal to winter in Northern
Newfoundland. A Mission doctor had worked on this north
shore for two summers now, and had reported a great need for

his services, and as much hardship as was in Labrador. In 1897, after a particularly severe winter and much sickness in the district, Reuben Sims's wife, a woman of better education than most of the settlers, had written to Grenfell asking that a doctor come to St Anthony and that the Mission help the people there. The trader Mr George Moore, whom Grenfell had stayed with when he called into the harbour before, urged that a hospital be built, for St Anthony was the jumping-off point for schooners leaving the island for Labrador, and there were often hundreds of vessels in the harbour and a great need for medical service for their crews.

Now Grenfell came to propose that the people in the settlement build their own hospital, and the Mission would keep it open during the winter months and until the fishing fleet had gone north. He and Beattie would stay in St Anthony that winter, to help with the building and to do what they could for the people. With the steamer stripped and laid up, Grenfell and Beattie moved into the trader's house and were given room for a surgery. Beattie opened a school in a building that the settlers had erected, and soon some thirty children were getting the benefits of his Oxford training and a touch of the Scottish dominie in the tawse Beattie hung conspicuously on his desk.

It had been Grenfell's ambition for years to stay in Labrador for a winter, an ambition he was never to realize; but now he could winter in Newfoundland, and he was delighted at the prospect. He took on the fisherman-trapper Reuben Sims as his servant and guide, and began to learn how to handle a dog team and komatik. During a holiday in Switzerland he had learned to ski, and now he brought his 'long' shoes, and preferred these to the skin-strung snowshoes the natives used. His early attempts to manage a team of eight to ten dogs and a 16-foot komatik often ended in a tangle of snarling, fighting huskies, the sledge overturned, and Grenfell head down in a snow-bank, or with half his team on one side of a tree and the others on the other side, with the komatik caught up against the trunk. But he learned quickly and took the accidents, a wetting when he misjudged the strength of the ice and went through to the water, as so much sauce for his pleasure. As with a boat, he could be over-daring and attempt what was learned only after long experience with a team and sledge; and Reuben Sims had often to check his pupil's too ambitious driving.

He loved the long journeys he had to make over the snow or ice to visit sick persons. When it was known that Grenfell was on the coast messages came from all over, asking his aid. His parish and practice extended as far as men could travel, and during this winter he made journeys of over sixty miles each way to Flower's Cove, on Belle Isle Strait, to Cape Bauld thirty miles away, and far to the southward. He never refused a call, and each journey was an adventure he welcomed. Nothing was ever to give him the satisfaction he got from taking a ship to sea, but winter travel had its own delights. The harnessing of the excited, leaping dogs, the jerk and motion of the komatik he rode or ran beside, directing the dogs with sharp calls and correcting them with a 30-foot lash as they spread out in fan shape on their long traces, had its own special pleasure. There was deep satisfaction when a long, muscle-wearying day was over and he sat with Sims, or anyone they met, over a fire in a settler's home or in a Government tilt on the trail; for then food had an extra quality, and a sleeping-bag was luxury.

He got to know the country in its majestic winter robe of white, the snow-contoured hills, the many ponds that were now gleaming medallions of ice, and the military array of spruce whose trunks seemed strained to hold the icy weight on their boughs. The coast took on a new grandeur as he drove his team close under the cliffs on the smoother ice there, and his challenging nature was stirred by the need for quick reactions to the obstacles each mile brought. It was an exhilarating experience for a man like Grenfell, and at the end of each journey reward came in reaching a sick person in time to help, or save a life. Then with the patient attended to, he would sit with the settlers and hear their tales of this northern land, the folklore and songs that had something of Ireland, Scotland, and France in their colour and swing. He loved those evenings with the fishermen and trappers, and gathered a great store of material for the articles and books he was now writing. At the end of each evening he held a service, for this was Christ's work he did, and he must tell people Who had sent him.

When he was not away on some mission he was bringing his

energy and inventiveness to serve the people of St Anthony, his declared purpose to brighten their lives. He took over a seldom used courthouse and its cells and made it into a cheerful club-room. The walls were papered with old magazines, and hung with the Bible texts Grenfell liked round him; a large Union Jack, a Stars and Stripes, and a Red Cross flag were stretched under the roof. Chairs were made from cut-down flour barrels, tables built by the settlers. A bagatelle table was made, the top covered with cloth from a wrecked steamer and the cushions improvised with elastic leg-bandage. The balls were sent up from St John's by the last mail-steamer of the year, with sets of draughts and dominoes. The settlers need no longer sit long hours in their dreary shacks, but came to read magazines or books, and to play games, some of them confessing to Grenfell that it was the first time in their lives they had played any game.

He organized more strenuous pastimes. A football field was marked out on the harbour ice, and with balls given to him by the pupils of Mostyn House School he taught old and young to play soccer. He held shooting matches, going with the men on long hikes to find fat eider duck and other game. When Christ-mas came he had a large tree erected and decorated, a treat the St Anthony children had never seen before. Sports were held on the ice on Christmas Day, with obstacle races where competi-tors climbed over a wrecked schooner showing above the ice and crawled under seal-nets. Targets were set up for the older men to show their marksmanship, and a greasy pole was erected for the agile. There were prizes or presents for every child, and the day ended with a concert.

His aim was not only to brighten the lives of these isolated people, but to bring them together as a community. As he found his own greatest happiness in having people round him and in sharing their lives, so he wanted others to feel the same. He continued this theme in trying to set up more co-operatives, and that winter he travelled long distances to talk to the fisher-men in other settlements, urging them to join together as the people of Red Bay had. There, at Red Bay, the settlers had been saved from the results of another poor season's fishing by their co-operative, for they got the best price for their fish and were learning where to buy their supplies. The co-operative had increased its dividend from 5 to 10 per cent., and the members bought what they needed in their own store at half the price traders demanded. Grenfell had visited the settlement during his cruise and found the people happy and without fear for the winter, their children decently clothed, and families with money for the first time in their lives. He wrote home to say, "Co-operation is now part of my religion."

He found opposition. Traders were now realizing that if the success at Red Bay extended to other settlements their profits would be less, and some of them were far from scrupulous in their opposition. To some Grenfell was not the 'angel' he had been called, but a dangerous character. He was accused of making money out of the co-operatives he proposed, and so he restrained his often impetuous speech by keeping carefully to a written explanation of co-operation to avoid being misquoted or having his words twisted by his opponents. He went to several settlements, gathering the fishermen together and explaining this 'copper,' as they called it, to them. Many were doubtful, many were afraid to go into such a venture, but that winter one more co-operative society was started at a little settlement, Braha, and Grenfell was jubilant. Soon the hateful truck system would be destroyed.

Towards the end of the winter his largest experiment in communal effort was carried out when Grenfell led a large gang of settlers inland to get timber for the new hospital. He stayed with them for two weeks, helping to fell, trim, and cart the timber by komatik to the hospital site, living in tilts the men built after digging down into the snow, and eating the same rough fare. Such work gave the energetic Grenfell satisfaction, but even greater satisfaction was in knowing that it gathered the settlers together in a common aim. By the time the ice was cracking in the harbour and the mail-boat could once again push close to the settlement 350 trees had been cut and brought in. The building could not be started yet, for the settlers had to prepare for the fishing, but it would be up next winter. Grenfell went to work to get the *Julia Sheridan* ready for the summer.

The ice was slow to leave the coast that year, and it was June 28 before the *Julia Sheridan*, with Grenfell on board, could sail for the North. Outside the harbour ice and fog made progress hazardous, and Grenfell had to wait with dozens of schooners on the Newfoundland coast for over a week. The Mission ship did not reach Battle Harbour until July 7, and the vessel had difficulty entering the tickle because of the ice. She had to be anchored outside for a time, and then, once in, was held by more and more ice. Grenfell reported to his Mission that schooners crammed the harbour and all movement was stopped. Not a patch of clear water could be seen from the island. The fishing would be a failure that year if these conditions continued. Vessels could not sail and nets could not be put out until the ice cleared. And there was no word of the *Strathcona*, or of doctors and supplies. Supplies of drugs and dressings were getting low at the hospital.

While Grenfell was still held at Battle the mail-steamer arrived with the precious stores and a new missionary, Dr MacPherson. MacPherson was at once packed off to Indian Harbour, but he was back in Battle again within a day, bringing a letter from the Master of the steamer, asking for help. The steamer's propeller had been knocked off by the ice, and she was in a dangerous position. Grenfell had steam raised in the *Julia Sheridan* and went twenty miles north, to tow the large ship to a safe anchorage and then to send word south for help. Grenfell was rightly proud of this service; it was no simple task for his tiny vessel to tow the large mail-steamer to safety.

This accomplished, Grenfell left for his cruise along the southern coast, but he was back in Battle in early August, to find the *Strathcona* alongside the wharf. This handsome vessel, steel-hulled, 97 feet long, and with a speed of nine knots, was his dreams come true, the answer to so many prayers and the reward for much effort. He went on board, to greet the crew of Yarmouth men who had brought her out under an experienced Master. She delighted him. Rigged as a ketch and with yacht-like lines, her hull reinforced for ice-pressure, and designed as a hospital ship, she would enable him to do so much more. She had a spacious hospital just forward of amidships, with the engine-room and crew's quarters aft and a saloon and two cabins in the forward part. The hospital had six cots, two of them slung, a proper dispensary, and X-ray equipment. There were luxuries in electric light, a bathroom, and other fittings never seen in a ship on this coast before. All her woodwork was teak on deck and polished mahogany below; brasswork gleamed everywhere—from her steering-wheel, with the words "Follow me, and I will make you fishers of men" engraved on it, as they were on the wheels of every Mission ship, to the galley fittings. Grenfell was the proudest man afloat. He installed himself in a cabin at the foot of a wide teak companionway between the hospital and the saloon, and felt himself a real shipmaster at last.

12

Preaching is not enough

GRENFELL's return to Labrador in 1899 was the beginning of a new life. From now on he was to detach
himself from the Mission in England, to give himself
entirely to the people of Labrador and Newfoundland. Soon
after his return he wrote to his mother: "I feel I have been
blessed in coming here, and feel sure that as in all things our
Father had a purpose in sending me." In 1900 he asked the
Council to let Dr Willway take over his duties in England for
another year, while he remained on the American side. The
Council could only agree. Mrs Willway was now gravely ill,
and Willway could not leave her. There was no other suitable
person to conduct the work in Labrador. Grenfell's title was
changed to Medical Superintendent, and Willway became
Superintendent in England. Two years later, when it was clear
that Grenfell's name was so closely associated with the Labrador

Mission, particularly in the United States and Canada, that support would be lost if he were recalled, the Council accepted the inevitable: Willway and Grenfell were made joint Superintendents. There was never again any attempt made to displace Grenfell from Labrador.

The Council could only hope that their enterprising and energetic servant would not bring them too many problems. They had enough already. In 1900 the Mission had a deficit of over £2000, and had to withdraw one ship from the North Sea for a time. Adjusting their work to serve the changing fishing industry meant building more mission halls and replacing the sailing-vessels with steamboats, and the Labrador Mission was growing bigger and more expensive than had ever been expected or desired. The Council, apprehensive of how far they might be involved by the impetuous Grenfell, could only warn him not to incur more expense. At the Annual Meeting in 1900 Dr Willway spoke somewhat wryly of his colleague. "Last summer," he said, "the Government of Newfoundland built a courthouse in the harbour at St Anthony, and last October a man landed from a steamboat and took charge of the courthouse. He took the judge's throne and turned it into a bagatelle board. I need hardly say that that man was my friend and colleague Dr Grenfell. What he is now doing none of us can tell. Those of you who know him are prepared for any news that may come home at any time from him."

The news, as it came during the next years, did nothing to ease the worries of those concerned with the Mission finances. Grenfell was expanding the work in all directions, seemingly with no thought for where the money would be found, but with a sublime assurance that it would be found. He went ahead with the building of the hospital at St Anthony, although warned by the Council that the Mission could undertake no new burdens. He got the Newfoundland Government to agree to contribute 1500 dollars a year towards the cost of medicines and doctors' expenses for this hospital, and he found a benefactor in the United States who would supply a heating system. A clergyman, the Rev. Jesse Halsey, who was also an excellent plumber, came to St Anthony to install the pipes, and local men blasted out a cellar to contain the boiler. The work dragged on for five years, each stage having to wait until money was found to advance again, and it was not until 1905 that the hospital was officially opened. But long before then patients were being treated, and doctors and nurses were improvising as best they could, carrying the water they needed from a stream and working with oil-lamps, ladders serving as stairways and beds set up where space could be found. How much this hospital was needed was proved each time the mail-steamer called in the harbour. Patients, as many as fifty at a time, came from as far south as St John's and from all along the shores of Belle Isle Strait for treatment.

In 1905, despite another warning from the Council not to undertake the work until at least half the money to pay for the building was in their hands, Grenfell began building the long since proposed hospital at Harrington, in Canadian Labrador. His petition to the Canadian Government had been rejected, the Government saying that they did not wish to start a precedent. Grenfell's Montreal committee had offered to find the money, and were promised 4000 dollars by a benefactor, but this money had not been received. Nevertheless, Grenfell proposed to go ahead, and he sent a married couple, a Dr Mather Hare and his wife, who had been missionaries in China, to Harrington to start building. When Hare, a Boston man, sent word that he could find labour Grenfell ignored the Council's caution and told him to go ahead. At the same time he sent a telegram to Montreal, asking for the money. Again his faith was justified: a reply came, saying that the money was there. Another benefactor presented Dr Hare with a steam-launch for his summer work, and a newspaper, the *Montreal Weekly Star*, which had been strongly critical of the Canadian Government for not helping, contributed dogs and sledges for winter travel.

The hospitals at Indian Harbour and Battle Harbour were enlarged in those years after Grenfell's return, and a house built for the doctor at Battle. A nursing station was established at Forteau Bay, at the eastern end of the Strait, where a nurse, Sister Bailey, lived and worked throughout the year, serving no fewer than eighteen settlements and travelling long distances by boat and komatik on her calls. Each year other nursing stations were maintained along the coast during the summer months, manned by volunteer medical students and nurses.

By 1905 there were few places on the coast of Labrador and

Newfoundland where a doctor did not visit at least once a year, either in winter or in summer. Grenfell himself covered over 3000 miles with the *Strathcona* every summer, and other, smaller vessels with doctors on board worked smaller sections. The number of patients treated annually reached and then exceeded 4000. The doctors handled every sort of ailment, from toothache to complicated brain tumours. They fought epidemics, amputated limbs, and tackled the new threat of beriberi, another nutritional disease, crippling its victims. They worked under every disadvantage, operating on kitchen tables as often as not. They had to improvise and invent instruments, teach husbands to administer anæsthetics to their wives, overcome people's fear of being cut. They carried on a campaign against dirt and ignorance, instructed the people in diet, and warned them of the dangers of spitting. Gradually they discredited the 'healers' and their dangerous cures and earned the people's trust. The day when the sick were at the mercy of anyone who pretended knowledge of healing was passing; a better service was available than a schooner skipper delivering a child with pieces of wooden slats as forceps. There were still not enough doctors or nurses to cover the coast all through the year, but that ideal was coming.

All this was not enough for Grenfell. He believed that in this clear-aired land there should be no diseases such as tuberculosis, typhoid, or smallpox. The cause of so much sickness was malnutrition, the poor diet and living conditions that debilitated the people and made them easy victims of every infection. The blame lay partly in the exploitation of the fisher folk, and Grenfell was fighting this through the co-operatives. There were four stores operating by 1905, and soon there would be double that number. In the North, where the settlements were too small for co-operatives, Grenfell financed fishermen who set up in opposition to established traders to break their monopoly. He bought furs from trappers, or carried them out to sell for their full market price and gave this to the trappers. He was friendly with most of the Hudson's Bay Company post managers, but he did not hesitate to advise the Liveyeres to demand detailed statements of their accounts from even this powerful concern, or take their catch elsewhere. He bought up the stock of trading schooners who had not cleared their holds on the coast, buying the goods cheaply and passing them to the Liveyeres at what he paid. Later, when the guest of honour at a luncheon given by the directors of the Hudson's Bay Company in London, he told his hosts bluntly, "I hold no brief for any company ... the brief I hold is for the catchers of the fur."

He realized quickly that the people's and the Colony's reliance on the two traditional activities, fishing and trapping, was dangerous. A poor fishing season or the periodic disappearance of fur-bearing animals from a locality could be disastrous. He had a dozen schemes for new industries. He believed Labrador to be rich in minerals, and urged the Canadian Government to send prospectors into the country. He believed that tourists could be attracted by the wonderful trout- and salmon-fishing and the hunting, and pressed for the coast to be properly surveyed so that larger ships could cruise them. He sent his own surveys and sketches of the coastline to the Royal Naval Hydrographic Department, drawings that are still there and have been included in charts of the coast.

Tentative efforts had been made to exploit the vast quantity of timber in Newfoundland and Labrador, but it was not until 1905 that the Anglo-Newfoundland Development Company, working in the interests of Harmsworth newspapers, built a newsprint mill in Newfoundland. Grenfell started on this industry as early as 1902, securing a grant of land in Canada Bay, south of St Anthony, a district notorious for its poverty, and launching a co-operative lumber-mill. The settlers had no money to buy shares, so Grenfell sank some of his own small fortune in the venture and wrote to his mother, inviting her to invest a hundred pounds. "These works are to me just as real and permanent a preaching as mere sermonizing," he told her. She could offer him only ten pounds, but with his own money and what little the settlers could offer he went ahead, buying machinery and an old schooner that was to be repaired and used for carrying freight for the several co-operative stores. A few years later one of the many experts coaxed to Newfoundland by Grenfell, without being offered fees, suggested that the land cleared of timber could be cultivated. Grenfell sent appeals for suitable seeds to his friends in America, and was presented with specially tested grain from an experimental farm in Alaska.

L

He found work for the women on the coast. He bought deer-skins from the Indians who camped in Hamilton Inlet every summer, passing these to the fishermen's wives to be made into moccasins and gloves. A thriving manufacture of sealskin boots began along the shores of Belle Isle Strait. When visiting the Liveyeres Grenfell noticed how the women tried to brighten their little homes with mats made from old sacking. They un-ravelled the yarn and coloured it with dye made from moss, then hooked the colours into sacking in crude and primitive designs. Immediately he decided that these specimens of native craftsmanship would sell in the cities, and he drew designs of sledges, dogs, icebergs, and other features of the country for the women to copy and supplied them with materials for a more finished product. In 1905 he carried this industry in native produce a step farther.

While on a lecture tour in New England he was taken to see what was probably the first organized attempt at occupational therapy ever made. A Boston woman, Miss Jessie Luther, had started this work, with a doctor she had met while a hospital patient. They had seen how those fellow-patients who occupied themselves with some hobby or handicraft were cured faster and were happier than those who were idle. When Jessie Luther and the doctor were discharged from the hospital they gathered support for their idea and opened a small workshop at Marble-head, in Massachusetts, where convalescents were taught weav-ing and other crafts. Grenfell was immediately impressed. When he had been shown round the workshop he said, "Yes . . . that's what we want. . . . When can you come and teach our people, Miss Luther?" Much though she was impressed by the dynamic Englishman, Jessie Luther had to explain that she could not drop her work like this and go to Newfoundland; but she offered to train any teachers he could send her. Grenfell found two women volunteers, and Jessie Luther gave them a few days' instruction. They went to St Anthony in 1905, with several looms Grenfell had found in a prison he visited; but they did not remain long in Newfoundland. They quarrelled for the few weeks they were together, and then left for home. In 1906 Jessie Luther found herself with three months' free time, and she wrote to Grenfell, offering to go to St Anthony and teach weaving. She received an enthusiastic reply, and made the long journey, by boat to the west coast of Newfoundland, the picturesque but wearying train ride across the island on the railway that had been opened in 1899, and from St John's, again by steamer, to St Anthony.

There she started what was to become an important part of the Grenfell story, an industrial department that was to extend and include hook-mat making, ivory- and wood-carving by disabled fishermen, the making of gloves, moccasins, and coats from deer and other skins, the cutting and mounting of a native stone, labradorite, and the potting of the many kinds of wild berries in which Labrador abounds. By this work fishermen's wives and daughters could add a little to the family income and be rewarded with badly needed clothing for their children and themselves. Jessie Luther stayed three months that first year, but was to return in 1907 as a permanent member of the steadily increasing Mission staff at St Anthony and one of Grenfell's most fervent admirers.

Meantime Grenfell was concerning himself with the welfare of the children. When parents died, breadwinners lost at sea or on the ice, the Liveyeres followed the Eskimo practice: neighbours took in the widows and orphans. Families were large in Labrador, often as many as fifteen to twenty children to a home, and seldom could the parents feed or clothe such numbers in decency. Their hearts were big enough, but the means to support extra children were small. Grenfell had come on many children whose chances of survival were slight while they remained in overcrowded huts and could share only the meagre rations of their foster-parents. He started collecting children, appealing to his friends in England and America to adopt them. He could seldom resist those sad, pale faces, and when a woman came on board his ship carrying two tiny girls who, Grenfell discovered, were both blind, he carried them south. A young girl had been frostbitten, and to save her life her father chopped both her feet off at the ankles with his axe. She was found and brought to a Mission hospital to be healed; new wooden feet were shaped for her by one of the doctors, and the girl was added to Grenfell's collection. In one of the rare cases of cruelty to children that he encountered as a Justice of the Peace he dismissed the stepfather who had ill-treated the child and claimed as his fee the child herself.

Some of these children he placed with families in England and America; but what he wanted was a home for them on the coast. In 1905 such a home was started at St Anthony with five children, and a local woman in charge. A year later an English lady, Miss Eleanor Storr, whose family had entertained Grenfell often, came to Newfoundland as an unpaid volunteer to look after the children's home. A new building was added to the many then rising at St Anthony; and now each time the *Strathcona* arrived back from her annual cruise, among the many trophies Grenfell had collected in bear-cubs, barrels of strong-smelling whale-meat for his dogs, caribou and polar-bear skins taken in exchange for clothing, lumps of rock believed to contain valuable minerals—there were always one or more bewildered and scared children he had collected, and now handed over to Eleanor Storr for their first real scrubbing and a new life.

Schools for these children and others on the coast were his next goal.

Grenfell believed that an educated people would not be so easily victimized by unscrupulous traders. There was little education on the coast. What schools there were were in the larger settlements, open only during the summer months. They were Church schools, and a wasteful system existed where in a settlement each church conducted classes of a few children each, the teachers chosen for their church loyalties rather than for their teaching qualifications. Grenfell disliked denominational schools, believing that they fostered rivalry and bigotry, and he planned to have Mission schools where all could attend. He began with volunteer teachers who came each summer, but his plans were more ambitious. He would build schools all along the coast and free the people from bigotry as well as poverty.

These activities did not please every one. While the missionaries had confined themselves to medical and evangelistic work they had been welcomed and praised, but as Grenfell launched his many schemes his popularity waned among the merchants. The success of his co-operative stores had put several traders out of business. His handing out of second-hand clothing, reconditioned guns, and food reduced profits and power. He was becoming a dangerous competitor. He was even proposing to start a co-operative stores at Battle Harbour, in competition with Messrs Baine Grieve, who had gifted the hospital building there and done much to help the missionaries. He was not always tactful, and it was not pleasant for the traders to know that he went to Canada and the United States and made them out to be some sort of ogre in his description of the 'truck' system and the prices they charged.

Even his attempts to bring a semblance of law and order to the coast were often an interference with powers the traders had possessed. In 1899 the Mission doctors had been authorized to act as Justices of the Peace, and Grenfell used this authority to fight illegalities that had been accepted or winked at for years. He was determined to stop the sale of illicit liquor to the fishermen, and he sought out and prosecuted mercilessly those traders who carried and sold drink. He succeeded in getting the Government to station a policeman on the coast, and now much that had been done with impunity became dangerous. With this interfering and far too active doctor, and Marconi wireless stations and telegraph stations being placed on the coast, the old isolation that had made investigation of crimes difficult was going. There had been a time when the more powerful traders and planters could ride roughshod over the independent fishermen, sending their men to remove the weaker man's nets and placing their own traps on the more rewarding berths. Now a squeal from the fishermen brought Grenfell on the scene to champion them, and when he could not handle a case himself because of limited power he carried it to St John's.

There had been strandings on the coast that were not always above suspicion, schooners wrecked or run on shore to be judged total wrecks by whoever happened to be on the spot, and the 'wreck' sold for a few dollars. If the buyer managed to refloat the vessel he acquired a bargain, and the only losers were the insurers. Lloyd's had had no representative on the coast to check these losses, and as early as 1893 they invited Grenfell to act as their agent there. He was willing enough, but the Mission Council disapproved, on the grounds that this would be stepping out of the missionary rôle and was liable to make the Mission unpopular. However, in the late summer of 1902 an English vessel, the barquentine *Bessie Dodd*, was reported wrecked at Smoky Tickle, at the entrance to Hamilton Inlet, and insurance claimed. The circumstances were so suspicious that Lloyd's cabled Grenfell, asking him to investigate.

The cablegram was handed to Grenfell when he returned from his cruise that year and was laying the *Strathcona* up in St John's. It was then November 15, and storms which had persisted all the season and caused the loss of six schooners were still blowing. But Grenfell could not resist an adventure such as this promised to be. He chartered a vessel, an English-built steam-trawler, *Magnific*, bought by Bowring and Sons of Newfoundland to see if bottom-trawling could be carried out in American waters, and, despite the bad weather and the imminence of winter, set out on the 800-mile voyage to the north. The ship encountered bad weather all the way, and as she went north the water coming on board froze on her decks and upperworks. The crew were kept busy chipping ice away and ridding the trawler of its heavy weight, and when she reached Smoky Tickle the trawler was sheathed in white from truck to waterline.

The *Bessie Dodd* was found, and it was at once obvious that a crime had been committed. The barquentine had loaded a cargo of dried fish at a trader's wharf, and had sailed, only to run on to a flat, sandy beach less than 150 feet from the wharf. She was undamaged, except for a broken steering chain, and her master had sold her and her cargo to the trader, a man named Gerry Jewett, as a total loss for 80 dollars. The ship was insured for 15,000 dollars, the cargo for another 20,000 dollars. The master and trader had conspired to swindle the insurers, believing that in this remote place and with winter near investigation was unlikely.

With magnificent seamanship the trawler's skipper, Captain Arthur Jackson, hauled the barquentine back into deep water, and towed her the long haul to St John's. The weather remained stormy, with wintry temperatures, and the voyage south was hazardous and difficult. In a gale off the coast of Newfoundland, the tow was almost lost, but the trawler's skipper got her to St John's, where Grenfell charged Jewett with barratry. The *Bessie Dodd*'s master was brought from England and confessed to conspiring with the trader. Jewett was tried and convicted. The grateful insurers presented Grenfell with a gold watch, and Lloyd's appointed him their agent for Labrador. He was more pleased at having removed Jewett from the coast, for the trader had been selling liquor, and Grenfell had long tried to get proof of this.

Grenfell's part in this incident did not add to his popularity among certain people, and there was a great deal of muttering against his prosecution of Jewett. He was stepping far beyond the missionary field, into affairs that should be no concern of a doctor or preacher. In November 1905 the opposition came out into the open. The St John's *Trade Review* printed an article, headed "Sactumettes, or Grenfell's Game." It read:

> This is about the time of the year that a gentleman known in this country as Dr Grenfell begins to publish in some of the local papers what he calls his 'Log.' As the matter contained in the Log is about as interesting as the back of a Bill of Lading and as original as a police-court summons, it is safe to say that not one man in a thousand reads it; but if the writings of the Doctor are not interesting no one can deny that the Doctor himself is an interesting man. He comes to us in the triple capacity of philanthropist, evangelist and trader, his special sphere of action being the rugged coast of Labrador. What he has achieved in the first two capacities is problematical, but there is no doubt about it, he has made considerable money by his mission. Clever man! There are but few men sufficiently gifted to successfully point to the Heavenly Jerusalem with one hand and sell old clo' with the other, but it appears that the Doctor is one of them. It is said that he can talk of the golden streets and dilate on the beauties of a five-dollar suit almost in one breath, enlarge on the better life and buy a consignment of skin boots at the same time (at the lowest possible price) without turning a hair. That a man of such exceptional parts shall make money on the Labrador is not to be wondered at, and we are not surprised to hear that he will soon retire from the Mission with what the sinful and vulgar would call "his whack of spondulics."

This article was the bugle sounding the attack for all those who disliked Grenfell. The St John's *News* published a letter from his Grace the Roman Catholic Archbishop of St John's, who, with other leading Churchmen, disliked intensely Grenfell's criticism of sectarianism and his preaching of evangelistic Protestantism. His intention to set up non-denominational schools was a threat to the Churches' influence, and, where they could, both the Roman Catholic and the Church of England bishops had opposed him.

Archbishop Howley now allied himself with the traders who had sponsored the attack on Grenfell. He sent a letter to the *News*, saying:

> If Dr Grenfell is ever overwhelmed with a spirit of humanity, of philanthropy, of Christian charity, could he not find ample fields for his overflowing zeal nearer home? There is nothing in the circumstances of Labrador that calls for extraneous help, or that our local government might not be able to cope with. Grenfell is not needed on that shore and his work is not only useless but worse than useless. It is demoralizing, pauperizing and degrading.

The Archbishop quoted figures to show that enough poverty existed in England for Grenfell to concern himself there, and said that the Mission, far from lessening disease on the coast, had caused an increase. Before the Mission came the death-rate in Labrador had been 9 per thousand, and in 1904 it was 20·52 per thousand.

One St John's paper, the *Herald*, defended Grenfell. His 'crime,' it said, was prosecuting Jewett, stopping illegal drink-sellers, and starting co-operatives. Far from making money, Grenfell had lost 2500 dollars of his own money in helping the co-operatives. The *Herald* fought this battle with lusty colonial vigour and no holds barred. The owner of the *News* was described as "That man of gall with his halo on . . . the greatest scoundrel who had ever entered the Narrows."

Grenfell answered his critics. He showed how the Archbishop's figures for the death-rate in Labrador had been chosen in a year when 56 Eskimos had died during an epidemic of *grippe*. These deaths deducted, the figure would be less than 10 per thousand. Clothing was not given away, except in cases of desperate need, and Grenfell made no apology for this. People had to pay for the clothing in work and service. He also started legal proceedings against the *Trade Review*, and its editor had to publish an apology, withdrawing every accusation. The Newfoundland committee supporting the Mission's work published a statement, saying they were entirely satisfied that the charges were false and that the work being done on the coast was valuable and for the good of all.

By the time the attack died down Grenfell had shrugged away his irritation. He had other matters to concern himself with, two great new ventures to launch. He was going to build the finest seamen's hostel in the world in St John's, and he was going to bring reindeer from Norway. The Mission had been offered an old sailors' home on the St John's waterfront, and Grenfell immediately and grandiosely decided to pull this down and build a better and bigger place. It was reckoned that 250,000 seafarers, fishermen and crews of visiting merchant vessels, passed through St John's every year and had nowhere to go other than the Water Street taverns. Hundreds of girls from the outports came to serve on schooners and were in moral danger in the poor lodgings they could afford, among the wild characters from ships. Grenfell was determined to build a hostel so attractive that men and women would prefer it to the taverns.

The suggestion that domesticated reindeer would be a benefit to Newfoundland and Labrador people was made to Grenfell by an American, Dr Sheldon Jackson, who had had much to do with importing these animals to Alaska in 1892. This experiment, carried out by the United States Government as a means of supplying food for the Eskimos in their territory, had been a great success, the original herd increasing tremendously. Grenfell was immediately enthusiastic. Reindeer would supply much-needed fresh milk, meat, and skins for winter clothing. They would displace dogs as a means of transport. Dogs were a necessity in the Colony, but also a liability, and could be a danger. There had been many occasions when hunger-maddened huskies had attacked and eaten human beings, particularly children. They were subject to a disease that killed them by the hundred, leaving the people with no means of transport during the winter. Feeding dogs could be a serious problem, for seal, whale-meat, or fish was not always available. Dogs had prevented the Mission doctors from keeping sheep and cattle, for they killed anything they could find when seeking food for themselves.

Reindeer would bring many benefits, and the multiplying herds would be a new source of income. Their meat could be exported. And they cost nothing to feed. They ate moss, and both Labrador and Newfoundland had plenty of moss. Grenfell asked the Mission's secretary in England, Mr Francis Wood, to find out how much a herd of 300 reindeer shipped to New-foundland, with Lapp herders to train the local men, would cost.

He was told that the cost would be around 15,000 dollars. The cost of the sailors' home at St John's as Grenfell planned it was estimated at over 100,000 dollars. Grenfell wrote to his increasing number of friends in America and Canada, and then set out himself to find this large sum. He had no doubt that it would be found.

13

Adrift on an Ice Pan

IN 1898, the year before Grenfell returned to Labrador, the cost of carrying on the Mission work there was £1750. In 1906 the total for the year was £5919. This was expenditure on the purely Mission work, medical and evangelistic, though it did not include the cost of running the hospital at St Anthony or what was being done at Harrington. These last were supported by a Newfoundland Government grant and direct contributions from the United States and Canada. Of the 1906 expenditure the Mission in England contributed £1694. The remainder came from North America and Newfoundland. With it came a great deal more, which went towards Grenfell's projects and 'special' funds he controlled and used to help cases of hardship. The total sums contributed and spent during those years cannot now be discovered, but they must have been very large.

The finding of this money was becoming Grenfell's main

task, and he was giving more and more time to touring and lecturing in America. His success was remarkable. In a single month he collected over 20,000 dollars in the United States alone, and a great deal more came in from the efforts made by others.

It was a personal success. Grenfell's impact on American audiences was astounding, for there was no reason why the people of the United States should respond to an appeal by an Englishman for the benefit of the people of a British colony. Yet respond they did, and it was not only Grenfell's "winning and forceful character" that won their support. He was not, as has been said, by ordinary standards a good speaker. He was far too discursive, talking for two hours or more and trying to cover too much in even this time. He had no extravagant gestures, no rhetorical tricks, though there were times when he did startle his audiences. At a meeting in Boston he introduced three children he had brought from Labrador, and, acting on a sudden idea, he auctioned these children, 'selling' them to foster-parents and adding the money he received for them to the Mission funds. He could shock with some outrageous utterance, as when he told one audience that Christian Scientists should have more sense than to spend a million dollars on a monument to a "silly old woman," or when his very acute sense of humour saw a joke even in the most serious moments. Sailing into the settlement at Cartwright one Sunday, he was asked by the Church of England parson there to read the lessons at the evening service. Stacked on the deck of the *Strathcona* where she lay near and to windward of the church were barrels of very ripe whale-meat Grenfell was taking south for his dogs. The smell of this whale-meat reached into the church, and while reading the lesson and in the middle of the sentence "The barrel of meal shall not waste" Grenfell got a whiff of the smell that diverted his thoughts. He said, "The barrel of whale . . ." then stopped and exploded into laughter. This sense of humour could be as disconcerting as it was delightful, and Grenfell could never resist its use. When a stout but wealthy businessman who might have contributed to the Mission funds asked the Englishman, "And what do you get out of all this work, Dr Grenfell?" Grenfell poked a finger into the other's overgenerous waistline and said, "Not this anyhow."

This mischievousness and utter lack of watchfulness of what he said gave him a reputation for eccentricity as well as a charm that attracted people to him. His stories of Labrador, chosen with his instinctive sense of drama, drew large audiences, but there was a great deal more than all this in his success as a speaker and personality. One of his greatest admirers and friends, one of the first of the young Americans who were to go to Labrador to share his work, a future United States administrator, the Hon. Francis B. Sayre, was to declare that what Grenfell achieved inside the United States was no less important than his work for fishermen. There can be no doubt that this is true. Grenfell's impact on people was as much as an evangelist as a missionary, for he made it clear always that he was engaged in God's service, his inspiration the example set by Jesus.

In his book *What Life means to Me* Grenfell says, "To me now any service to the humblest of mankind is Christ-service." He accepted the truth of Christianity absolutely, and saw this as a vast pattern of continuity that made man immortal and as one. It was a creed that involved man beyond himself, with all other men as with God, enlarging him to the heavenly pattern. "I believe," he wrote, "absolutely in the socialism of Jesus... 'fraternity in action,' it has been called, because it dignifies and adds a *raison d'être* for being alive; viz, permitting us all 'to descend into the abyss of sorrow and sin and help to bring out entombed comrades.'" This was his simple but vast creed, and all the man-added trappings of sectarianism, of formalized ceremonial in the organized churches, merely blurred and complicated the truth, even when they did not falsify it. He believed the intellectual testing of Christianity was futile, for the truth was evident in the happiness and certainty faith gave. "The theory of Christianity," he said, "would not convince the heathen of the Congo that religion is desirable, or make a Russian Jew wish to adopt Russian Christianity."

It was in this faith that Grenfell lived and worked, and his attraction and influence was in the simplicity and directness of his acceptance of what he believed. He was rare in his world because of this, and so the ordinary mortal whose beliefs were more complicated, whose willingness to be absorbed was less, and whose values were more selfish felt himself in the presence of some one abnormal, some one in the mould of what they saw as the quality of saintliness. When a hard-headed American businessman said, "If Wilfred Grenfell came through that door now I would feel that Jesus Christ had entered the room," he was not being blasphemous, but was expressing the remarkable effect Grenfell had on so many. To those touched by the fear or greed of competitive society a man so dedicated, so utterly simple in his certainty of truth, would either be adored or be crucified.

It was perhaps fortunate for Grenfell and for those he served that in the early years of his work he chose to seek help more in America than in Britain. Despite their hard-headedness in many things, Americans are less watchful of their emotions, more eager for the idealistic than many of the older societies. Grenfell was what many Americans aspired to be, a man of vision and a man of action. His mixture of strong masculinity and faith was in their pattern and understanding. Particularly to young people, both in America and in Britain, his appeal was tremendous. This Christianity he spoke of was no censorious or melancholy and thwarting affair of restrictions on high spirits. "Following Christ," he told them, "has given me more fun and adventure than any other kind of life," and he advised his young listeners that "When two courses are open, follow the most venturesome." He gave religion a chuckle and brought it into the winds of life, giving it reality in showing it as service and love. He asked no young men or women to sit and hear a sermon, but to live an adventure, as he was doing.

He brought out of America men and women who wanted to share his adventure. Young people of all classes gave up their vacations to go to Labrador and Newfoundland to work for nothing at any task they were given. Known as 'Wops' and 'Wopesses' (workers without pay), they were navvies, ditchdiggers, builders' labourers, hospital assistants, boats' crews, schoolteachers, and fuel-gatherers. Many of these volunteers were the children of wealthy parents; others made great sacrifice to find their fares to Newfoundland. Traders on the coast said enviously that people who would not work for them for five dollars a day would work for Grenfell for nothing. A young man who had been offered a position by a famous fur-trading company refused, writing to say, "I am afraid I would spend more of your money than you would wish, because since I have been with Dr Grenfell and seen the people I cannot go up and rob them." Not only the young, but many who were famous in their profession—doctors, surgeons, dentists, experts on horticulture and other subjects—accepted Grenfell's invitation to "come and help." Many of the doctors and nurses on the Mission permanent staff were unpaid; those who did receive a wage could have earned ten times as much elsewhere. It was a remarkable proof of Grenfell's effect on people and a justification of his faith.

As the Mission expanded and Grenfell's projects increased in number, as he moved across the United States and Canada and back and forth to Britain, he was becoming famous. He was writing voluminously, publishing book after book describing his work and the people of Labrador. His 'Log,' a detailed record of his *Strathcona* voyages and the winters he spent in St Anthony, was being syndicated in America and England. His Canadian supporters started their own magazine, *Among the Deep Sea Fishers*, in 1904, and Grenfell contributed to this and to the British Mission's *Toilers of the Sea*. He was already the subject of many articles in magazines and in the Press on both sides of the Atlantic, and in 1905 a biography, *Dr Grenfell's Parish*, and a fictionized portrait, *Dr Luke*, both written by the American author Norman Duncan, were published.

He was being sought out by the highest. Theodore Roosevelt's secretary wrote, inviting him to lunch and saying, "they could talk over many things that interested the President." As he moved from place to place he was the guest of the most famous and wealthiest, seldom failing to bring away something for his people, as he brought away 3000 books for a travelling library from a visit to Andrew Carnegie. In Canada, as in America, he had almost ambassadorial status, his hosts the Governor-General or the governors of states. In England he was called to Buckingham Palace to talk to the King about his work, and he was consulted unofficially by the Colonial Office on Newfoundland affairs.

In the King's Birthday Honours list of 1906 Grenfell was appointed a Companion of the Most Distinguished Order of

St Michael and St George, and in 1907 he was taken by Sir Frederick Treves, knighted after performing one of the first operations for appendicitis on King Edward VII, to be presented to the King and invested with the insignia of his Order. That same year Oxford University presented him with the first Honorary Doctorate of Medicine ever granted by the University. The faculty of Princeton Theological Seminary invited him to be lecturer on missions, and in the following years honours came from many American and Canadian universities and professional bodies, including the American College of Surgeons. A remarkable tribute was paid to him when he was appointed to be a member of the National Academy of Social Sciences of America, a body limited to two hundred and fifty men and women who had specially distinguished themselves in medicine and social science.

If Grenfell gave these tributes any value, it was that through the great and wealthy he would get more help for his people. He found no pleasure in attending functions or in Society drawing-rooms. In England, he preferred to go to Parkgate to be with his beloved mother and to join his brother in the sort of mischievous teasing and verbal sparring they both loved and excelled in. He preferred the company of fishermen in their ships and trappers in their tilts to any other. Banquets and correct dressing were a bore. When he did attend these occasions he was as likely to appear in anything but the correct dress, or arrive late because he had been absorbed in some new idea or had encountered something interesting on the way. He appeared very late at one banquet given in his honour in New York, explaining to his hosts that he had navigated from his hotel by the stars, but something hadn't worked out quite as it should have.

His life was being forced into a mixture of missionary and publicist, with more and more calls on him as a publicist. He enjoyed telling about his work, but he loved being with the fishermen and on board the *Strathcona* a great deal more. There he could forget the problems of money, the irritations of opposition to his great schemes, the need for administration. He could be the sailor he loved being. Each year he was discovering more and more of the coast, steaming as far as Cape Chidley and exploring every inlet. He took the *Strathcona* into many places where she should never have been, bumped her over many rocks and shoals a more cautious navigator would have kept away from, remarking as she came clear that he must remember to put the rock or shoal on the charts he was making. He hated following the same course twice, and once his Newfoundland mate had to threaten mutiny if Grenfell insisted on trying a channel between two islands the mate believed to be foul. Weather never stopped Grenfell, and, indeed, he found it yet another challenge. Settlers joked about this, telling one another, "Wind is blowing powerful hard . . . this will be sure to bring Dr Grenfell." His crews, mostly made up of young undergraduates with little if any sea experience, and his passengers were laid low as the *Strathcona* justified her nickname of the "Holy Roller" in weather more exciting than safe, Grenfell utterly happy and thinking it a great joke when only his engineer, his mate, and himself were able to manage the ship. The loss of the *Strathcona* was predicted many times, but Grenfell was sure the Lord had too much work for her to do to allow this to happen. "I don't really take chances with my ship," he claimed, "except that I do carry a voluntary cook from Harvard or Yale, or some other university. Maybe that is one of the greatest risks I ever took."

The ship was all-purpose. As well as being a hospital ship, she was lifeboat and tug when needed. With her Grenfell rescued the passengers and crew of a sinking mail-steamer, the s.s. *Viking*, salvaging much of the cargo and loading it on to a scow to tow to safety. She was a survey ship, and in 1908 Grenfell carried out valuable hydrographic work with the then Governor of Newfoundland, an ex-Naval officer with survey experience, Sir William MacGregor. That same year severe storms wrecked thirty-five vessels of the Labrador fishing fleet, and in one harbour where the *Strathcona* was sheltering sixteen schooners were cast on shore. Grenfell used his ship to haul the least damaged to safety and salvage some of those on the rocks. With the *Strathcona* he acted as scout for the fishermen, locating places where fish were plentiful and guiding or towing schooners there. With all this he carried on his missionary work, healing, operating, and holding religious services. Dr Willway, watching his energetic colleague from England, wrote in the Mission magazine:

M

Dr Grenfell is captain of his ship, Lloyd's surveyor, wreck commissioner, peripatetic magistrate, and Poor Law commissioner as well as evangelist and missionary, from the Belle Isle Straits to Hudson's Bay. In his leisure (?) he botanizes, makes charts (not always wise to follow them implicitly), hunts and fishes for his larder, carries on a voluminous correspondence, much of which is written on odd scraps of paper, and engages in literary work. I think it would be inside the mark to say he is actually at work eighteen hours a day.

Grenfell's energy was tremendous. The famous Arctic seaman the Newfoundlander Bob Bartlett, as a young man, thought to test this tenderfoot Englishman on a hunting trip, only to find himself and an experienced guide having difficulty in keeping up with their guest. When they reached the lake where they were to set up camp the guide broke a small hole in the ice to get fresh water. Grenfell promptly enlarged the hole so that he could have a dip in the icy water. Bartlett had thought himself tough, until Grenfell backed him against a shed wall and told him to open his mouth. He held the sailor against the shed, while he removed Bartlett's tonsils, which had been bothering him.

A voyage with Grenfell on board the *Strathcona* could be both stimulating and exhausting for his amateur crews and for those guests he had invited to "come and see for yourself." Both guests and crews found themselves hauled from their bunks at an early hour, to join their host in a swim. He seemed immune to the cold, and climbed from the water on to ice pans to shout that "the water is fine." He climbed aloft to dive from the cross-trees, or to race his admiring young followers over the masthead. He was without fear, sure that no harm would come to him until he had carried out the task set him by God.

On shore he was as energetic. With the ship anchored, he was away to find those who needed his doctor's skill or other help. The *Strathcona* was never long anchored before her sides held a cluster of boats and visitors were on board, many coming long distances to be treated, to put some complaint before Grenfell, to seek his advice, or just to see "t'Doctor." He held his Justice of Peace courts on the ship's deck, upholding his dignity as a judge by dressing up colourfully, and interpreting the law in his own often humorous way. He divorced one ill-suited couple, although divorce was not then legal in Newfoundland, and for one particularly beastly crime he far outstepped his powers by having the culprit lashed to the *Strathcona*'s mast and whipped.

He expected his guests to share every task and to be no less energetic than he was. They found themselves toiling as steve-dores, dragging logs and loading them on to the ship. They became anæsthetists at an operation, sweated on halyards as Grenfell experimented with new sail arrangements, became cooks and dishwashers, animal attendants when Grenfell brought on board some creature he had found. They helped to raid illegal stills, and Grenfell sought these out with special determination. His hatred of strong drink had increased with the years, and he was steadily driving it off the coast. In H. G. Wells's novel *Marriage* a trapper introduced into the Labrador phase of the story is made to say, "Doctor Grenfell was a very good man, a very good man, but he made brandy dear, dear beyond the reach of the common men altogether on the coast." Grenfell and his guests and undergraduates toppled many a hidden still into the sea.

Grenfell tried hard to spend every summer on board the *Strathcona*, and as much of the winter as he could at St Anthony. This place was rapidly becoming the largest of the Mission stations, more and more buildings clustered round the hospital. Most of the medical work was now left to a brilliant Boston surgeon, Dr John M. Little, who joined the Mission in 1907, and Grenfell was able to give his time to developing his many schemes—there were at one time as many as forty of these—for the welfare of the settlers. His activities ranged from shipbuilding at Canada Bay to bottling native berries, and each time he returned to St Anthony he had another idea to set into action. He was never idle. In the evenings he joined the doctors and staff in their common room, livening the place with his joking, teasing the young women volunteers, dressing up and acting some part. He appeared once in the magnificent robes of his Oxford Doctorate, with a top-hat, and in blue jeans and sealskin boots, to show how he looked as a gentleman. He read aloud from books he liked, called on Dr Little to bring out his banjo so that they could all sing his favourite Sankey hymns. He loved to set an argument going, exercising his own agile brain in a game where he excelled. The place seemed empty when he was away, though there were times when his doctors wished he were less energetic or stimulating. He could sweep away the work of months in insisting on some new idea being carried out, and he would waken his doctors up long before dawn to tell them of some wonderful scheme he had evolved. He was able to do with very little sleep, and was out prowling round the rooms or carrying out some task that gave little rest to others.

When, in January 1908, the steamer *Anita* was worked into the ice as near St Anthony as she could be taken to land a herd of 300 reindeer Grenfell had a new and absorbing occupation in training the animals. He was away when the deer arrived, so missed the excitement of their landing. They had to be got on shore over the harbour ice, and a gangway was built against the ship's side. Lapp attendants, who had been engaged for two years to teach the Newfoundlanders how to herd the animals, coaxed the deer down this gangway. The strange place and the crowd of settlers and their families who had come to watch this show frightened the animals, and they scattered in all directions, two bolting on to the loose ice and being drowned. The Lapps, picturesque in their long fur coats, trimmed with red cloth, and high, four-cornered cloth hats, gathered the herd together and took them away from the settlement, camping beside them and showing great patience and solicitude for their charges.

When Grenfell returned to St Anthony he was eager to train the deer for their future work, and was annoyed when the Lapp herders said the animals must have at least a month's rest after their long voyage, to acclimatize themselves. When, at last, Grenfell was allowed to see them drawing the light sledges, pulkas, the Lapps had brought with them he was disgusted to find the pace far from the swift, dashing movement he had thought it would be. Instead of flying over the snow Grenfell sat on the pulka while the Lapp driver walked ahead of the deer on skis, leading the animal at a sedate pace. Now and then the pulka was tipped over and Grenfell was deposited into the snow. The expedition ended when the deer entangled itself in its trace, and in its struggles sank itself and its driver neck-deep in the snow, a churned-up mass of struggling bodies.

Grenfell was determined to do better than this. With a companion, and without a Lapp, using a komatik instead of the pulka, he set out. He hitched on two deer, and, dressed in a gorgeous costume of white deerskin jacket, blue sash, red cap, grey trousers, and high, yellow skin boots, attempted to drive the deer as he thought they should be driven. This did not please the deer. In turn they looked round and, as Grenfell was to declare, "made faces at us," opening their mouths wide and gasping their indignation. But they would not run. Grenfell managed to get them to trot for a time, but he came back to the settlement disgusted with his new means of locomotion.

That same year, 1908, this impatience almost cost him his life. He had taken morning service at St Anthony Church on Easter Sunday, April 19, and on coming from the church found two men waiting for him. They had travelled sixty miles from Brent Island, in Hare Bay, south of St Anthony, to tell him that a boy he had operated on for acute osteomyelitis was gravely ill. The parents had treated the wound incorrectly, and there was danger of blood-poisoning. Grenfell was upset by this news and said he must go and save the boy. He would leave immediately after the midday meal and would travel alone. The messengers would rest their dogs and themselves, then follow and meet him on the southern shore of Hare Bay to guide him to their island.

Grenfell was advised to wait until the men had rested and eaten. As he had to meet them on the trail there seemed no sense in his going ahead. Also, this was a bad time of the year for travelling. The winter was almost over, and the weather might change suddenly, the snow surface become difficult and dangerous. Grenfell was not a fully experienced winter traveller, and no one, unless he had no alternative, made such long journeys alone.

Grenfell would not wait. He brushed aside all warnings, and ordered his seven best dogs to be hitched to a komatik. Immediately after lunch he set off. He took his retriever, a black spaniel named Jack, with him for company, and, with this dog leaping excitedly ahead of the team, Grenfell headed upward to follow the trail over the range of hills that lie irregularly along the coast. Dr Little and Jessie Luther watched from the hospital, seeing him reach the highest part of the trail, where he turned and waved to them before heading downward and disappearing. Weather-wise settlers shook their heads over the doctor's foolishness, but consoled themselves in knowing that he had only eighteen miles to travel to reach his first stop, the settlement of Lock's Cove, on the northern shore of Hare Bay. From there he would follow the Bay round, keeping close against the land, to where he was to meet the Brent Island men.

It rained in St Anthony that night, and the wind rose strongly from the east, from seaward. When Jessie Luther, who describes these days in an unpublished manuscript, came out the next morning she found a changing scene. The harbour ice was cracking, being drifted through the narrows and driven with a grinding sound against the shore. Water was dripping from the eaves of every building with heavy plopping, pitting the snow. Objects which had laid unseen for months were rising starkly from the hidden earth—fences, barrels, piles of lumber, rubbish tossed out of the cottages. The snow was soft and treacherous underfoot. This was Jessie's first winter in Newfoundland, and she was thrilled by the change, the first signs of spring.

The local men were less thrilled. They thought of Grenfell and how this weather would delay him. They discussed his chances of 'getting on' in the thaw and strong winds, and one old man declared, "T'road be wonderful heavy to-day. 'E won't stir out." It was the general opinion that Grenfell would have to remain at Lock's Cove until the weather changed again. It changed that afternoon. The wind veered to the westward, the temperature dropped, and the snow hardened. The old men then decided that Grenfell would be able to travel. " 'Tis civil weather for t'Doctor," one said. " 'E'll 'ave a fine run this evening."

That night the wind increased, and it froze hard. Jessie Luther was awakened early by the noise of the harbour ice driving against the rocks, setting up a crashing and growling that was her first experience of ice moving to high winds. She went outside to enjoy the sight, and with the first light of dawn watched the drama below the staff house. The whole harbour was in motion, pans tilting and seeming to struggle in a wide, formless battle. Great masses of ice seemed to grow upward, mounting on others and hanging there, to collapse and sprawl in pieces. The wind was driving the ice out, and there were veins of water almost to the wharf. A soft haze hung over the hills on the far side of the harbour, and shadows were a delicate violet. A few birds sang against the clash and crack of the ice. It was an exciting thing to watch, but it was cold. Very cold. Jessie went back to her warm bed.

She was not long there before she heard a door bang and some one calling. She got up again and opened her door, to hear a young lad, Steve Pilley, telling Dr Little that "t'Doctor's adrift on an ice pan in Hare Bay." Within seconds the whole staff were gathered round the boy. A man had travelled from Lock's Cove with the news, Pilley told them, stopping at the deer camp. Then the man himself arrived and told his story. Grenfell had reached Lock's Cove in good time on the 19th and stayed there that night. When morning came and the weather had softened, as it had at St Anthony, he had been advised to stay where he was. He would not. He was impatient to reach the sick boy and must go on. The Lock's Cove men warned him not to attempt crossing the Bay ice, but to follow the coast round, keeping close to the shore.

That evening a man had gone to the headland that shelters the settlement from the south-west to look for seals. He had seen dark figures on a small pan some two miles from the shore, and put his telescope, the only one on the coast, on them. He had seen a man and five dogs on the pan, the pan hardly bigger than "a kitchen floor." Immediately he returned to the settlement, but by then it was dark, and nothing could be done. Men were to keep a look-out from the headland all night, while others were digging a boat out of the snow for a rescue attempt if the pan and its burden were still in sight the next morning.

No one believed a rescue could be made. The wind still blew strongly, and would be carrying the pan out of the Bay and to the open sea. Once in the rough water it would break up. Even if he could be reached the man would not live through this freezing night. Jessie Luther remembered that at the service he took on that Sunday Grenfell had chosen Psalm 23 for the lesson. The words he had spoken had a poignant and ominous meaning now: "Yea, though I walk through the valley of the shadow of death, I will fear no evil."

That day passed slowly at St Anthony. The doctors and nurses attended to their patients, men went into the woods to fetch logs for fuel, Eleanor Storr set her children to their lessons, Jessie Luther tried to teach women weaving. But every one moved quietly, spoke seldom, and looked upward at the trail often. Reuben Sims, Grenfell's servant, boasted of the Doctor's strength and stamina. He could live on an ice pan for a week, the loyal man swore. " 'E 'as 'is bread-bag with 'im," he said, "and some one's sure to pick 'im up." Two men arrived, travelling from the southward. Reuben spoke to them, and came to tell Jessie Luther, " 'Twasn't the Doctor at all, miss. 'Twas some one else comin' from t'other way. Th' Doctor 'ad George Read's b'y [the invalid] with 'un, and 'e'd never take chances wi' a b'y in 'is care." He clinched the argument by saying that there had been only five dogs on the pan and Grenfell had seven. Reuben shook his head sorrowfully. " 'E's perished, whoever 'e is," he added; " 'e couldn't live through the night." Others were not so sure it was not Grenfell. They gathered in groups to discuss the tragedy. "Ef the Doctor's gone," one old fisherman said, "dat's the end o' the French shore and St Anthony. 'Twill all go down. . . . 'E's the one keeps us all goin'." All doubt went when another messenger arrived from Lock's Cove. The figure on the ice was Dr Grenfell. The man who sighted him through the telescope had recognized him. The Lock's Cove men were waiting for daylight to attempt a rescue.

With the dawn, men on the headland above Lock's Cove were peering down on the water and scattered ice drifting past. At first could see only the pans and open water flecked with white where waves were breaking. Then the pan with its tiny black figures was sighted, several miles seaward but still inside the Bay. Between it and Lock's Cove ice drifted in scattered fields, obstructions to any boat attempting the rescue. The fishermen never hesitated. A crew of five was already waiting, the elderly George Read, who had first sighted Grenfell, his two sturdy sons, and two others, George Davis and George Andrews—"five as brave hearts as ever beat in the bodies of human beings," Grenfell was to describe them. Each man knew that they were risking their lives. They would have to work their boat among ice pans that the wind was driving together and where the boat could be caught and crushed. If this happened the rescuers would share Grenfell's fate. "It was for the Doctor," one of the men said years afterwards. "His life was worth many. We wouldn't let a man like that die without trying. We all felt the same."

The boat was launched, the men stripping to their shirts for the struggle ahead. George Read was skipper, steering while the four others rowed. They had the wind behind them and made good progress, but were brought up by a barrier of ice. They scrambled to the pan and hauled their heavy boat over to another open lead, then went on. They were almost nipped a dozen times, having to leap on to the ice and drag their boat up before the pans closed on it. They forced the boat through soft sish ice—snow packed together by the wind—Read's eyes assessing each danger. At last they could see Grenfell clearly. He was standing up, waving some sort of flag, the dogs round him. The fishermen hardly recognized him. He looked so old, and his face was a queer colour. He watched them solemnly, this man who always greeted them with a joke. No one spoke as Grenfell was helped into the boat and given tea from a kettle the fishermen had brought, and now Read turned the boat for home. She faced the wind and weather now, and the fishermen had to strain their muscles to drive her ahead.

Grenfell began to talk. He spoke contritely, saying how sorry he was to have brought them into this mess. He seemed unable to stop talking, telling the men how he had followed the coast round almost to the end of the Bay, then, believing he could cross the ice, he had headed for the far shore. He was more than half-way across when the komatik sank into sish ice, and he and the dogs sank through and into the water. Grenfell got his knife out and cut the traces, and the dogs swam to a small pan of packed snow and ice, and he followed. The pan was tiny, and he realized it would not hold together long. There was a larger pan some twenty yards away, and Grenfell tied the dogs' traces into one long rope, making this fast to his leading dog. He tried to urge the animal into the water, so that it would swim to the other pan, but it would not budge. He picked up a piece of ice and threw it towards the larger pan, then told his well-trained retriever to 'fetch.' The dog leapt into the water, then swam to the other pan. The komatik dogs followed, and Grenfell swam and was dragged through the water and broken ice by the rope he had made fast round his wrist. He got on to the pan with the dogs, wet through, his boots full of water. He knew his clothing would soon freeze hard, and he must have protection from the cold wind. He had to decide who would live, himself or his dogs. He made the decision that was to torment him all his life. He killed two of the dogs and skinned them, using their skins to make a rude coat for his chest and back. In darkness he cleaned the dead dogs' leg-bones, and tied them together to make a short staff, and when morning came he took off his shirt and tied this to his grisly staff. He told this story, half in wonder, speaking sorrowfully of the dogs he had killed.

When the boat reached Lock's Cove Grenfell was taken to a hut and given dry clothing and food. He did not realize his feet had frozen, until the pain of returning circulation went leaping through his body. But he said he must get back to St Anthony to relieve his friends' anxiety. The fishermen said he was not fit to travel, but he turned on them angrily, demanding to be given a team of dogs. He did not want help and would go alone. He was furious when the fishermen insisted that he lie on a komatik for the journey.

He was equally angry when he arrived at St Anthony and Dr Little ordered him to bed. His friends were amazed by his appearance, for they hardly recognized him. His face was a curious dark red, his eyes bloodshot, and he had aged to an old man. His hands were so swollen that he could hardly use them, his voice hoarse and weak as he insisted on describing what had happened during his twenty-hour ordeal. He told how he had waited for death, but had not been afraid. He had heard a hymn being sung, "My God, my Father, while I stray ... Thy will be done," and he wanted this sung. He insisted on his improvised flag and staff being brought to him so that he could describe how he made them.

Little gave him a strong sedative, for he would talk. The hymn persisted in his brain, and with a flash of humour he told Jessie Luther that he knew now that Heaven is not a cold place. His hands and feet still pained, and he had been bitten twice by the dogs. Jessie made a cradle to raise his feet and packed him with hot-water bottles, and at last he slept. But he was awake as early as ever the next morning, complaining at being kept in bed. He wanted to get up and meet all the people who had come from distant settlements to see him and to say how happy they were that he was still among them. He abused Dr Little for giving him morphine, then got out of bed and sat beside the stove, restless and talkative. He began stuffing a puppy-dog skin with his thickened fingers, making up a team for a model komatik. He did not notice two of his dogs that came into the room and ate his stuffed puppies, and was furious when he discovered this had happened. He wanted to get his whip and thrash the culprits.

On the 25th, four days after this terrible experience, he was proposing a trouting picnic, though he still had to hobble and use a stick. On the following Sunday he took the church service and sang the hymn he had heard that night on the ice pan. After the service men, women, and children gathered round him to tell him how happy they now were.

He dictated the story of his experience to Jessie Luther while he was still suffering the effects of exposure, and this story was to become famous. *Adrift on an Ice Pan* was his best-selling book, and brought in subscriptions and gifts from every part of the world. Once the story reached the outside world he was headline news, and when he lectured the next winter in England his audiences were bigger than ever. He presented each of his rescuers with a gold watch, and placed tablets, commemorating the dogs he had been forced to kill, in the Mission hospitals and in the church of Mostyn House School.

Wherever he moved now he was known, the man who had lived on an ice pan. His enemies declared that the whole adventure was a publicity stunt, but a young American girl who met him on board the *Mauretania* in May 1909 could only be impressed. He was taking his mother, now seventy-eight years of age, to the United States, where she could watch him being presented with honorary degrees at Harvard University and Williams College, and he was attracted by this handsome and regal-looking young woman whose name he did not know. He sat with her on deck, and began to lecture her on the uselessness of her life as a young Society lady. She was indignant. "You don't even know my name," she retorted, "and talk to me like this." He grinned then. "Your name doesn't interest

me," he told her; "it is what it is going to be that interests
me."

That same year, in November 1909, he married her in
Chicago.

14

The International Grenfell Association

GRENFELL'S visit to England in the winter of 1908–9 gave the Council of the R.N.M.D.S.F. an opportunity to question their elusive Superintendent on what exactly was happening in Labrador and Newfoundland. He had been appointed to conduct a medical and evangelistic mission, but seemed to be spending most of his time organizing co-operatives (there were eight of these now), running industries, from ship-building to berry-potting, touring the United States, or annoying people in St John's. He was collecting money—a great deal of money—but the Mission saw little of it. Grenfell had half a dozen 'special' funds which he kept himself and controlled, or which were held by the American committees for him to draw on. The Council had always been strongly against this method of finance. It was more orderly and businesslike for moneys to be paid into the Mission funds and handled by their finance committee.

Grenfell, too, was becoming something of an autocrat in his assumption that the Labrador Mission was now his special property. When he was questioned about his ventures outside Mission work he retorted bluntly that these were no concern of the Council. Rules, too, seemed not to apply to him. He did what he thought should be done, then informed, or did not inform, the Council. He ordered expensive alterations to the ships, approved hospital extensions, introduced dozens of volunteers from America, carried guests on board the *Strath-cona* every summer, even after getting the Council to forbid others having guests on the coast. It all added up to a great deal of money, and even when the volunteers and guests paid their own fares to Newfoundland they had to be housed and fed by the Mission. That many of them presented Grenfell with large sums of money did not make the arrangements any tidier or Grenfell's methods less unsatisfactory.

Far too much was happening casually and according to Grenfell's whims. The purely Mission work was being swamped by dozens of other activities, and control of the whole organiza- tion was slipping from the Council's hands. Grenfell, too, was changing the character of the work—or, rather, its direction. At the Mission's Annual General Meeting in 1907 Sir Frederick Treves, introducing Grenfell to an enthusiastic and cheering audience, referred to the change. "His work seems now to have little to do with deep-sea fishermen," Treves said. It was splen- did and praiseworthy work, but now mainly being done for the good of the people on shore, the Liveyeres and the Newfound- land settlers. Doctors and nurses still served the schoonermen in the summer, but more and more the work was among the settlements. This had not been the Mission's original purpose.

The Council were finding they could do little to control this trend, or their Superintendent. He was either on the coast and beyond their reach or tearing across America. They heard of him rather than from him, and were reaching a state when they wished themselves out of the whole Labrador effort. As early as 1905 Grenfell was informed that the Council would not object if his American supporters wished to take over the management of the Labrador Mission.

The Canadian supporters had proposed this in 1904. There had been trouble over a nurse, a Canadian, who was charged by one of the doctors with ill-treating patients. She was dis- missed, and, as a protest against the dismissal, Miss Julia Greenshields, the Toronto lady who had presented the Mission with the *Julia Sheridan* and whose energy and efforts had built up and maintained Canadian support for Grenfell, resigned with all her committee. Grenfell induced her to continue, and she did so. But she wanted Canadians at least to share control of the work on the coast. She believed that much greater support and help would be found if the Mission were administered from their side.

The Council were agreeable, but laid down certain conditions. Any new organization would have to be an affiliated branch of the R.N.M.D.S.F., guarantees would have to be provided for the continuance of the work, and the British Mission protected from any future liabilities. The Council were to continue to appoint a Superintendent and to pay all salaries; the aim of the Mission in Labrador must continue to be "the spiritual and temporal welfare of fishermen"; and the Canadian committee must abide by the teachings and beliefs of the Protestant Evangelical Church.

Nothing came of this proposal. In 1905 an attempt was made to control, or at least have some sort of check on, expenditure on supplies. The Mission secretary, Francis B. Wood, came to Newfoundland, and a managing committee of prominent local men was formed. An agent was appointed, and now all stores and supplies for the Mission were to be ordered through him. He was directly responsible to the Council in England, and the goods purchased would be paid for from a fund kept in a St John's bank and maintained by subscriptions sent in by the Mission, United States and Canadian supporters, and the Newfoundland Government. Cheques had to be signed by this agent, or Grenfell, and one member of the managing committee.

While he was in St John's, Wood told Grenfell that the Council would not object if his American friends wished to take over the administration of his work entirely. Grenfell wished this also. He believed he would be given a much freer hand by Americans, less irritating supervision. But when he suggested this to them he found the Americans far from eager. They were more than willing to help with money, goods, and volunteers, but not to undertake the management of what was now a large organization.

So things continued as they were. The Council tried to control Grenfell, Grenfell more and more did what he thought should be done, and the unfortunate agent tried to carry out the Council's orders and to please Grenfell at the same time. It was a state of affairs that might have continued if Grenfell had kept to the rules and had been content with even this amount of organization. But he could not be restrained. He began to find this attempt to keep the Mission on a businesslike footing irritating. He had liked the agent at first, and had, indeed, recommended that he be appointed Superintendent of the new sailors' home when it was completed; but by the time the home was ready Grenfell was less pleased, and he had found some one else for this position.

In 1907 the United States supporters put their house in order. Until then, since Grenfell's first visit to America in 1896, what organization there was for the collecting and distribution of funds had 'just growed.' In Canada there were some fifteen committees, held together by the trusty Miss Greenshields, and affiliated to the R.N.M.D.S.F. This affiliation was possible in a British dominion, but not so easy in the United States. There Grenfell's friends and admirers had banded themselves into committees, known vaguely as "Supporters of the work of Dr Grenfell." In Boston the Rev. Dr Carpenter and Miss Emma White conducted campaigns, and were supported by influential people like the banker Estabrook. In New York the Delanos, father and son, had gathered strong help in philanthropists, heads of universities, and other prominent people. There was an increasing number of other 'Grenfell' committees throughout the United States; almost every American university had its 'Grenfell Society'; schoolchildren had banded themselves into supporters; and organizations like the Needlework Guild of America were sending clothing. Contributions from all these were sent to the New York Committee, who contributed to the St John's bank account, financed some of Grenfell's 'special' ventures, and sent goods and volunteers to St Anthony. It was all somewhat haphazard, and there was one serious drawback. Large sums were being given to endow certain parts of the Mission, the St John's sailors' home, certain hospitals, and the upkeep of ships. It needed a properly incorporated body to hold these endowments, and to relieve the committee, who were a collection of private individuals, of what could be a heavy responsibility.

In 1907 the Grenfell Association of America was formed and incorporated according to the laws of the State of New York. At the same time a New England Grenfell Association was formed and named, though not incorporated until 1914. The Mission Council were not very happy at the use of Grenfell's name, and their secretary, Wood, who had been invited to New York to discuss the forming of these associations, stated the British views. Grenfell himself said that there seemed no alternative. His name was widely associated with the work of the Mission in Labrador, and also the use of the word 'Royal' might not be helpful in the United States. Who first suggested naming the associations as they were named is not known, but named they were, and the 'Grenfell Associations' were legally born.

By 1908 Grenfell had got himself involved in a quarrel with the St John's agent. The records for what was happening at this time are not complete, and those that remain available are somewhat bewildering. What is clear, however, is that Grenfell wanted to shift the complete administration and financial control from St John's to St Anthony, and he had found some one he believed would be more useful to him than the agent. Grenfell always preferred the volunteer to the paid worker, and he had met an American named Webster, a man wealthy enough to work for nothing, and in Grenfell's view "an excellent businessman." Grenfell was hardly qualified to judge the abilities of any 'businessman,' but when he met people who impressed him he was apt to invest them with qualities they might not have. Now he was all for his new friend, and the Mission's representative in St John's could do nothing right.

This representative had been handling some of Grenfell's 'private' affairs as well as the Mission business, and among these were the accounts of the co-operative societies. A number of creditors who had supplied goods to the co-operatives pressed for payment, and the agent had to inform Grenfell that there was no money to pay them. Grenfell was shocked. He believed that the co-operatives were in a strong financial condition. He blamed the agent for not keeping him better informed, and asked his friend Sir Edgar Bowring, head of Bowring and Sons,

N

and one of Grenfell's most loyal and powerful supporters in the Colony, to have the agent's books examined. Sir Edgar called in a local firm of accountants, and a young man, H. R. Brooks, investigated. He found that the accounts were correct, but suggested that the method of keeping them could be improved. The agent kept single entry books and had lumped in the accounts of all the co-operative stores as one. When Grenfell heard of this he blamed the agent for making a mess of these accounts, and asked the Mission Council to discharge him. This the Council refused to do, and a far from happy time resulted, with Grenfell getting angrier and angrier because he was being frustrated.

He had brought Webster to St Anthony by now, acting from there as though St John's did not exist. In the next year Grenfell's "excellent businessman" involved him in some remarkable examples of his abilities. Grenfell gave Webster a power of attorney, and he collected a cheque for 7000 dollars from Dr Little's sister in Boston, money she had worked hard to gather to pay for enlarging St Anthony hospital, with another 1000 dollars collected by the Grenfell Association in New York for the same purpose. Webster paid this money into an account in his own name at the Bank of Commerce in Halifax. Then, as "Agent for the Grenfell Mission," he proceeded to spend about 5000 dollars in purchasing large quantities of goods that were to be dispatched to St Anthony. His, and Grenfell's, idea now was to buy Mission supplies in Canada, where they were cheaper than at St John's. But Grenfell had never guessed his deputy would do what he did. Grenfell had to appeal to the Association in America for another seven thousand dollars to clear the hospital debt.

Webster's next performance was to call for quotations for timber for the Mission, and then give the order to Roddickton Mill, Grenfell's co-operative venture in Canada Bay. The St John's agent immediately accused Grenfell of overcharging for this timber. Webster retorted in terms that the other man considered slanderous. He threatened legal proceedings. Grenfell meantime had not helped matters by depositing the money he had received from the American Association, to clear the hospital debt, in a St John's bank and immediately drawing cheques against it, which he handed to some of the co-operatives' creditors. These cheques were for a total of almost 7000 dollars, but were not to be presented until Grenfell gave the word. Some were presented, and the fat was really in the fire.

It was all a beautiful mess, and the St John's agent was making the most of it. Grenfell, hearing criticism of his and Webster's actions, was indignant. He wrote to England, demanding that Wood be sent out to investigate the whole matter. Wood did come, but seems to have acted no less foolishly than the others. He heard the agent's story, then went to St Anthony while Grenfell was away, ignoring a telegram Grenfell sent ordering him to a meeting at St John's. Instead Wood further infuriated Grenfell by going to Montana on other business. Grenfell said he would have nothing more to do with the secretary, but would come to England to meet the Council and straighten out the whole matter.

From what can be learned from the existing correspondence the whole unfortunate affair was Grenfell's own fault. His business methods were shockingly casual, and he had listened to Webster and seen a way of getting the Mission business shifted to St Anthony, where he believed it could be handled more efficiently by his 'business manager' and Dr Little when he was away. He had thought to save money by buying in Canada instead of St John's, and he had given Webster far too much power. There had been dishonesty nowhere, neither from St John's, Webster, nor Grenfell, but just a pathetic demonstration by three men, none of whom had the slightest notion of being businesslike—Grenfell least of all.

Not for one moment did anyone believe that Grenfell had acted for his own profit. Years later, when another worried man wrote to Wood for advice on another crisis, the Mission secretary answered him from his past experience:

> I believe in laying bare the situation as it appeared to me. In 1910 I did Dr Grenfell the best service a man could possibly render another, staved off, I believe, a condition of affairs which must almost inevitably have ended in sorrow and scandal. ... I have never regretted the steps I took, even though an old and valued friendship became strained and can never, I suppose, be restored to its former footing.

Wood then gave his advice, and ended his letter:

In conclusion may I remind you and all associated with Dr Grenfell that you have a man to deal with of peculiar temperament, whose vices, paradox as it may seem, are his virtues. His extraordinary personality and his steam-power driving energy are his God-given virtues, which have led to his accomplishing an enormous amount of good ... the gift of balance and judgment having been denied him, his strong personality and driving force result in his making errors and possessing methods and aims which an ordinary man would perceive, and in littleness would avoid. But whatever errors Dr Grenfell makes and however wrong his methods may appear, judged by ordinary standards, you must never lose sight of the fact that his actions are prompted by the highest motives.

This was generous tribute from a man Grenfell had handled very roughly during their differences. Grenfell himself, in the end, realized that Wood, no less than himself, had acted "from the highest motives." He sent the secretary a cable:

My DEAR WOOD,

Thanks for your letter. Tear up anything I wrote to you, and believe me I am ever

Yours very affectionately,
WILFRED GRENFELL

Webster disappeared back into the United States.

But the trouble had disclosed a state of affairs that set Grenfell's supporters thinking. A friend in New York wrote to him, "Delano ... He loves you dearly, but does not always approve of your business methods." It was clear that some one was needed to handle the Mission's business affairs, and Grenfell had realized this himself. In a long, far from polite, and somewhat incoherent letter he wrote to Wood, and where he defended his actions during the trouble, Grenfell declared:

If you knew the number of endless things I have to remember and saw my floor at the present moment littered with dozens of unread and unanswered letters and remembered that I only came in from sea at 1 o'clock this morning and that it is Sunday, and that we expect the mail to-night at nine o'clock, you would understand that if my explanations don't always agree it's not because I want to shuffle my responsibilities on to anybody else, nor is it exactly that I am either a fool or knave, but because I want a business manager as I have been saying for ever so long.

I am putting it to you again and to the New York committee, who are getting a copy of this letter, that if I don't get one whom I can rely on, whether it's Peters, Wood or Webster, or some one, my days of usefulness to this mission will soon come to an end. How can a man keep up with surgery and medicine, with navigation, literature, correspondence, religious work, and have that sympathy which alone makes his work useful to the individual, if he can't be relieved of these business intricacies.

The New York committee were convinced Grenfell was right, and by now they were realizing too that they had to take more than a benevolent part in the work they had helped to enlarge with American money. They had a big stake. Contributions from the United States in 1909 amounted to 71,000 dollars, and by now the Mission staff was becoming more and more American. Most of the summer volunteers came from that country. It was not enough to hand out the money, or send volunteers and supplies, and leave others to manage them. In January 1911 Grenfell carried a letter to England from the American association. In it the Americans offered to take over the management of the Mission in Labrador. W. F. A. Archibald, Chairman of the Council, replied within a few days, saying, "This proposal might result in much benefit to the poor people on the coast, by the amalgamation of the whole of Dr Grenfell's enterprises under one head." The Council's only concern was for the continuance of the spiritual side of the Mission on the Protestant Evangelical basis.

> We consider it should not get into the hands of the Roman Catholics, nor drift into Unitarian lines. Probably this object might be secured by some provision to the effect that as far as possible all doctors and nurses and persons in a position to exercise spiritual influence should be engaged in the character of real medical or lay missionaries holding religious opinions of the nature I have indicated.

Grenfell was at the meeting held in New York to consider Archibald's letter. By now he had found a true and capable adviser in William R. Stirling. Stirling, a partner in the banking firm of Peabody and Houghteling, of Chicago, was a great friend of the now Mrs Grenfell's family, a shrewd and sincere adviser, and a generous contributor to the Mission's funds. He had accompanied Grenfell to London to lay the proposal before the Mission Council, and now he stood by to act for his friend and explain the British views to the American committee.

The committee passed a resolution:

> It is the sense of this Board that the Grenfell Association of America assume control of the Labrador Medical Mission, subject to such conditions on the points indicated in the letter from Mr W. F. A. Archibald ... as may be formulated by the special committee already appointed.

Another resolution was passed:

> That the temporary Chairman, Mr Eugene Delano, be authorized to employ Price and Waterhouse, Chartered Accountants, to go over the accounts of the Mission and other properties connected with Dr Grenfell's work in Labrador and Newfoundland, whether operated under the name of the Mission or independently.

Price, Waterhouse and Company were a New York company that had originated in England, and it was felt that such a company would be approved in England. These accountants sent a young man named Cecil Ashdown to Newfoundland, and from his visit another scandal was to be uncovered and the American plans changed.

The sailors' home in St John's was opened on June 22, 1912, a much-anticipated ceremony that Grenfell almost missed. He had been on the coast with the *Strathcona*, and was making for St John's, when he was met and asked for help by some fishermen. Their schooner had been wrecked and sunk off Cape York, near the eastern end of Belle Isle Strait, on southern Labrador, the previous year, and had lain under the ice all the past winter. The fishermen had returned with the spring, and by superhuman effort raised their vessel and patched her as best they could, sealing the holes in her hull with bags of soaked ship's biscuits, cement, and planking. They had sailed her sixty miles southward, but at a harbour they entered a number of other schooners' skippers, acting as insurance adjudicators, declared her unfit for the passage to St John's, the only place where she could be repaired properly. The skipper of this indomitable crew asked Grenfell to help, for the schooner was his own property, and without her he would be ruined. Grenfell risked the realization of a ten years' dream, the seeing of one of his greatest ambitions, and towed the schooner the 300 miles to St John's. He arrived there the day before the opening ceremony of the sailors' home.

This handsome four-storeyed building of dull-red brick and excellent design was now to be named the King George V Institute for Seamen. After returning to Buckingham Palace from his Coronation in June 1911 King George had pressed a button that carried a signal through the transatlantic cable to St John's and announced the laying of the building's corner-stone, a gracious act that brought wide publicity to the Mission. Pictures of the new Institute and articles describing it were published in many countries.

Grenfell was immensely proud of his newest creation, and rightly so. Situated on Water Street, across the road from the very spot where Sir Humphrey Gilbert had landed and taken possession of Newfoundland in the name of Queen Elizabeth I in 1583, thereby founding England's overseas empire, and on land presented by Sir Edgar Bowring, the Institute was a notable achievement. It had cost almost 160,000 dollars, and contained cubicles for men and women, dining-halls, snack-bars, games-rooms, a hall seating 300 people, a cobbler's shop, a laundry, where the visiting fishermen, seamen, and schooner girls could repair their wardrobes, a hairdresser's shop, lounges, and a large swimming-bath. Grenfell was praised and con-gratulated by governments and rulers for providing this build-ing, letters coming from H.M. King George, Queen Alexandra, President Taft, and many others. Now the thousands of sea-farers entering St John's need not be tempted into the public-houses, nor girls be in moral peril when they waited to go on board the schooners. The sailors from foreign ships would have a place to go where they would not be robbed.

Grenfell went to England after the opening of the Institute, and it was while he was with his mother and brother at Park-gate that the next blow fell. The accountant Ashdown, while investigating the Mission finance, had discovered an irregularity in the Institute accounts. A young American whom Grenfell had appointed to be superintendent of the Institute had defal-cated, and the accounts showed that 1000 dollars was missing. Grenfell was greatly upset. This was a blow that came on top of others. He had found himself greeted far from warmly by certain members of the Council in England on this visit, and had learned that Wood, acting on information passed to him from St John's, had again called in the young accountant Brooks, to investigate the Mission affairs. Brooks had reported back, advising that a properly trained manager be appointed. When Grenfell heard of this he had been furious. Now he had been let down again. The young manager of the Institute had given up a position with the American Y.M.C.A. and a salary of over 4000 dollars a year to work with Grenfell for half that sum. He had travelled round the United States with Grenfell, acting as his secretary, and the two men had become very fond of each other. Grenfell felt himself betrayed. He instructed the Mission committee at St John's to prosecute, and the young manager was arrested.

There were many in St John's who thought Grenfell was unnecessarily harsh in prosecuting the young man, and said that the blame for his crime was as much Grenfell's as anyone's. If the Mission affairs had been run properly and if Grenfell had kept a better grasp on these affairs there would have been no crime. The American's family repaid the money, but he was found guilty of misappropriating Mission funds and sentenced to six months' imprisonment. Grenfell attended the trial, and when the culprit had been sentenced the two men "shook hands and wept," in a frank display of their emotions.

This tragedy, and other discoveries Ashdown made in his investigations into the Mission affairs, caused the United States supporters to reconsider their decision to take over the Mission. Ashdown had found "Dr Grenfell's work in a marvellous state of efficiency" as far as the hospitals and other Mission activities were concerned, but he found the business methods lamentable. The Americans decided that

> it would be unwise for us here in New York to assume the business control of the Mission. In the first place, we are not equipped for such work, and there is no one on our board able to give sufficient time to the work to ensure its proper management. Then, too, we feel that we are far removed from the seat of action.

By then, 1912, the Mission in England too were having doubts about their decision to hand over all their properties in Newfoundland and Labrador to an American organization. Still, something must be done to control Grenfell and put his work on more businesslike lines. The council of the R.N.M.D.S.F. made another suggestion. They suggested that an incorporated company be formed under the Newfoundland Company Act, this company to take over any property held in trust by Dr Grenfell, including the Roddickton Mill, schooners, reindeer, etc., and to take over on loan all hospitals, institutes, and other buildings that were the property of the Mission in England, under a trust deed to carry the work on for five years, when the whole position could be reviewed. The English Mission would contribute £2000 annually as its share of the cost of running the Mission in Labrador and Newfoundland. The several supporting associations, Canadian, American, and British, would appoint two directors each to form the board of governors of the new company.

So the International Grenfell Association was formed, and was to continue. A Grenfell Association of Newfoundland was incorporated, and became part of the larger organization. Legally the I.G.A. was a Newfoundland company, though its activities were to become more and more directed from the United States. Grenfell was retained as Superintendent, in charge of the Mission work and with large powers. Like so many who met Grenfell and found themselves associated with his work, the accountant Ashdown—now appointed Chairman of the new company's finance committee—was to remain and give a great part of his life to this service. So was the young St John's accountant Brooks, who served the Mission as Treasurer in Newfoundland for many years and did much to gain support there and to defend Grenfell from future attacks by his enemies.

15

Marriage: More Attacks

GRENFELL was married in Grace Episcopal Church, Chicago, in November 1909. His bride was Miss Anne Elizabeth Caldwell MacClanahan, only child of a successful lawyer who had served as Provost Marshal with the Confederate Army in the American Civil War. The father died when Anne was a child, and she had been brought up by her mother, a New England lady, in Chicago's most fashionable district, Lake Forest. The girl inherited a considerable fortune from a relative, and was educated at Bryn Mawr College. After graduating as Bachelor of Arts she accompanied the wealthy W. R. Stirling and his family on a three-year tour of Europe, and was returning from this tour when she met Grenfell on board the *Mauretania*.

Grenfell brought his bride to St Anthony in January 1910. It was dark when the mail-steamer *Prospero* pushed her way through the ice as far as the narrow entrance to the long, hill-surrounded harbour. The Mission staff and settlers had prepared a royal welcome for the couple, and as the steamer's searchlight fingered at the ice to find its weakest parts rockets soared into the sky, signal cannon boomed, men stationed along the shore fired off their guns. Green flares were set alight on the hospital jetty, to tint the hills, the ice surface, the Mission buildings, and the flag-decorated *Strathcona* still embedded in the ice. A komatik decorated with red and white cloth and streamers went out from the jetty, its driver using his long whip to urge the dogs to a dashing pace. People streamed after the komatik, a long black line of figures going to welcome their benefactor and his wife.

They saw little. Two figures, muffled against the freezing wind, came down the ship's accommodation ladder, to sit on the komatik and be driven to the settlement. Grenfell escorted his wife to the staff house through a triumphal arch and under a long banner made of bed sheeting with "Welcome to our noble Doctor and his bonnie bride" painted on it. The fishermen and their families lined the path, but were oddly silent. Only now and then some of the younger people shouted a welcome or gave a cheer.

The Mission staff, with Dr Little as their leader, greeted the couple inside the staff house. Grenfell looked "twenty years younger," despite the white hairs now mingling with the brown above his ears, as he introduced the tall, handsome girl he had married. Jessie Luther, in her unpublished manuscript, says that Mrs Grenfell wore a fashionable hat with a short veil over her face and had a beautiful speaking voice. She was as tall as her husband, and seemed taller because of the hat and her hair piled up loosely in the style of the time. Jessie Luther, like every one else at St Anthony, was intensely curious about the newcomer, wondering how she would fit into their close and isolated community. American newspapers had made a wonderful story of "the sacrifice that Miss Anne MacClanahan is making in leaving her luxurious home in Lake Forest for the privations of Eskimo huts at Battle Harbour in wintry Labrador," and "Society gasped" when she said she was following her famous husband to the North. One New York paper published a picture of her future home, a tiny log hut that was really the deer-herders' shelter.

In actual fact, even while Society gasped, a handsome residence was being built for the couple at St Anthony. Placed under the hill above the Mission buildings, it was far from being an Eskimo hut. It was a two-storeyed house built of local stone and enclosed on three sides by a glassed-in piazza, its rooms lofty and spacious and with every modern convenience in plumbing, central heating, and electricity. The local men who had built it were determined to give their doctor the finest home on the coast, and had taken great pains to achieve this. They had even set pieces of beautiful blue labradorite into the granite of the fire surrounds, but, never having built a proper fireplace before, they omitted hearths, and almost caused the house to be burned down when fires were lit. Eleanor Storr, Jessie Luther, and the other lady volunteers covered the walls in brown burlap, and the doctors helped to carry in the furniture that Mrs Grenfell had sent from Chicago. Despite great effort, the house was not quite ready when the couple arrived, and Jessie Luther, seeing this fashionably dressed young woman, was clearly doubtful of her ability to manage. Jessie wrote, "It is unfortunate that so many problems await solution and so much adjustment seems necessary. It will be hard for her."

Jessie need not have been concerned. The new Mrs Grenfell was well able to handle most problems. The morning after her arrival she was borrowing an apron and directing the furnishing of her home with a cool and composed authority. She was demanding a cook and solving the problem of a leaky roof in a manner that made the Mission staff realize that a new personality had arrived. They were to find, in the months that followed, that Mrs Grenfell was not only capable but fully conscious of being consort to one who was almost a king in this northern land, and intended to make this clear. The new house became something of a seigneurial hall, where people did not drop in in the easy manner of the coast, but were invited. The men of the settlement, Reuben Sims, Grenfell's servant and oldest friend at St Anthony, Edgar MacNeill, whom Grenfell looked on almost as a son, from the day MacNeill's mother brought him as a boy to the doctor and said, "Edgar will work ten hours a day for you if you will give him one hour's teaching a day," and who with this start had become the

Mission's most admirable Crichton, designing and erecting all the Mission buildings, no longer came along at any hour to consult Grenfell on some problem. The, to them, grandeur and formality of the new house made them feel awkward and ill at ease. With the doctors, nurses, and lady volunteers they came every Sunday evening after church service, to have a weekly 'mug up' of cocoa with cream and buns, and then to sing hymns.

That summer Grenfell carried his wife on board the *Strathcona* to show her his beloved Labrador and introduce her to his friends along the coast. She stood up to the experience courageously, but with little enjoyment. She did not share Grenfell's pleasure when he was presented with barrels of half-rotten whale-meat for his dogs, or enjoy being shipmates with piles of dried and salted fish. Her idea of social entertainment was not sitting in a smoke-filled tilt or being entertained by somewhat odorous fishermen on board their schooners. Grenfell gave little thought to food, but he had a fondness that his wife could not share for the glutinous mess that is boiled cods' heads, and Labrador's favourite 'browse,' soaked ship's biscuit mixed with cod and served with crisped pork fat. Mrs Grenfell preferred less colourful dishes and more ordered surroundings.

She was happier and more at home when Grenfell took her and their first child, the three-months-old Wilfred junior, to England in 1911. They travelled on board the ship where they first met, the *Mauretania*, and spent much of their time in one particular place Grenfell called "Pop corner," where he had proposed to Anne. She wrote from London to tell her mother of all the famous people they met on board the liner. Madam Melba sat in the deck-chair next to theirs, and "notables kept Wilfred talking for hours." She was delighted to tell how "all London is crying out to meet us," and reported proudly how King George had sent for her husband and kept him talking almost an hour, discussing whale-hunting, local justice, and other features of life in Labrador. She shared her husband's warm reception when he addressed a large audience in Queen's Hall, London, with the famous explorer Sir Ernest Shackleton as chairman, and at a reception given for Grenfell by the Royal Geographical Society. She met Count Marconi, who was giving the *Strathcona* a wireless installation, was entertained by Lord

Strathcona, and stayed at Windsor with Sir Frederick Treves. To the young Chicago lady this was a thrilling experience. She was intensely proud of her descent from Scottish chieftains, and loved telling people so. British aristocracy was her ideal. She was now part of it.

Those who knew Anne Grenfell intimately loved and admired her. Those who knew her less intimately often disliked her. Although she and Grenfell could be like merry children inside their own home, and being with them was a delightful experience for those who shared that home, she seldom unbent to others, even Grenfell's best and oldest friends. Her appearance and manners were regal, and she lived up to them. She could tell a Customs officer who asked if she had any spirits to declare, "My husband does not allow strong drinks in his colonies," and not seem pretentious. She loved the social conformities, and achieved them magnificently. Her assumption of 'consort' status, her insistence on her husband being recognized as the founder and principal figure of the Mission, annoyed many, particularly some of the Mission staff who had worked in easy friendliness with Grenfell for years. Her affection for and pride in him was maternal, despite being twenty years his junior, and very often in acting to protect him from spending his time and energy she offended his old friends. These friends were often to receive graceful but firm little notes, to tell them how sorry Wilfred was in not being able to meet them, but "he has not a moment to spare."

She was steadily to take over the management of her husband and his affairs outside Labrador. She handled his mail, arranged his appointments, and instructed the young men who, in turn, accompanied him on his lecture tours as secretaries. She became his literary collaborator, displacing his brother Algernon, who had helped him to edit his books until then. When the publisher Houghton Mifflin, of New York, wrote to congratulate Grenfell on a story, *Suzanne*, he had sent to *The Atlantic Monthly*, and said, "Count Tolstoy would have been proud to write it. You have his genius, but he never had your supreme faith in the abiding love of Jesus Christ," Mrs Grenfell told her mother, "I am much interested in it, as I did a great deal about it myself. I did all the polishing and worked for days over it." Soon she was sharing the Mission work. She took over the marketing of the products of the industrial Department and set herself to raising a fund for sending children from the coast to schools in the United States and Canada.

Her service and usefulness to the Mission was to be very great, even if it lacked the warmth of her husband's passion and humanitarianism. She was a dominant personality; a natural and insistent manager who had now found scope for her qualities. She realized from the beginning of their life together that Grenfell's importance to the Mission was now in being the binding inspiration behind the work, and while he must continue to be on the coast he must also be where his brilliance as a publicist and his personality gave the Mission world prominence. Her purpose was to move him in that direction.

Much that he had done in the past could now be left to others. In those years before the First World War and onward Grenfell was being supported by a team of outstanding men and women. Dr John M. Little had made the hospital at St Anthony famous by his brilliance as a surgeon and his ability as an organizer. He was one of the greatest surgeons of his day, and was to make medical history in several directions. He made a special study of beriberi, and was to do much to clear that disease from the Labrador coast.

The other hospitals were only a little less fortunate. Dr Mather Hare was still at Harrington, travelling his long stretch of coast, winter and summer, and with his wife making the Canadian hospital an important part of the Mission. Dr Wakefield was at Battle, adding to his ordinary medical work a campaign against the causes of tuberculosis. He lectured the Liveyeres on cleanliness and simple hygiene, on a more balanced diet, gradually achieving a new standard in the fishermen's homes. A young Englishman, Dr Harry L. Paddon, was rapidly shaping what was almost a second mission in the northern half of Labrador. Paddon, as a schoolboy, had heard Grenfell lecture at Repton School, and been inspired to serve as Grenfell served. He had become a doctor, and after working for the R.N.M.D.S.F. in the North Sea had come to Labrador. He took over the hospital at Indian Harbour, enlarging it, and then establishing a winter hospital, first at Mud Lake and later at North West River, deep in Hamilton Inlet. Like so many other Grenfell doctors, Paddon married a Mission nurse, and was to bring up a family in Labrador, one son taking over his father's work when the time came.

These were only a very few of the many who now carried out the actual work on the coast. Six doctors and three times as many nurses were permanent members of the Mission staff, with a rapidly increasing number of volunteer ladies like Eleanor Storr, whose children's home now contained thirty orphans. In the summer this staff increased to twenty doctors, many of them well-known specialists, and up to 150 Wops and Wopesses. By 1914 there were four hospitals and six nursing stations along the Labrador and Northern Newfoundland coasts, and the number of patients treated annually had passed the 6000 mark. Grenfell need not now be worried by the financial or management side, for a finance committee of the International Association handled the large sums coming in and what was now an annual disbursement of 66,000 dollars. The Grenfell Mission was a large and expensive organization, and its founder was most valuable as a means of finding money for its needs.

It was in helping her husband in this task that Mrs Grenfell excelled. Alone he would have been content to carry out his lecture engagements without any special flourish, staying wherever he found a room and avoiding so-called Society or irritating ceremonies. His wife had other ideas. She took charge, and the Grenfells travelled in state, the handsome and regal Anne commanding the private homes and hotels where they lodged. Hosts and hostesses found themselves swamped by Grenfell's restless if stimulating presence, his wife's royal appropriation of their homes. Telephones were monopolized, rooms taken over for secretaries or where Grenfell could write. Wherever they were pulsed with their energy and presence. Anne tolerated no interference with her husband's work, and all had to recognize his importance and be there to serve him. If she was dissatisfied with the arrangements for his meetings she swept him away. She used her own and her husband's high social positions to attract the snobbish, flatter the aspiring leaders of provincial Society, and with Scottish shrewdness found out who were the wealthiest and saw to it that they were given prominence.

She set herself to make him what she believed he should seem as well as be, a famous world figure. His carelessness or whimsicality in dress was taken in hand. With his thoughts chasing one another he was liable to pick up whatever garment was handiest, or dress to some mischievous fancy, appearing in odd-coloured socks, even odd shoes, or some favourite old suit. Jessie Luther reported that when in 1909 she escorted his mother to the hall when Harvard University was presenting Grenfell with a degree he appeared on the platform beside his soberly and correctly garbed hosts wearing his magnificent Oxford robes with a golden tweed suit and bright yellow shoes. He was chided by Court officials for appearing at Buckingham Palace incorrectly dressed, though neither the King nor the Prince of Wales demurred. The Labrador Doctor was permitted these eccentricities.

His wife urged him to more conventional dress. His older friends found him in formal morning clothes with a top-hat, explaining that "Anne told me I must dress properly because the people expect it." His friends thought he looked rather ridiculous in such correct garb, and he was obviously much less comfortable than when he wore his favourite tweeds. But he adored his young wife, and nothing she did could be wrong. If she was not there to watch him, however, he lapsed sadly. The young men who acted as his secretaries and had been instructed by his wife to see he dressed properly and kept appointments, and did not miss trains, aged in their efforts. His hosts found themselves sending on clothes he had left behind, or rushing after him to boats or trains with tickets, and even his passport, he had forgotten.

His friends lamented some of the changes they found in him, and blamed his wife for being a snob and making him what they sometimes felt was not his real self. They believed she wanted to shine in Society and was using her husband to achieve this ambition. This was not so. She did aspire to the heights, but it was for her husband and, for his sake, the Mission itself. To her he was the Mission, and she demanded that this truth be recognized.

The outbreak of the First World War in 1914 was to bring changes and new problems. This was a sad year for Grenfell, apart from the War, for in the spring one of the worst disasters of the Colony took place. Two sealing-vessels were caught and

o

foundered in the ice, with a loss of over two hundred men. The Seamen's Institute at St John's became a hospital and a mortuary. That same spring Grenfell lost two of his dearest friends and oldest supporters: Lord Strathcona died in England, and Miss Julia Greenshields in Toronto. The death of this loyal woman affected Grenfell a great deal, and he was to say that he felt he "never wished to visit Canada again."

Grenfell visited Lord Strathcona just before his death, seeking help for the beloved *Strathcona*. The ship was lying helpless in St John's, her sorely tested boilers burnt out and condemned by the surveyors. Lord Strathcona said he would pay for new boilers. He died a few weeks later, but his daughter remembered his promise, paying for the boilers, and continuing to send the thousand dollars every year, her father's annual gift to the Mission.

The War brought a change both in the personnel and the spirit behind the Mission in Labrador. On the outbreak of hostilities extra work was loaded on to the Mission when the Moravian missionaries of German birth were deported. Some of the British doctors and nurses left to join the forces. Wakefield came from the north to offer a company of 150 Legion of Frontiersmen he had raised, then to join the Newfoundland Regiment. Eleanor Storr became an Army nurse, as did other Mission sisters. Newcomers came, but they were not the evangelistic missionaries of the past. Many of them wanted, no less than their predecessors, to make a better life for the fishermen and their wives, but were content to do this with medical service and social and industrial work. There was less need for evangelistic preachers on the coast now, for more clergymen were being sent there. The doctors could leave the people's spiritual welfare to these Churchmen. Grenfell, for the time, did not mind. Indeed, he never did insist on his doctors being religious, and there were men and women of all denominations working for the Mission. Grenfell's perfect Christian was the Good Samaritan, and he believed that if a person served others he or she was living Christianity. He welcomed even freethinkers. Dr Little never made any pretensions of being other than what he was, an ordinary churchgoing Christian who had no desire to evangelize. Neither had a newcomer, a sturdily built young Bostonian, Dr Charlie S. Curtis, who came to St Anthony in

1915, and who was to influence the direction of the Mission's effort hardly less than Grenfell himself.

Grenfell left these able men and women in charge while he went to war. He joined the Harvard University Medical Unit in 1915 and crossed to France. He did not stay more than a few months. Younger men offered themselves, and Grenfell was recalled. He was then fifty, though fitter than most young men. He volunteered to serve with the Royal Army Medical Corps, but was told that there was no shortage of medical officers.

This brief war interlude over, Grenfell returned to his work for the Mission, his mind teeming with ideas for his people's welfare. He had met an American businessman and convinced him that there was a great future in breeding fox for their pelts. The Mission had conducted a small fox farm at St Anthony for some years, and Grenfell was certain that the industry could be expanded. The American established a breeding farm in Sandwich Bay, with a young man named Clarence Birdseye as manager. Out of this an interesting story was to come. Birdseye watched one of the Mission servants catching trout and immediately thrusting them into a snow bank, then moving them to a snow-packed hut where the dogs could not get at them. Months later he saw these fish thawed, and found that they were as fresh as when they were caught. He took this idea back to the United States, and evolved a method of 'deep freeze' that was to make him wealthy and his name known throughout the world.

Grenfell tried to interest the Hudson's Bay Company in fox-farming, but the Company preferred to continue as it had for the past two hundred and fifty years. Its directors invited Grenfell to be their Honorary Surgeon on the coast, and to make an investigation and give any advice he thought useful on their trading methods. Company post managers were finding strong competition from the French Revillon Brothers, and from an increasing number of small independent traders. Clarence Birdseye was financing trappers, and had made a coup in 1914 when the Hudson's Bay Company and Revillon Brothers stopped buying furs on the outbreak of war. Birdseye bought all he could and cleared a large profit.

Grenfell advised the Company to trust their managers more than they did, and not to restrict them to prices decided on in

London. He quoted instances where the Company had lost fur because their managers on the spot could not bid against smaller men with less capital. Grenfell, despite his dislike of book-keeping and his somewhat haphazard methods, was a shrewd and imaginative businessman when he chose to be so. He gave money no value and lost much of his own in trusting people too much, but his schemes were usually sound in themselves. His letter advising the Hudson's Bay Company on their methods of trading is an excellent summary and wise council.

In 1916 he was the target for another uproar of abuse from those who had suffered from his shrewdness on others' behalf. Those traders who had gone out of business, or whose profits had been reduced and their prices forced down, through the success of the co-operative stores and Grenfell's other activities against their monopolies had tried several times since the first attack in 1905 to discredit him. They forced a Government inquiry into Grenfell's 'gun-running' in 1912, the guns being reconditioned weapons sent from England by Grenfell's brother. The inquiry had cleared Grenfell, but regularly the Newfoundland papers printed criticisms of his methods. Now they believed they could do him a great deal of harm.

This new attack came after a Canadian newspaper, the *Montreal Gazette*, had reported incorrectly a speech made by Grenfell at the Ritz Carlton Hotel in that city. He had been describing conditions in the North Sea at the time the R.N.M.D.S.F. had been formed, and said that fishermen spent their time in drinking-hells and contracted diseases fatal to themselves and to their families. The newspaper reported this as having been said about Newfoundland and Labrador fishermen. Another paper, the *Montreal Star*, which did not even have a reporter at the meeting, featured the matter prominently. Immediately the St John's traders opposing Grenfell leapt to the attack and protested against this vilification of the fishermen. A great deal of indignation was roused against Grenfell. The manager of the St John's Institute, Sheard, telegraphed him, telling him of the campaign being raged, and asking if he had said what he was accused of saying. Grenfell was bewildered. He sent a message back, "Utterly unable to understand. Have never felt or expressed anything but unbounded admiration."

He asked for an inquiry to be made into the whole affair and wrote a long explanation of what had happened. The *Montreal Star* accepted this explanation and printed an apology. Grenfell admirers in the United States and in Newfoundland came to his defence. Dr J. F. Andrews, a famous Californian ophthalmologist who had given his services free to the Mission for many summers, published a letter saying that Grenfell was the most unselfish human being he had ever met. Dr B. H. Allen, of Massachusetts General Hospital, said Grenfell would do anything for his people, even to endangering his own life, and that to meet him was to become a better man. A long letter was addressed to the St John's *Evening Telegraph* by a fisherman. He described Grenfell's coming to the coast in 1892, and the service he had done to the schoonermen. "He gets the salt brine in his eyes, for he is out in all weathers," this fisherman wrote.

> Let those who speak ill of him follow after his heels. Very surely it will be different from sitting in an editor's chair. Not only do the people of Labrador look for Grenfell, but forty thousand fishermen look for him sooner or later . . . they know the magnificent work he has done . . . all those fiddle-faddle tales about him are not worth the paper they were written on . . . there is not a fisherman I know nor a fishing skipper that sails a vessel to Labrador has anything but good to say of Grenfell or his work, and it would be to our shame if one of us could not give Grenfell our everlasting gratitude.

But the traders and merchants who had lost money because of Grenfell's activities were out to make the most of this opportunity. They petitioned the Newfoundland Government, listing their grievances and asking for redress. For many years, they claimed, they had

> silently acquiesced in the competition of charitable organizations in the interests of the poorer class of fishermen who had derived benefits from the mission; but a misrepresentation that the Dependency of Newfoundland is largely composed of paupers had roused the charity of the generous public of the United States and brought benefits in money and kind that have now become a menace to all other mercantile concerns on the coast, who have to pay duty and freight upon materials they use or vend.

The petitioners demanded that the privilege extended to the I.G.A., successors to the R.N.M.D.S.F., should either be curtailed or abolished, not only on account of the above reason, but seeing that it is affiliated to certain stores trading on the coast, and thereby having an outlet for the sale of duty-free merchandise introduced under the caption of "foods for charitable purposes."

The Government appointed a commissioner to investigate these charges. He held an inquiry at St John's, where Grenfell was questioned, with many fishermen and settlers. The Commissioner travelled north, examining the co-operative stores' accounts, the hospitals, and the many other Mission works, and his report vindicated Grenfell completely. He was unable to find any connexion between the co-operatives and the Mission, except that Grenfell had advanced money of his own to buy shares and had lost heavily in doing so. He had given his shares away to the fishermen and settlers.

This, that Grenfell and the Mission profited from the stores, had been the merchants' main charge, but the Commissioner went on to praise the Mission for what it was doing for the people, and even commented on the complaint from High Churchmen. There was no religious bias, he said; the Mission was undenominational, but all were welcomed; both parsons and priests helped.

This was to be the last open attack on Grenfell for a long time, but the results of the inquiry did not make him any more popular in Water Street, the St John's merchants' headquarters. He was to be sniped at often, remarking dryly, "The St John's newspapers seldom have a good word for me."

No one would have dared attack the Mission after 1918, for its value and the nobility of its staff were proved during the influenza epidemic that swept across the world soon after the War ended, causing the deaths of over two million people. How many died on the Labrador coast then is not known, but the figures for some of the settlements tell how Labrador and Newfoundland were ravaged. At Okkak, in the north, every man died, and only 39 women and children survived out of a population of 270. At North West River 67 people out of 75 went down with the infection, including Dr Paddon. A quarter of the population at Cartwright died, and some 40 children were orphaned. In isolated places, where no medical help was available, whole families died, and their huts had to be burned over their bodies as a pyre. When an old settler and his daughter died at Cape Porcupine his widow and son had to leave the bodies freezing in the cabin while they kept themselves alive by eating starfish, jellyfish, and even their puppy dog. A woman saw her husband, two sons, and another woman die, leaving her alone. She dared not light a fire because of the bodies, and lived for eleven days with this grim company, afraid to open the cabin door because unfed and now ferocious huskies would have attacked her. They howled and flung themselves at the door in attempts to get in. In an Eskimo settlement the dogs did attack the sick and dead. The only survivor in this group of natives was a seven-year-old girl. The dogs did not molest her, and she lay among them for over a week, getting warmth from their bodies. When rescuers arrived they were amazed to see the girl coming towards them, and they fled in terror. She lived alone with the dogs for another three weeks, until men came to shoot the dogs that had acquired a taste for human flesh, and so must be destroyed.

The doctors and nurses of the Mission, with the clergymen of all denominations working on the coast, seldom saw their beds or homes during these terrible months. Dr Paddon, despite being weakened by the influenza, travelled ceaselessly, going as far south as Cartwright, 200 miles from his headquarters, to help the Church of England parson there, the Rev. Henry Gordon, save those still alive. Grenfell was at St Anthony, and he remained there, sending Dr Curtis round the coast with the *Strathcona*. Like the others, Grenfell was tested almost beyond his remarkable endurance. With the hospital crammed, he and his helpers carried blankets and bedding to the homes of the stricken, until the whole settlement was a hospital. When the epidemic was over the Mission had the task of gathering in the orphans and giving them a home. Dr Paddon and the Rev. Henry Gordon found the means to build an orphanage near Cartwright for their 40 parentless children.

16

The Changing Scene

THE winter of 1918–19 was the last Grenfell was to spend in St Anthony. The need for more and more money to carry on the Mission was making even greater demands on him as a lecturer and publicist. The War had sent prices soaring, and, even with many of the staff unpaid volunteers, and those who were being paid receiving little more than pocket money, the cost of running the ever-expanding Mission was leaping upward at the rate of 10,000 dollars a year. It was over 90,000 dollars in 1919, and this did not include disbursements for new buildings and gifts sent to Grenfell for his special funds that he used as he thought fit.

Greater expenses loomed ahead. Some of the Mission buildings were in poor condition, or too small for the increasing number of patients and expanding activities. St Anthony hospital had been built with green timber, and heating it in the winter had warped and split planks and beams. Draughts came in from every joint, floors were unsafe and walls sagging. The building had been patched and propped as much as it could be, and in 1919 Dr Curtis—in charge at St Anthony after Dr Little left the Mission in 1917—told the I.G.A. Council that "work could not continue" there much longer. A new building of stone or concrete was needed. It was reckoned that such a building would cost 80,000 dollars, not including the cost of its equipment.

The children's orphanage was in no better condition, and was now far too small. It contained some sixty children, and after the devastation of the influenza epidemic there were many more parentless children to be cared for. The Rev. Henry Gordon and Dr Paddon were trying to raise 20,000 dollars to build their orphanage and school for the children of Sandwich Bay, and the Grenfell Mission contributed 9000 dollars for this cause.

There were a dozen other major calls on the Association's finances. A new hospital was needed at North West River, a nursing station at Flower's Cove, Cartwright, and elsewhere. The Mission was caught up by its own usefulness and the need to expand, and Grenfell went ahead impulsively, urging expansion. The Mission fleet now numbered half a dozen vessels; most of them had been presented to the Mission, but all had to be maintained. The *Strathcona* was in poor condition, her plates rusted and dented, her frames rotting through. She leaked so badly that her crew and passengers had often to eat their meals and sleep in her deck-houses; unless a large sum were spent on her she would soon be unfit to go to sea.

These were only a few of the urgent needs; and the Association was finding itself with a deficit at the end of each year. The future of the Mission was worrying its supporters, for they could not all share the faith that made Grenfell so sure that God would see to it all. Grenfell was getting no younger. The time was coming when he would not be there to charm and coax money from the people of the United States and elsewhere, and no one knew better than the members of the I.G.A. that it was Grenfell's personality and energy that brought in money and supporters. No one was ever likely to do what he could do. Some sort of insurance should be taken for a future when he was not there.

The Council decided to raise an Endowment Fund for "the perpetuation of Dr Grenfell's work," and he was asked to devote himself to the task of finding a million and a half dollars, the interest on which would supply part at least of the Mission's costs. It was a gigantic undertaking, and would mean that Grenfell must spend months in America and Britain. "It seems almost absurd," Grenfell wrote at the time,

> but the decision to reconcile myself to the facing of this task was perhaps the greatest effort I had ever made.... The long fall cruise I had hoped to make in a renovated *Strathcona* must be abandoned, and the work on the sea I love must once more for the time give place to the raising of money.

It was a sacrifice, but he had to make it. He was being edged farther and farther away from the actual work on the coast, into a world where he would never wish to be.

It also meant having a home in the United States, for it was there that the bulk of the money would be found. The Grenfells already had a house at Swampscott, on the New England coast, but now they moved to a more convenient place. A house was taken in Brookline, a Boston suburb, and Mrs Grenfell was not sorry to make the change. She had never liked living through the winters at St Anthony; and now she had a family to be educated. There were three children: the nine-year-old Wilfred junior; Pascoe, born in 1912; and a girl, Rosamond, born in 1917. Until now they had been in the care of foreign governesses, their training organized by their mother. She was bringing them up according to her ideas of how the children of a famous man and an English gentleman should be trained. They were not allowed to mix with or to meet the fishermen's children at St Anthony, but were walked out daily, in proper dress, by their governesses. They had to speak French inside their home, for Mrs Grenfell, an accomplished linguist herself, considered foreign languages a social necessity. She intended that her children should go to English schools, to become English in every way. For the time being Boston seemed nearest to this ideal.

Grenfell himself took little part in his children's training. He saw them only briefly, during his short stays at home. He hardly noticed that their training was not the same as his had been, and that they could not, as he had done, make friends with all or develop themselves in adventurous games. They had to remember they were the children of their famous father. Grenfell rather shocked his eldest son by his own boyishness when they did meet, but fascinated the children by his stories, invented as he told them, of rabbits and other creatures that he acted and imitated. But Grenfell's real children stretched along a thousand miles of coastline and included some thousands of people. His own family had to take second place. Mrs Grenfell had her child in her restless and unpredictable husband, and could give only direction to her children's training, leaving their care to governesses and her mother.

Neither Grenfell nor his wife was to have much time to devote to their family in the years that now followed. They were away from their home for months at a time, travelling thousands of miles round the United States, Canada, and Britain. On these tours Grenfell addressed audiences almost daily, often two or three times in one day. He spoke in halls crammed with thousands of people, in churches, at receptions, before the many women's organizations and men's conventions that are a feature of American life, at luncheons given in his honour, and at the homes of wealthy individuals he canvassed.

His success was remarkable. America was experiencing a trade recession in the early twenties, and money was not plentiful. Dozens of other appeals were being made: in Canada McGill University was asking the public for five million dollars; in the United States President Hoover was asking aid for starving Europe. In one city Grenfell visited no less than eleven other appeals were being made, and in New York four of his most important meetings were cancelled because they would have clashed with other charitable efforts. There could hardly have been a worse time for the Grenfell Association to launch this campaign.

Yet in the first three months of the campaign for an endowment fund Grenfell gathered in half a million dollars. By the end of the first year 790,000 dollars had been subscribed, and other moneys had come in for the ordinary maintenance of the Mission work, the ships, and for the new buildings. Everywhere he went Grenfell drew large audiences; the halls he spoke at were filled to their doors, and many were turned away. With money, offers of help came to the Association from hundreds of young men and women who had heard Grenfell speak. Grenfell's faith was justified again; his magic was working.

He was perhaps too eloquent. He saw his people's hardships too vividly, felt the tragedy of their lives too deeply. He could never be complacent about suffering, particularly the sufferings of those he had made his own. He drew his pictures through his own sensitivity, enlarged them with his own pity, and coloured them with his indignation. That the people of Newfoundland and Labrador had suffered their often grim lot for generations, their condition an accepted part of the Colony's history, could not, for Grenfell, mute a tragedy or condone a crime. Many in Newfoundland, however, accepted as normal what horrified him, and considered his descriptions and accusations wild and false dramatization. Until the Mission came Newfoundland had no social services, and its people lived and died as best they could without outside help. "Toil," one of the Colony's historians wrote, "which rapidly changed young housewives into old women, and reduced strong men to invalidism, was the price of existence." Many became defensively proud of this 'independence'; those who might have worked to ease the people's hardships looked away, or defended the system. Many disliked Grenfell because he exposed what they knew in their hearts to be wrong. That he carried his pictures to other countries was a stinging rebuke and accusation against themselves.

They believed that he harmed the Colony's good name. In 1921 he was attacked again. His attacker this time was Newfoundland's Prime Minister, Sir Richard Squires. Squires had visited the United States to try to raise a loan for his Government and to ask the United States to relax tariff restrictions on Newfoundland imports. He had failed, and he blamed Grenfell. He asked if he might attend a meeting of the Grenfell Association of Newfoundland, and when he appeared at this meeting he demanded that a vote of censure be passed on Grenfell. He had, Squires said, gone to a foreign country in the service of the Colony, and everywhere he went he "came upon the bloody trail of a man named Grenfell," who was ruining the Colony's reputation and credit by his stories of a people destitute and exploited, a Government dishonest, and merchants willing to degrade their own countrymen to make money. Grenfell, he said, was blackmailing the consciences of generous-hearted foreigners with his lurid tales and should be ordered to stop his libellous campaign.

Grenfell was at the meeting, held in Government House, and replied to the accusation. He had been shown a cutting from an American newspaper where one of his speeches had been reported. The journalist, Grenfell claimed, had exaggerated and twisted his words to make a sensational story. He was supported by some in the hall who had heard him speak in America. A fisherman, George Whiteley, whose family had been supporters and admirers of Grenfell ever since he came on the coast, and to whom Grenfell was the saviour of his kind, got up and defended his hero. The meeting refused to censure Grenfell. Squires then attacked him through the local Press, and once again the hunt was on. Grenfell was challenged to a meeting in St John's, where his speeches would be discussed. He was at St Anthony then, and would have accepted the challenge if Dr Curtis had not warned him that such a meeting would be packed by his opponents and he would be discredited. The then Governor of Newfoundland, Sir William Allardyce, with whom Grenfell had formed a deep and sincere friendship, arranged a dinner-party where Grenfell and Squires could meet and sort out their differences. The trouble, the last open attack Grenfell was to suffer, was smoothed over, though many in St John's were to carry their grudge for a long time.

These attacks hurt Grenfell, though he was more bewildered than contrite. That he had some small feeling of guilt comes out in a letter he wrote to his champion, George Whiteley:

> Thanks a thousand times, my dear George, for your splendid help when the Prime Minister was attacking me. I am not the saint I ought to be—but I have tried to do what I thought the Master would do in my place—and if I have failed it is not because I purposely tried to mislead as Sir R. Squires believes. I love the coast, I love the fishermen. I am older than I was, and I know I might have been wiser—but I have tried—and had great joy in it.

When he could he turned from these complexities of the civilized world to find relief and understanding in the simpler world of the sea and those who lived on it and by it. Here, on ships and on the waters, he was free of conventions he would never understand or wish to learn. A load lifted from his shoulders when he stepped on board the *Strathcona* and was in the company of his fishermen and the adoring young Americans and Englishmen, more and more of them the sons of other young men he had inspired years before, who had come to share his great adventure. He could be himself here, wear what odd or colourful clothes he wished, and not have his beloved Anne telling him he must dress correctly because "the people expected it." He could forget that there are times for meals, and no agitated young men would be reminding him that trains ran to a timetable, that a meeting opened at eight o'clock, or that he had an appointment to keep. The sea was a vast, soothing balm, giving freedom from petty irritations. It was not free, of course, and Grenfell's faults as a seaman were that he never would recognize this, even with the *Strathcona*'s many dents as reminders. But the eye could lift to a distant horizon, and the only problems were the challenge of the elements.

He went to the coast as often as he could, but each year his voyages were shorter. Always there was a date when he must be somewhere else, always the crying need for more and more money. The War had brought prosperity to the Newfoundland and Labrador fishermen, but it was a prosperity on shaky foundations. The impoverishment of those European countries which had bought the Colony's main produce and the general deflation of prices that followed the war-time inflation brought disaster to an economy that had never been sound. The price of fish tumbled until it was not worth while catching them. The great fleets of schooners dwindled, and fewer and fewer Newfoundlanders came north each summer. The conditions of the Liveyeres became desperate. Traders, even large and old-established merchants, who had carried debtors for generations went out of business, and there were not even the hard bargains of the credit system to maintain the people. Those who might have fished for what reward there was could not. Torn or lost nets could not be repaired or replaced because the fishermen did not have the twine to work with. They could not buy salt, or any of the other supplies they needed.

Once again starvation and destitution was the common lot. and the diseases of malnutrition ravaged the coast. The Government gave what relief it could afford in offering flour and molasses to those who cut timber for wood-pulp and pit-props. Often these were cut and never collected, lying until they rotted, and the men who had cut them starved. Grenfell had many grim tales to tell his audiences when he lectured. "My last patient to-night," he wrote in one of his 'Logs,'

> was a woman of thirty-four years of age. She looked fifty. With two barefooted, naked children she came with a cough and pains in her chest. Pale and haggard, she sat in my cabin without one word of complaint. She had been on dry white flour and molasses all winter; her little girl of two years showed it only too clearly. Her two older boys had worked at pulp-wood but had been unable to make enough for sufficient food.

Men literally crawled because their limbs were swollen with beriberi; yet they had to make some effort to feed their families.

Grenfell and the Mission workers did what they could. The hospitals were crowded. At every stop Grenfell made with the *Strathcona* he found a procession of miserable people waiting to be treated and to be helped with clothing and food. In two weeks of one voyage he treated over 300 sick people, and every other doctor and nurse on the coast had the same experience. Grenfell's heart was sore, his pity boundless. He went on shore at one place to visit an old fisherman who had sustained himself by cutting timber for the *Strathcona*'s boilers, to find the man half-starved and without a warm garment. Grenfell stripped off the suit he was wearing and gave it to the fisherman; then, as his boat had returned to the ship, he swam back to the *Strathcona* in his underwear. Passengers on board the ship, friends Grenfell had brought with him to show them the coast, found their wardrobes depleted when Grenfell's supply of old clothing was used up.

The people were losing heart again, returning to the indolence and hopelessness of the past. They would not help themselves, even when they might have done. The co-operatives were failing because of this, and soon only two remained in business out of the eight Grenfell had started. At Red Bay William Pike kept the store there prosperous, saving the settlement from the full effect of the general disaster. The co-operative at St Anthony would have failed but for the efforts of Dr Curtis and an Englishman, Mr Alfred Blackburn. Gren-

fell had given all his shares in this store to settlers, and they
had promptly decided to sell up and claim their part of what it
brought. Blackburn prevented this; he turned the store into a
spot-cash co-operative, and it began to prosper again. The
lumber mill at Canada Bay was losing heavily, partly through
the people's indolence. One by one the other stores collapsed,
one of them ending when its manager absconded with the
funds and 10,000 dollars he was given to buy a schooner. He
disappeared to the United States and was never found. Grenfell
tried to reorganize these co-operatives, finding a young English-
woman, Margaret Digby, of the Horace Plunkett Foundation,
whom he sent to Newfoundland to report and advise, instructing her to "call on the Governor, stay at the Institute and carry
a tin of Keatings," and leaving the rest to her. She located the
trouble easily enough, the people's lack of experience, a poor
system of education, and the rivalries of sectarianism destroying
a community spirit; she made recommendations, but by then
the experiment had failed and the people were in no heart to
try again.

Desperation was affecting the people's moral values. Grenfell
was often cheated. He was sold billets of wood for his ships'
boilers that were the property of the Mission's mill at Canada
Bay. After every gale log dams were reported carried away, and
it was these logs Grenfell bought from their finders. He was the
easiest victim for anyone with a hard-luck story, and not all who
came to him were deserving cases. There was always some truth
in the accusation made that he 'pauperized' the fishermen, for
some were only too willing to be pauperized, and Grenfell
wanted so eagerly to help. His great reindeer experiment had
been ruined by those he was trying to help. While the Lapps
were there to watch over the herd it increased from the original
300 animals to over 1500; but when the Lapps went home in
1915 local men took over their task and allowed the animals to
stray and be shot by the settlers. Grenfell had tried to get the
Newfoundland Government to erect fences to confine the deer,
but no one was interested, and to many of the Colony's administration anything Grenfell asked had to be opposed. Grenfell
and his doctors, as Justices of the Peace, punished those settlers
who were caught shooting the deer; but in a land where few
had money to pay fines, and without gaols, punishing was

futile. By the end of the War only 150 reindeer survived. These were taken over by the Canadian Government and re-established on the mainland.

Grenfell forgave every crime. He seemed blind to the faults of these people he had made his own. When he was told of tricks played on him he shrugged the information away. He believed that people have no original sin, but are made in Christ's image. Their flaws had been impressed on them by the conditions enforced by the selfish and ambitious. He would no more blame his people for spoiling his dreams than he would blame a storm for damaging his ship. So he went on working for them, in the winter pleading for money and other help, and in the summer cruising with the *Strathcona*.

His ship, like himself, was getting older, and she had been sorely tried. In 1922 a north-west wind and heavy sea finished her. She was crossing Bonavista Bay, on the Newfoundland coast, when her weakened frame and rusted plates were finally overstrained by the waves and she started filling. Grenfell was not on board. When the water was above the engine-room plates and the engineer had to wear thigh boots to carry out his job her captain, William Sims, asked a passing schooner to stand by. The schooner's captain came on board to survey the ship, and he condemned her at once. The crew got away to the schooner with difficulty, and half an hour later the *Strathcona* fell over to port and sank. She had served Grenfell for twenty-three years, and he had asked much of her. He was upset and saddened by her loss. "How many busy days we have shared together," he wrote,

how many ventures we have essayed. How many times her decks have been crowded with our brethren seeking healing of the body —relief from pain—counsel in anxiety. Babes have been born on board her; helpless children saved and carried to the permanent care of loving hands. Some have been married and others have died in her accommodating shelter.... Once she towed nineteen shipwrecked crews to safety; once saved from a wreck nearly two hundred persons. Five times she has been on the rocks herself.... Many have gathered in her cabin for worship and praise ...a thousand times the sound of her whistle and the flutter of her flags have brought to eager, waiting hearts the message of hope and help.

P

She was to be replaced, but no other ship was ever to mean so much to Grenfell or to the people of Labrador. She was part of the Grenfell legend.

Her intrepid and often reckless commander was also feeling the strain of ceaseless effort and age. He had received a sad blow when his "adored and wonderful" mother died in 1921. In 1924, after four years' continuous labour on the coast and travelling in search of money and help, it was clear to his medical friends that he should ease up. He was sixty now, and he set a pace too fast for that age. The directors of the I.G.A. urged him to take a holiday and presented him with the cost of a tour round the world for himself and his wife. "We hope," the directors told him, "you will drop all care and seek the enjoyment offered by this extensive trip, coming back rested in mind and spirit." Grenfell and his wife travelled to England, then across Europe to Egypt and Palestine, before visiting Persia, India, China, and Japan. The tour was to have lasted a year, but Grenfell was back in America after nine months. He had given himself little rest in those months, keeping fully occupied in studying the social conditions of the countries he visited, carrying on a voluminous correspondence to keep in touch with Mission affairs, working with his wife on a book about his travels, *Labrador looks at the Orient*, lecturing to universities, and being entertained by officials and missionaries who wanted to meet him. His holiday became something of a triumphal but tiring tour, though he enjoyed seeing places like the Holy Land.

He spent the last month of his 'holiday' on a course of orthopædic surgery under Dr MacKenzie Forbes in Montreal, then, after lecturing for a few months, went to St Anthony to see how the new hospital there was progressing and to inspect the new Mission ship, *Strathcona II*. This ship, a converted steam-yacht, had been purchased in England with money given by the Hudson's Bay Company. She was smaller than the first *Strathcona*, but Grenfell was well pleased to have his own ship again.

The new hospital was rising. Wops had cleared the site and built the foundations, and now, with local help and professional guidance, they were raising the walls of steel and concrete. The new orphanage was already built, a large, three-storeyed steel-and-concrete building with forty-two rooms, paid for mainly by thousands of children responding to Grenfell's appeal for "twenty-five-cent bricks."

The Association's finances were being strained at this time. Expenditure for 1925 reached the huge total of 140,000 dollars, and there was a deficit for the year of over 15,000 dollars. Grenfell seemed, for the time, to have reached the limit of American and Canadian generosity, and the directors decided to send him to Britain, to raise support there. Out of 80,000 dollars contributed by the five associations forming the I.G.A. in 1925 the English member, the R.N.M.D.S.F., had contributed only about 3000 dollars. It was felt that Great Britain should do more. At a meeting of the board of directors in June 1926 Grenfell was instructed to

> carry on, for the period of one year, a campaign in Great Britain and Ireland, at no cost to the R.N.M.D.S.F., to increase interest in the work of the I.G.A. For this purpose a special office and a special worker to be selected by Dr Grenfell, and all moneys raised as a result of this campaign shall pass through the hands of the R.N.M.D.S.F., to the work carried on by the I.G.A.

Grenfell, as always, interpreted his instructions as he thought fit. He came to England with his wife, a young American as his travelling secretary, and a Miss Katie Spalding, who had been a volunteer worker on the coast for several years. Completely ignoring the officials of the Mission to Deep Sea Fishermen— indeed, not bothering to tell them what he was doing—he opened an office and announced a brand-new organization, the Grenfell Foundation of Great Britain and Ireland. Using all his high-placed connexions, he formed a committee of sponsors, including the High Commissioners of Canada and Newfoundland, two Archbishops, two leading nonconformist churchmen, the Chief Rabbi, Lord Southborough, who had been Mr Francis Hopwood and the originator of the Labrador Mission, his own kinsman Lord Desborough, and other distinguished people. He then opened a whirlwind campaign, travelling round Britain in a second-hand car that cost thirty pounds and which broke down as often as could be expected.

He was, as always, successful in arousing interest and getting support from people of all classes. He achieved, among other triumphs, the remarkable feat for a missionary of filling the

London Polytechnic Hall twice a day for two weeks. "His manner," one newspaper reported, "is jerky, his sentences have the doctor's quick, commanding note, and he makes no attempt at consecutive thought.... The congregation, which included hundreds of young people, listened as with one heart and soul to the great doctor's narrative." His unexpectedness and impulsiveness delighted these young people, as when he leapt from a platform he shared with the American temperance campaigner, Pussyfoot Johnson, and helped to throw rowdy interrupters out of the hall. Hotels he stayed at did not present any bill when he ended his stay; porters and waitresses handed back the tips he gave them and asked him to put the money in his Mission funds; professional typists he engaged worked for nothing. As in the United States and Canada, young men and women came to him to ask how they could help, and many were to go to Labrador as Wops. Again his own vast generosity and dedication of self inspired others to serve, drew people to him who wanted to follow in his footsteps. In the six months Grenfell remained in England on this visit his name became as famous in his own country as it had been in America for years.

The Council of his old Mission, the Royal National Mission to Deep Sea Fishermen, were naturally somewhat bewildered to find themselves ignored and a new association formed to do what, as far as they were aware, was their job. They invited Grenfell to meet them and explain exactly what he was doing and what his new association was. He appeared before the Council in December that year, and from the detailed verbatim report of the meeting it is obvious that he was feeling neither guilty nor apologetic. His replies to many of the questions put to him verged on the truculent. When he was asked what was happening to the money he was collecting in England he answered, "I am not carrying it in my pocket." When one member of the Council objected to the Chief Rabbi being part of a Protestant body Grenfell retorted sharply, "His doctrine is not any bar."

He remained short and outspoken to the point of rudeness throughout the meeting, and it is clear that he wished to end his connexion with the R.N.M.D.S.F. and to have his own organization in England. He had not been authorized to do this by the I.G.A., and he had taken little trouble to assure the legality of what he was doing. When it was pointed out that the British Mission might be held responsible if anything went wrong with the venture he answered, "If God Almighty says 'Go' we must have somebody go wrong sometimes." Nor was he concerned when he was told that as his 'Foundation' was not a properly incorporated body his distinguished patrons might find themselves held responsible if anyone were to bring legal proceedings against the organization. "We know your enthusiasm," the Council chairman warned him, "and how you are apt to entangle people and infect them with your own enthusiasm, but it does not always work well." Grenfell had never stopped to consider if anything he started would work well. He knew that it would. "Start something," he told one of his Mission workers; "somebody will always finish it." This was not cynicism but infinite faith. The new association would be successful. All those fears and fussing over legality and details did not concern him, and showed a lack of trust in God's all-seeing care.

So the Grenfell Association of Great Britain and Ireland was born, and a final break made with the R.N.M.D.S.F., though two of its members were to be on the board of the I.G.A. for some years. The directors of the I.G.A. approved the new organization, now that it was an accomplished fact. The R.N.M.D.S.F. granted the I.G.A. a ninety-nine year lease on their properties and buildings in Newfoundland and Labrador at a nominal rent, and in a few years' time handed over the titles entirely. The only connexion between the two Missions was to be the mother Mission passing on income from endowments collected for the work in Labrador.

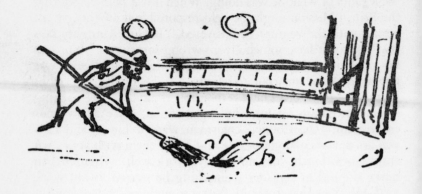

17

The Approaching End

HIS new association off to a flying start, the loyal Katie
Spalding remaining in England to guide its course, Grenfell returned to Labrador. He was becoming conscious
that "life is short—we have so little time to do things," and had
a reminder of this when he had his first bad heart-attack while
climbing a hill in Labrador that year, 1926. It was a warning
that Grenfell, as a doctor, must note, even if he refused to let it
interfere with his work or slow down his breathless pace. He
still drove his ship through gales, still called all hands to share
his morning swim, and defied old age and his heart condition
by leading his young Wops over the masthead as an exercise.
He was delighted that he could still beat his sons at squash,
walk his guests off their legs over the hills.

He wrote as much, though now he was passing on his religious faith and philosophy rather than describing his adventures
in action. He had published thirty-five books and hundreds of
articles, though his wife did most of the revising and enlarging
of his autobiographical *Labrador Doctor* for reissue as *Forty*

Years for Labrador, just as she contributed other writings under his name. Also, she saw, as he could not see, the end of their labours coming, and she built a house on the shore of Lake Champlain, in Vermont, to where they could retire. She herself was far from well and often in pain. As early as 1919 she had been treated for what was believed to be a tumour, and again in 1925 she had treatment at Boston. Whether or not she suspected cancer is not known. She was the sort of woman who would keep such suspicions to herself. She must have guessed something serious, but never complained or mentioned her condition. With her loyal and devoted friend Miss Eleanor Cushman—the Grenfells' unpaid secretary for ten years—she lived only to look after her husband and to advance his cause.

In 1927 Grenfell could mark up another achievement of his long task; the new hospital at St Anthony, a handsome brick building designed by Mr William Delano, with the latest equipment, and classed with the best hospitals in America, was completed and ready for use. A Royal Naval vessel, H.M.S. *Wistaria*, brought Sir William and Lady Allardyce to perform the opening ceremony, and another ship carried a company of distinguished guests. Grenfell almost missed this important occasion. He had been north with *Strathcona II* and been delayed by turning back in response to an appeal from a fisherman whose wife was ill. Heading south again, the ship encountered fog and got off course. She ran on a rock at full speed and listed heavily. She was being pounded badly, and it seemed that she was lost. She was abandoned and fell almost on her side, still being beaten on the rock. Grenfell, in one of the boats, stayed near to watch her end, but miraculously she slipped clear and floated again, though listing heavily. She was boarded and found to be seaworthy, though sadly battered. Inside she was a shambles, furniture and fittings smashed by the violence of her pounding. Coal from her bunkers clogged the pump inlets, so passengers, including several women, helped the crew to empty out what water was in the ship with buckets. Steam was raised, and she reached St Anthony the day before the opening ceremony and in time for Grenfell to join his guests in climbing the hill behind the Mission buildings to unveil a tablet in memory of Dr John M. Little. Little, who had continued to work for the Mission as a director while practising his profession in Boston, had died the previous year. Now his ashes were to be buried near a large granite outcrop high above this place whose people he had served so well for ten years of his life.

The next day, Monday, July 25, St Anthony celebrated as it never had before. The ships in the harbour were dressed over-all; British and United States flags flew from every building. The Church Boys' Brigade, the Mission's Boy Scouts and Girl Guides, paraded with a guard of honour from the warship. Salutes were fired from the ship, and the Governor appeared in full dress uniform. Even Grenfell did not protest at being 'dressed correctly' by his wife for this proud and important day. When Sir William Allardyce had formally opened the hospital he announced that His Majesty had been "graciously pleased to confer the honour of Knight Commander of St Michael and St George on Dr Grenfell." Grenfell was now Sir Wilfred Grenfell, K.C.M.G.; his wife was Lady Grenfell.

A year later Grenfell went to Buckingham Palace to receive the accolade. The following year, 1929, he was again in Britain, to be installed as Lord Rector of the Scottish St Andrews University. He thoroughly enjoyed the traditional student welcome when his carriage was drawn through the streets of St Andrews by red-gowned, boisterous, and admiring young men. In con-ferring on Grenfell an honorary degree of Doctor of Literature, an honour he shared with Sir William Allardyce and his old friend Henry Richards—now knighted for his services to edu-cation—Professor Blyth Webster ended his oration: "Labrador had been said to mean Land of the Labourer. I present as Rector-elect for laureation the Labourer of Labrador, toiler of the deep, tiller of human soil, helper and healer of the lives of men." Grenfell, who was succeeding as Rector the famous explorer and humanitarian Dr Nansen, gave as his address "St Andrew," patron saint of fishermen, as well as of Scotland and the University, a man after Grenfell's own heart in his loyalty to his trust and in his impulsiveness.

Grenfell's election was commented on to a remarkable extent in the Press. He was hailed as a "worthy successor to Nansen." *The Times* gave him a long editorial, saying:

> At first it is a little difficult to think of him as Rector of a uni-versity, since never was a man of intellect less academic. But St Andrews University—true, as Sir Wilfred Grenfell suggests, to

the spirit of its patron saint—likes men of adventure for its rectors. Education, moreover, does well to honour him, since he has served her no less gallantly than he has served religion and health and wealth and craftsmanship and every other human activity.

The editorial ended:

> Labrador has the peculiar privilege of giving the world something more than any material advantage. . . . It has been the lamp whence a great light shined . . . the light of practical ability fired by spiritual vision.

Other papers were no less laudatory. "British businessmen," one said,

> who would not recognize a ministering angel if they saw one, have listened and been impressed with his story. They are beginning to realize that Labrador, too, is coloured red on the map and that its products may be important to the British Empire.

This last was a comment on Grenfell's efforts to interest British capitalists in Labrador. His "Gospel of pills and poultices" had long since replaced the mere handing out of tracts and preaching. Now even pills and poultices had taken second place. "The whole difference between this mission and the ordinary medical mission," Grenfell was to write,

> is that I don't personally regard the hospital work as the first work of the mission, and never did. I am far more interested in making a new man than a new body. The message of the love of God to my mind lies in the orphanage and dock and industrial work and in the gardens more than in the hospitals. This is the attitude to God that makes the mission appeal where others don't.

He was now calling on his native land to develop Labrador so that its people would have this new life. With that shrewdness he possessed, so contradictory to other sides of his character, he laid out his arguments: the control of vast mineral deposits, for which there was a market of gigantic proportions in America, the control in British hands and with settlements in Empire currencies not weakening the nation's foreign-exchange position. There were almost inexhaustible timber resources, great waterfalls for the supply of cheap electricity, and Labrador and Newfoundland were the obvious sites for the air terminals that must come with the growth of air travel. Grenfell was eager that the benefits of all these should come to Britain, for, despite what he called his "amphibious nationality" and his admiration and affection for Americans, he always remained a staunch Englishman. Now, for the good of his country as well as for the good of the people of Labrador, he would pour wealth into his countrymen's pockets. He came to England more and more in the next few years, urging this investment. He spoke of it at a luncheon given in his honour by the Lord Mayor of London, appealing to the City, to the Hudson's Bay Company, and to other great interests. He pointed out that if it had been worth the Canadian Government's while to offer a hundred million dollars for Labrador after the British Privy Council had supported Newfoundland's claim to the territory in 1927, then Labrador must surely be of value.

He was listened to and admired. He was loaded with new honours, presented with the Livingstone Gold Medal, made a Fellow of the Royal Geographical Society; Lloyd George presented him with two prize boars for the Mission farm at St Anthony. Sixteen London chefs selected Labrador salmon as the best of an unlabelled group. The Colonial Secretary listened to his views on how to solve Newfoundland's now desperate troubles. He was received by the Royal Family as a friend, the most sought-after man in London, and with his wife was entertained in most of the great homes in Mayfair. Duchesses organized and ran flower-shows and concerts to help his funds, and his appeals for money were responded to generously. But British capital remained unimpressed by the prospects in Labrador. The slump had hit the United States, and the whole world was depressed. What response Grenfell might have found a few years earlier was not now forthcoming. His greatest success, apart from his personal impact, the money he gathered, and the establishment of a Grenfell Association in Britain, was inducing the Admiralty to send a survey ship to the coast. But when Labrador's mineral wealth was exploited it was to be with American capital, not British.

Grenfell was carrying on this strenuous campaign, travelling almost ceaselessly in Britain and America, holding meetings and seeking out rich supporters, while he was far from well. He had another, more severe heart-attack in 1929, and was to have recurring attacks from then on. Lady Grenfell urged him to take things easier, and he and she both suggested to the board of the I.G.A. that his work be confined to lecturing in larger towns, to talking on the radio, and interesting influential and wealthy people. His New York doctor, Dr Beeckman J. Delatour, who was also an old friend and a director of the I.G.A., reported Grenfell's condition to the board. Its members resolved "That it is the earnest desire of this board that both Sir Wilfred and Lady Grenfell lay aside all responsibilities of the Mission for the coming summer in order that they may devote themselves to complete rest and relaxation." Lady Grenfell acted on this advice by resigning as head of the educational department of the Mission, though she continued to work for the industrial side.

Grenfell took little notice of the second warning he had received, though he did not lecture so often. He worked, instead, to interest wealthy and influential people and did succeed in interesting men so different as Henry Ford and the British Prime Minister, J. Ramsay MacDonald. Grenfell was still a hero-worshipper and admired those who had achieved. He gave his admiration to such diverse men as Admiral Byrd and the racing motorist John Cobb. His choice of friends was nothing if not catholic, and he had neither political nor religious prejudices. He admired the idealistic and theatrical socialist and the captain of industry equally, writing to tell a friend that MacDonald was "splendid" and that "If this man Ford had charge of Newfoundland he would make it smile with wealth."

He was cultivating British political figures, partly to get them interested in opening up Labrador for development, and partly to do what he could to save the Colony from complete disaster. He was even working with his old opponent, the Prime Minister of Newfoundland, Sir Richard Squires, who asked him to act unofficially on the Colony's behalf. Newfoundland was coming to the end of its financial resources and credit by now. The Government had undertaken burdens it could not manage, trying to ease the people's desperate condition by road-building, a new dock at St John's, jetties at outports, and other works. It had to take over the railways when the private interests running them were unable to continue operations, and this meant rebuilding most of the line and roadbed. The now world-wide depression had worsened the value of what the Colony had to sell, and in 1931 Grenfell could have what satisfaction there was in learning that a mob of angry Newfoundlanders had chased Squires and actually 'treed' him outside the Government buildings. This might have made Grenfell laugh, but it gave him no real pleasure.

Exactly how much Grenfell had to do with the action the British Government took to save the Colony is not known. He was not invited in officially, and what he did was by personal contact and was not recorded in the Government archives. But in his letters to friends, particularly those to George Whiteley in St John's, he tells how he was "seeing the Prime Minister often, and keeping in close touch with Lord Amulree" on the matter. He had opposed strongly the Canadian effort to buy Labrador from Newfoundland, and now he was as strong for a Commission Government. "I believe that the only way to save the Colony is by commission government," he told Whiteley;

> say, three men who know their business, advised by just as many as you like. Secondly, we must have a Civil Service founded on merit, where, whatever happens, a scamp, like so many Government officials are, is immediately and fearlessly reprimanded and kicked out.... The Government officials that I have been connected with on the Labrador coast have so many of them been not merely incompetent but many of them criminal.

There was talk of Grenfell becoming Governor of Newfoundland, and this appointment was mentioned in newspapers. British papers said, "No better man could be appointed," but Grenfell told George Whiteley, "I am too old a dog for that job." Again, there are no records of any such offer being made to him by the British Government, and it is certain that many in Newfoundland would have disliked having him as Governor.

He did meet the Commissioners who were sent to investigate the Colony's affairs and recommend a solution, advising them on whom to consult and warning them of others who, he believed, could not be trusted. It is difficult to tell how much influence he was able to wield, but that he did have a great deal to do with the final decision the British Government made is almost certain. In 1933 the Commission of Inquiry recommended that self-government in Newfoundland be suspended and the Colony ruled by a Commission of three Newfoundlanders and three Britons under the chairmanship of the Governor. The Colony's legislature had no choice but to accept this drastic cure for its ills. As a modern Newfoundland historian says, "In 1934, the light that was lit in 1855 with the granting of Responsible Government went out." Commission Government was to continue until after the Second World War, when, in 1949, the people of Newfoundland voted for union with Canada.

By then, in 1934, Grenfell had reached the end of his active work on the coast. He made his last summer voyage in 1932. In 1931 he had accompanied an American-sponsored survey party —the Forbes-Grenfell Expedition—to help carry out one of his greatest ambitions, the charting of the coast. He had asked the British Air Ministry for an aircraft to carry out a survey, but the economies cutting down the British armed forces prevented this help being given. Professor Alexander Forbes, of Harvard University, owned a small aircraft and a yacht, and gathered a team of undergraduates to carry out the survey. The Geographical Society of New York offered to produce charts from the information supplied. Grenfell acted as pilot to the expedition, with the *Strathcona II* as supply vessel. The next year the Royal Naval survey ship, H.M.S. *Challenger*, came on the coast, charting and marking, the need for this proved when the warship found one rock by running on it.

This survey, incomplete though it was, was another triumph for Grenfell to add to his many others. He saw the start of the tourist trade he had advocated for so long when the Clarke Steamship Company of Montreal began a series of summer cruises to Labrador, and there was an earnest of things to come when an Italian air squadron under General Balbo, and Colonel and Mrs Charles Lindbergh, with other pioneer aviators, used Labrador as a stopping-place on their world flights.

Grenfell saw, too, the changes that were coming to both the fishing and the Mission. Motor-boats were displacing the oars and sails of the past. Each year there were fewer schooners, foretelling the day when none would come north. Cod-fishing was declining altogether, partly because of a loss of markets and partly because the Labrador fishermen would not move with the times and improve their methods of curing to compete with Icelandic fishermen. Salmon was becoming a more important catch than cod, as the Hudson's Bay Company introduced better ways of preserving these fish for carrying. With the decline of the fishing fleets the Mission became more and more for the Liveyeres. Dr Paddon was now established permanently at North West River, deep in Hamilton Inlet, and Indian Harbour was made a summer station. When the hospital at Battle Harbour was burned down in 1930 it was not rebuilt. Instead a new site was chosen at St Mary's River, on the mainland. Cartwright was made an important Mission station, with a hospital and a large school and orphanage to replace the station built by the efforts of the Rev. Henry Gordon and Dr Paddon, which had burned down.

The need for the Mission's services had not decreased. Indeed, with the continued depression in fishing the need was greater than ever. Those destroying diseases, tuberculosis, scurvy, and beriberi, still took their toll, and epidemics ravaged the settlements. Dr Curtis and Dr Paddon set out to fight them with an increasing emphasis on their causes, malnutrition and incorrect diet. A gift of a large greenhouse enabled Dr Curtis to grow thousands of cabbage and lettuce plants at St Anthony, supplying ample vegetables for the hospital patients and passing on young plants to the settlers for replanting in the gardens they were urged to make. Both Paddon and Curtis were proving that all kinds of crops could be raised at their farms at St Anthony and North West River, that cattle could be bred successfully. Mrs Curtis lent the fishermen's wives machines for canning berries and vegetables, and gradually the people were taught to use their land and improve their diet.

In those last years of active work Grenfell was able to see the effects of the efforts he had begun so long ago. Children he had found half starved, dirty, and without hope were now grown to men and women and a better life. The two blind girls he had lifted from their mother's arms—saying jokingly that he would probably drown them—had been sent to the United States for education and training and were now good-looking young women, supporting themselves by working for the Mission's thriving industrial department run by William Pike's sister, Minnie, at Red Bay. Many other children who had been sent to America by the educational department were now the Mission's engineers, carpenters, hospital servants, teachers, or were prospering outside the Colony. If he had achieved nothing more, in saving these hundreds of children from the cruelty of poverty and the threat of disease, giving them the opportunity to grow up healthily and with an education, Grenfell had done a great service.

He had done no less for many born to better conditions and opportunities. There are times when the observer marvels at the fame Grenfell earned for giving his life to a comparatively tiny section of the earth, and for the welfare of a relatively small community. He had made the world conscious of Labrador and its people's condition, but if size is the measure, then many men and women have achieved a great deal more without attracting half the attention Grenfell did, or receiving the honours he received. But, as has been said earlier, his work was outside Labrador and Newfoundland no less than in the Colony. There were now thousands of men and women who had followed him to Labrador, who had been inspired by him to serve their fellows and were better and happier people for having known him.

There had been failures among those whom he sent to the coast. Grenfell was never critical, and welcomed anyone who said they wanted to serve with him. To him, offering young men and women an opportunity to work for others was an important part of his Christian duty, and he did not stop to consider if those he welcomed were suitable for the work. Most of the young Americans and Britons who came to the coast during the summer months were sincere, and even if they were not professing Christians they burned with the ideal of service. They worked hard, and many of the tasks they were given were far from pleasant. Even Grenfell, who accepted hardship and discomfort as a challenge and enjoyed them, and who expected those who worked with him to stand up to anything he could take, was shocked to find the young Wops working to lay a water-pipe line for the hospital at Cartwright being tormented almost past endurance by clouds of black flies rising from the swamp where the work was being done. The story of the Grenfell Wops deserves its own recorder, for without them the Mission would not be what it is to-day. Indeed, it would not exist. Those who now control it, manage its affairs, and maintain it in its present vast usefulness began their service as volunteers on the coast and have made the Mission part of their whole lives.

But, as has been said, there were failures. It became the 'thing' for young university undergraduates to serve for a summer with the Grenfell Mission, and some of them made themselves a nuisance and a trial for the hardworking doctors and staff. Parents with difficult sons—young men who drank too much, some who were drug addicts—asked Grenfell to allow their sons to go to Labrador, where there would be no temptation. Grenfell was always delighted to help, and the Mission doctors found themselves with some odd characters on their hands. The doctors could only ask Grenfell to be more careful of those he sent, but he paid little attention. He would not deprive youth of its chance.

This matter of the Wops was one of several where Grenfell's doctors often wished he would be less impulsive and big-hearted. It was they who had the task of handling the problems he so often tossed into their laps. His impulsiveness and forget-fulness landed him into troubles, as when he appointed two doctors to one post, then had to recompense one of them with 1000 dollars. He never realized that with the Mission's growth the old ways had to go, that rules had to be made and kept to, that organization was essential. He picked up children and brought them to St Anthony, with no thought for the fact that the orphanage there was already overcrowded and that, no matter how eager the staff were to save more children, there were physical limits. He just dumped the children on the wharf and left some one to 'finish the job.' He had a royal row with one nurse whose station he visited. She had five cases of a contagious disease and had isolated them in a hut, covering them with her oldest blankets. She arrived, to find Grenfell coming from her storeroom, his arms piled high with her newest and best blankets, and when she asked where he was going he said the poor chaps in the hut needed the blankets. She protested, telling him to return the blankets. He refused, demanding if she knew to whom she was speaking. She was firm, insisting that he do as she said and reminding him that this was her station. He was furious, and dropped the blankets on the floor and strode off. Five minutes later he was teasing her about the incident. But he was equally annoyed when he was stopped gathering up armfuls of clothing from the store at St Anthony. The young woman in charge of the store explained that there was a new order, and that no clothing could be taken without a list being made and a receipt given. Grenfell hurried to Dr Curtis, to tell him to "Get rid of these women."

Grenfell was, often enough, not an easy man to serve, but no one was more beloved. Dr Little thought the world of him, though his patience was tried sorely when Grenfell descended on St Anthony, a whirlwind of energy and new ideas, to upset something Little had spent months organizing and making work smoothly. Children were brought to the orphanage at St Anthony and Grenfell did not know their names, and had forgotten where he found them. A man he brought to the hospital seriously ill died there, and no one knew his name or where Grenfell had picked him up. He was buried in the Protestant graveyard of the settlement. Soon afterwards Dr Curtis received a letter from a much-worried woman who wanted to know how her husband was progressing. This was the man who had died, and he was a Roman Catholic. The body had to be taken from its grave and re-interred.

Grenfell's memory was notoriously bad—or, rather, with his mind fully occupied with new ideas or engrossed in what he was doing, he could not be bothered with remembering small details. The doctors at St Anthony found themselves apologizing to guests, many of them important figures in the outside world, whom Grenfell had invited on a cruise and forgotten all about. The doctors found, too, that they had to take over patients their restless chief had been treating. If a case interested him he would operate, then leave the after-care to others while he responded to yet another idea or the urge to be off on a journey. His assistants had to clear up many a trail of work he had started.

But he was forgiven. No one among those who worked with him retained a grudge, nor ceased to love him. He had only to appear and his omissions and crimes were forgotten, for his smile and obvious happiness in seeing them again made it impossible to bring up some grumble or annoyance that Grenfell himself had so clearly never wished to cause and over something he had long since forgotten.

In an organization so large and in conditions that could be

Q

trying to the most equable tempers there were inevitably disagreements and troubles. Doctors and nurses had their arguments and jealousies, there were grumbles and worries. Grenfell came and charmed away every irritation. The adoration in which he was held both by his staff and by the people on the coast astonished outsiders. A volunteer doctor who had tried vainly to convince a Liveyere woman that she should open a window and let fresh air into her home was amazed when Grenfell entered the house and, having learned of the woman's obstinacy, pushed his elbow through a window to settle the matter. The woman never protested. If Dr Grenfell did it, then it must be right.

This was his highest reward, a far greater reward than the long list of honours he possessesd . . . the people's love and trust. Few men have had so many friends. They were kings, presidents of great nations, statesmen, ministers of every religion, toilers by hand and brain. They extended over the whole of the earth, and an hour with Wilfred Grenfell was their cherished memory.

By the end of his active working life many sores had been healed, and the man's sincerity and selflessness were recognized by even his old enemies. He and the higher Churchmen had learned to appreciate each other better. The *News*, the Newfoundland newspaper that had attacked him so virulently in the past, published an editorial, "By Their Work Ye Shall Know Them," where Grenfell and the Mission were praised and thanked for all they had done for the Colony. Other St John's newspapers repeated the tribute. Grenfell could leave the coast, and there was only sorrow and regret for his going.

18

Last Years

GRENFELL was sixty-nine when he was forced to withdraw from active work; not a great age, and, except for the threat from his faulty heart, he was physically able enough. The danger was in overstraining the heart by too much exertion, and, though the end was inevitable, Grenfell, like anyone else in his condition, could prolong his life by reconciling himself to physical inactivity and avoiding all excitement. To a man like Grenfell this was impossible.

He had a cerebral hæmorrhage in 1932, but recovered and continued his lectures and deputation work, though less strenuously than before. His appearances were fewer and only in the larger cities. He crossed to England late in 1934, to attend the performance of a Jack Hulbert comedy that was organized as a Royal Matinée in aid of the Mission funds and that was under the patronage of T.R.H. the Duke and Duchess of York, soon to be King George VI and Queen Elizabeth and to extend their patronage to the Grenfell Association of Great Britain and Ireland. Apart from Their Majesties, Grenfell's sponsoring committee for this matinée reads as though he had enrolled most of Debrett. In his appeal printed in the handsome programme Grenfell asked for £10,000 to be contributed towards the Mission's annual costs of £40,000, and was able to say that the four hospitals and seven nursing stations on the coast had treated over 12,000 in and out patients during the previous year. He remained in England until the following spring, lecturing and gathering more support for the Grenfell Association of Great Britain and Ireland, then visited Germany, where he was treated as an important visitor by the Nazis. He was not deluded, and wrote to a friend some shrewd and warning comments on this "land of the free (?)."

This was to be Grenfell's last visit to England. His brother Algernon had died that year, and, with his mother gone, there was little to hold him in his native land. Except for a few old friends like Sir Henry Richards and Edwin Sibley, who had been one of his East End club boys forty-five years earlier, and the host of new friends he had made, his interests and the people he knew best were in the United States, Canada, and on the coasts of Labrador and Newfoundland. Even Parkgate, where his nephew had taken over Mostyn House School, was no longer the same. Cheshire was becoming Liverpool's dormitory and the countryside covered with trim bungalows. The silting of the Dee estuary had continued relentlessly, and now only the highest tides reached the red stone revetment. The fishing-boats had almost all gone. Grenfell could still call on those villagers who had been children with him, but he was no longer a part of their lives, only an honoured guest.

Lady Grenfell no longer wished to enter English Society, nor have her children British. Her eldest son had gone to Oxford, the second son, Pascoe, to Cambridge. The daughter, Rosamond, had been educated at an English school. For a time Lady Grenfell had urged them to become British, but with their father's illness she advised them to return to America. Wilfred junior was then teaching at an English school, but he came to the United States; Pascoe had never wished to live anywhere but in America; and Rosamond preferred to finish her education at McGill University, in Canada. With her husband clearly

happier as close to the work of the Mission as he could go, Lady
Grenfell gave up any plans she had to live in England. Her task
now was to prevent her husband overexerting himself, protect
him from his own restlessness and the importunities of those
who would have worried him with their troubles. She knew
now that she had cancer and might not live long. What time she
had left she would continue to dedicate to her husband.

To many suffering from Grenfell's ailment the house Lady
Grenfell had built on the shore of Lake Champlain, Vermont,
would have been a perfect retreat. This part of New England
has a soft, reassuring beauty, reminiscent of parts of Southern
England. It is gently rolling country, where cattle move lazily
on pasture greener than most in America and the lanes away
from the main highways have the winding, hedge-walled
character of Grenfell's own land. The towns and houses have
a trim, well-kept cleanliness that speaks of permanence and of
people with a quiet, sure pride in their country. Vermonters
have the slow, assessing friendliness of English village people,
an unaggressive self-sufficiency, moving unhurriedly, satisfied
to be outside the haste and impatience of so much of America,
and Grenfell felt at home with them, as much as he would ever
be at home with those who were not sailors.

Kinloch House, the Grenfell home, was hidden away from
what human movement there was. Within eight miles of the
town of Shelburne, where the family could attend church, and
within walking distance of a tiny hamlet, a store and a few
wooden houses at a crossroads, it stood a hundred yards or so
above the lake shore and among spruce- and fir-trees that
screened it from the few who might have wandered this far.
The house was a typical steep-roofed, white-painted, wooden
New England building, with pillared entrance, spacious rooms,
and a large, wide, glass-enclosed and marble-paved piazza overlooking the lake. Here the 110-mile-long Lake Champlain was
only a few miles wide, and on the far shore the Adirondack
Mountains lifted themselves in a noble background. A small,
tree-clustered headland formed a small cove in front of the
house, where boats could ride in safety, and half a mile off
shore a tiny island stood, shiplike, with its trees as sails.

The place was, perhaps, too sheltered and untroubled for a
man like Wilfred Grenfell, to whom combat and challenge

soothed as well as stimulated. He could sit in the large drawing-room, where a huge polar-bear skin, hook mats, and carved ivory from Labrador characterized the furnishing, or on the piazza, and watch glorious sunsets as the sun burned its way down behind the mountains across the lake and poured gold and colour on the water. He could watch fierce winds swell the lake into white-crested waves that dashed and were broken against the black, slaty rock of the shore; but these only re-minded him of vaster seas, wider horizons, and struggles he had shared with the *Strathcona*. Here he saw yachts heel past and the daily passenger steamer seem to pump itself along as the beam of its old-fashioned steam-engine rose and fell and turned its paddles. But these were mere toys, a playing at boats to one who had watched fleets of hundreds of smacks and schooners engaged in their hazardous toil. There was a lack of urgency in this tangless, pleasurable little world. Grenfell would have been happier, less restless, poised on a cliff-edge from where he could have watched a harsher, wider world and share, in imagination at least, the voyaging of passing sea traffic.

This was a place to rest, and Grenfell was incapable of rest-ing. He must be occupied every hour he was awake. He had to lie down for an hour after lunch, but during the remainder of the day he found something to do, often testing his weak heart far too much. He sailed his son's 16-foot boat on the lake, taking out young men who visited him and teaching them to sail without a rudder, using their weight as ballast. He fished from a motor-boat, dived and swam in the lake every morning, then sunbathed, very proud of his tan, as he was of his still thick but snowy-white hair and his excellent teeth. He chopped down trees to improve the view from the house, planted bushes sent to him from England, helped to build a jetty for the boats and a large study away from the house. He became a familiar figure in the lanes, cycling miles on a red-painted bicycle and visiting the near-by village, Charlotte, to talk with the storekeeper there. He would wander along the lake shore, or in the woods with his sketch-book, or a hand-net to catch butterflies to bring home and mount.

He was as busy during the evenings. He took up hobby after hobby, making models of komatiks and boats, learning pot-tery, or shaping figures with lobsters and shells. He still loved to read aloud to his wife, or to the many visitors who made the pilgrimage to his home, and to sing hymns. "Making a joyful noise before the Lord," he told his family when they suggested his voice was more powerful than musical. He liked chess, and tried to teach his family to play, but they avoided games if they could. When he lost he was upset and got excited. He avoided defeat by elaborating on another favourite game, Chinese checkers, introducing new rules until no one could win but himself.

He still wrote articles for the Mission magazines, and maintained a voluminous correspondence, until his doctor forbade him to write. His articles were becoming long and rambling discursions, repeating much he had said before, harking back to the past that meant so much to him. He wrote to those closest to him, to his wife when she was away, his daughter, to Eleanor Cushman, now working for the Mission in New York, and to Katie Spalding, secretary to the vigorous association in England —whimsical, humorous letters that were mostly drawings of himself as a fat little sailorman getting into all kinds of trouble and predicaments. Neither age nor sickness dulled his sense of humour; he wrote to his wife:

> I took off my shoe, and what do you think I found? A large hairpin! Now I know why I have lumbago, and I want to know why you put it there? Was it part of a conspiracy to keep me from walking about? Of all things I despise conspiring pins—I have sent the pin to the police, and they will no doubt unmask the source. The specialist in hairpins has the matter in hand.

Much of his correspondence was to his friends in the North, asking for news of the coast and making suggestions to improve the people's lot. His mind still teemed with ideas, and he wrote to George Whiteley at St John's, suggesting new ways of offering cod to the market, urging him to keep up his efforts to drive all strong drink off the coast, and to go and see the commissioners who were now governing Newfoundland and get them to build roads and establish airfields. He wrote to William Pike at Red Bay about the co-operative, and making more suggestions. On the impulse of a memory, he would send a cheque to some fisherman whom he remembered and who might need help. He interested himself in every new scientific discovery, and was greatly excited by experiments being carried out in atom-splitting. When he read about a new plastic glass he immediately saw this invention as a boon for the coast and wrote off for information. He was told the plastic would withstand any weather and admit most of the sun's ultra-violet rays, and he decided that this was the very thing to hasten plant-growing at Dr Curtis's farm in St Anthony, and for solariums for tubercular patients. He contributed 500 dollars from his Discretionary Fund so that two scientists could go to St Anthony and demonstrate the new glass, then was surprised when Dr Curtis wrote to tell him modern research had proved that direct sunlight was harmful to sufferers from pulmonary tuberculosis. Grenfell's correspondence with people on the coast and his tumbling showers of suggestions and ideas were not always welcomed. Neither were his gifts of money looked on with approval by those who now conducted the Mission. He was still, nominally, Superintendent, but others had to carry out the work. Inevitably they were shaping it to their own ideas and methods. To have some one, no matter how beloved and admired, intruding and disturbing their task with what were sometimes extravagant and expensive suggestions could only be an irritation. This voice from the past spoke of what was gone, for the Mission was changing. It was still a dedicated service, conducted by men with a humanitarianism no less than Grenfell's, but not always with the same evangelistic fervour. It was a practical humanity, the saving of life and the improvement of the people's conditions, but without the colour and drama Grenfell instilled into it. The work was now for the planner, the able administrator, not the dreaming idealist. Experience had shown that there had to be a limit to what the Mission could do, or should do. Except for Dr Paddon, for whom, as for Grenfell, the work was part of a Christian faith and way of life, the doctors rarely carried on religious instruction, but left the people's spiritual welfare to the Churches. They found enough to keep them busy in managing the now large organization.

No one—least of all those on the coast who had worked with him and who knew how much he had achieved—wanted to shut Grenfell out entirely from the Mission. This, even if anyone had wished it, would have been impossible, for he was still too vivid in the memories of every family on the coast; his spirit

impregnated and inspired every one who worked there for the
people. This inspiration would never die, and is as much alive
to-day, when this book is being written, as when Grenfell sailed
the *Strathcona* among the islands. It still calls nurses from
England, young men and women from America, as it holds in
brotherhood middle-aged and elderly men and women who
knew the man and shared his work. No one wished that spirit to
go, or to be forgotten, but the hard facts of everyday problems
had to be accepted. Grenfell was gone and could no longer thrust
and inspire new schemes. For better or for worse, the Mission
had to be what those who now ran it made it. It could not be
run from beyond its place, nor with Grenfell intruding new
ideas that could not be worked.

There had to be changes. Grenfell's sole right to choose and
send volunteers had caused a great deal of trouble for the
doctors on the coast, and as early as 1932 he was asked to give
up this right. He registered a protest, but accepted the directors'
decision, writing to them:

> It would be the negation to me of the whole spirit of foreign
> missions if we do not send young men and women, as we do,
> into places where danger is great. We can only bring out good in
> people by trusting them. . . . Do not think that I am bearing any
> *arrière pensée*. It is obviously the opinion of every single director
> —and my wife is of the same opinion—that this law is a good
> one and that I ought to consult Willmer or Curtis before I send a
> W.O.P. down and there should be some law preventing me doing
> it. That, I think, may be perfectly right because at my age my
> judgment may not be good.

That same year the directors suggested he relinquish his
position as Superintendent, but Lady Grenfell refused to allow
him to resign. She knew that while he remained Superintendent, even if only nominally, he would feel close to the Mission, and that without this he would be lost and unhappy. The
directors, who had made the suggestion from the best of motives
and to spare Grenfell from the work involved, withdrew it at
once. There was then no question of his usefulness to the
Mission being ended, for he was still the personality who
attracted support and was still able to address meetings and
interest wealthy people.

Lady Grenfell's opposition to the proposal was an earnest of her intentions to maintain his position and to defend him from any attempt to displace him. She did this, fiercely and effectively. When a too zealous member of the board of directors wrote and asked Grenfell to give 2000 dollars from his Discretionary Fund towards the cost of research into tuberculosis on the coast Grenfell refused. He believed it was the Newfoundland Government's duty to carry out such research, not the Mission's, and he was upset to learn that the proposer of this suggestion had been able to discover the amount of money in the Fund, moneys given to him personally to use as he thought fit. Lady Grenfell was away from home when this correspondence was going on, but she was told of it by Grenfell's male nurse-companion. She immediately wrote to the chairman of the finance committee, Mr Cecil Ashdown, asking him to see that her husband was never again approached on this or any similar matter. "The whole thing was a great worry to Wilf," she wrote.

> His blood pressure went up to 185, the highest that Beeck [his doctor] has ever found it. He was distressed.... Reading the minutes, I cannot feel that the directors were so terribly keen on this project or they would have deferred other work and paid for it. In any case, I wanted you to be fully posted as to what I have done. [She had also written to the proposer of the idea.] Wilf had a bad heart-attack last night. I do hope with all my heart that he will not be worried by such requests from anyone. The administration of the private fund is about all the fun and interest now left to him.

She was equally watchful that Grenfell did not bring troubles on his own head, nor do anything to lessen his reputation and importance. When he sent a long, disjointed, and repetitive article to the Mission magazine she wrote to the editor, asking him not to print it. She arranged for her secretary to bring all the household mail to her first, and she withheld any letters she believed would worry her husband. His own letters were also intercepted, and not allowed to go if they contained anything she thought would do him harm. She prevented what might have annoyed the Mission directors by holding back two letters Grenfell wrote to the R.N.M.D.S.F., offering his old mission the Seamen's Institute at St John's. With the decline in shipping into the port and the disappearance of most of the schooners, this once valuable amenity was no longer being used, and the directors had offered it to the Commission Government of Newfoundland. This annoyed Grenfell, and he acted on the impulse and wrote to his old mission, asking them to take over the building.

Living with the Grenfells had always been a delightful experience for the secretaries and close friends who knew them best, for Grenfell bubbled over with a puckish sense of humour and loved to tease. He had a gift of nonsense, to which his wife responded with quick appreciation and laughter that rang through their home. They were, her secretaries said, "like two children together," happy in each other's company and with complete adoration on Grenfell's part. He was always gentle and considerate with those who worked for him. But there was a period, between 1936 and 1938, when his disease and high blood-pressure affected his brain and he was not always quite sane. In those moods he became suddenly furious with people and liable to act on some wild impulse. When Lady Grenfell was at home she could watch for these moods and restrain him, but she was not always at home. During one of her absences he visited a judge at the near-by town of Burlington and was told about a dispute over some land his wife was having with a neighbour. He was immediately up in arms, threatening to go and tear down fences and take the law into his own hands. He rushed off to a local newspaper to offer a series of articles on the dispute and other subjects. His nurse wrote off hastily to Lady Grenfell, and she wrote to the judge, asking him never to discuss business with her husband, and to the editor of the newspaper, asking him not to accept the articles.

She had to be everlastingly on the watch, and all this time she was suffering severe pain from her ailment. She was given a far too powerful X-ray treatment and suffered torturous after-effects, and the disease brought on secondary illnesses to pester her further. Time after time she had to enter hospitals. She wrote to a friend:

> This has been a very thin summer for both of us. I have a good deal of pain, which of course makes me a delightful companion in the household. I was thinking this morning it would be a good deal better, if it weren't for Sir Wilfred, if I could go to some rest home and not inflict my presence upon the family.

Yet not until the very end did she cease to watch over her husband or lessen her efforts for the mission he had created. She travelled to New York to help in organizing operas being performed by famous singers for the Mission funds, and she still continued her work for the industrial department. Two "Dog Team Taverns" had been opened, one within ten miles of Kinloch House, where tourists could lodge or get meals and see and buy the produce of Labrador. An old church beside this tavern was made into a "Grenfell Museum," and Lady Grenfell appeared and helped there often. Shops had been opened in New York and other cities for the sale of Grenfell handicrafts; stalls were taken at exhibitions. With the work involved in all this, in handling her own and her husband's correspondence, in watching over him, cultivating wealthy philanthropists who might help the Mission, she left herself little time to think of her own sufferings. She did a great deal for the Mission in these years. From one rich woman she was to be instrumental in getting half a million dollars and another million dollars willed for the Endowment Fund. On top of all this labour Lady Grenfell set herself the task of collecting together her husband's favourite pieces of prose, and extracts from his own writing, publishing these as *A Labrador Logbook*, under his name.

Her life in those last years was an amazing demonstration of determination and loyalty. That she was the type of person who must dominate cannot lessen what she achieved and what she suffered to do what she did. She was truly the "Queen Mother" Eleanor Cushman named her, in a noble and royal disregard for the pain she suffered and in the dedication of her last years to her husband and his mission. That she saw it as her husband's mission cannot attenuate the grandeur of what was a complete ignoring of her own painful troubles.

By 1938 both Grenfell and his wife were very sick people. Lady Grenfell was suffering great pain all the time, and Grenfell was badly crippled. He indignantly refused a wheelchair, but had to hobble round on crutches. His forced inactivity rode his patience sorely, and he was not easy to handle. He decided he must go to Labrador once again, and wanted to make the journey on board a tourist ship. His wife was worried and distressed, asking Eleanor Cushman to help her discourage him from the idea. He did not go. Indeed, his health was now so poor that he had finally resigned as Superintendent of the Mission in 1937, the board informing him that he would "hereafter be referred to as The Founder, and whilst any suggestions or ideas would always be welcomed from him, it was thought better that these should come to the board through the Secretary, Cecil S. Ashdown, and that he should not correspond with other officials of the organization." Dr Charles S. Curtis, already virtually in command, was appointed Superintendent in succession.

In October 1938 Lady Grenfell's doctors advised another operation. Grenfell with his male nurse and secretary, Wyman Shaw, a young medical graduate, accompanied her to Boston and were installed in a small, quiet hotel. She was operated on, and Grenfell wrote to his old friend, Francis B. Sayre:

> Anne had to go through an abdominal operation on Wednesday, and I have been here ever since. I know you will rejoice with me that all is well. . . . I'm sitting here alone and Anne is in pain, but I feel so happy and grateful because that will soon pass and we will have time for work yet.

He was not told his wife was dying. Wyman Shaw tried to keep him amused by taking him to football matches, and he could visit and be visited by his many friends in this city that was a second home for him. He was not allowed to see his wife as her end approached, but he crept up to her door one night and slipped a letter under it, asking if she remembered a ship called the *Mauretania* and a spot called Pop Corner, adding a sketch of the little fat sailor kneeling before a tall regal lady on the deck of a tiny ship. A few days later he was called to her bedside for the last time. To this last day she had held to her task, reading every letter that arrived and dictating replies before she died.

Grenfell took his great loss calmly. He had always been sure that death was not extinction, but a passing on to a heavenly continuation. He had accepted this in his early days as part of his Christian faith. In his paper on Immortality, written in 1914, he said: "As with my love for life here, so it is with my faith in immortal life here and hereafter. Now that I come to write it down, I find that the chief reason that I believe in it is just because I am sure of it." Later, and particularly during his illness, he liked to rationalize his belief. Writing in a letter about two scientific books he had read, he said:

> They both say that no longer is there any controversy between religion and science. Both agree that matter is freely convertible, and when broken up leaves nothing but a mathematical equation, but with us, when our bodies are gone, there is still something to be accounted for.

But Grenfell needed no scientific reassurance. Answering a letter of condolence from Edwin Sibly, he said:

> Yes, thank God, I know she lives, and I know I shall rejoin her. I believe increasingly she now fashions more than ever my daily actions and thoughts and work. She said at the last, "I am slipping away from you.... I shall never be far from you.... Love like ours can never be parted." We sang Bunyan's hymn of his arrival to serve the Master.

His health improved in the months following his wife's death. He went south to St Simon Island, in Georgia, where he and Lady Grenfell had spent most of their last winters together; then to Miami, to join Dr Kellog's "aristocracy of health" on a diet of roasted "protos" at Kellog's clinic. While in Miami he was well enough to address 4000 of the Pan-American League on what was one of his favourite themes—the need for close friendship between the United States and Britain—though he wrote to a friend:

> I gave the address, but found it difficult to keep my thoughts together. Indeed, I was quite nervous the night before, and I never had been that way before until lately. What is happening to my old think box I do not know, but I forget words. I have never had such a fight to give the message I wanted.

There were still times when he was not altogether rational, and he was missing his wife sorely. He believed she remained close to him, as she had promised, and he wrote to Frank Sayre, "I read a little portion of her book each day and she surely speaks to me." But without her he clung more and more to the Christ he had followed so long, speaking of religion a great deal and with a lessened tolerance for the sinner. "Who," he demanded, "can think of Christ with a glass of champagne and a cigarette in their hands." He swept a tray of glasses with his

arm when it was offered to him at a reception, and he made
loud-spoken comment on anyone who was drinking in restau-
rants. In an excess of religious zeal he wanted to give all his
possessions away—even Kinloch House.

His family were worried by his behaviour, and knew that he
must have some occupation to distract him. His eldest son
suggested that part of the grounds of Kinloch House be turned
into a camp for boys, and Grenfell was delighted with the suggestion. He said he would not mind staying in Vermont for the
summers now, but when he discovered that the boys who came
to the camp were not from city slums but from well-to-do
homes he lost interest. His family then took a calculated risk in
the hope of helping him to better health. They proposed that he
carry his wife's ashes to St Anthony for burial. He was delighted and excited by the prospect. Lady Grenfell had asked
that her ashes be either scattered on the sea or buried at St
Anthony, a last loyal gesture to her husband, for she had always
hated the sea and never liked living at St Anthony. She knew
he would be made happy by this choice of a resting-place.

In July 1939 Grenfell sailed from Montreal on board one of
the tourist ships cruising on the Labrador coast, accompanied
by his daughter, Wyman Shaw, and a friend who had been his
and his wife's host in Georgia. He was carefully protected from
the many tourists who, thrilled to find that their fellow-passenger
was the famous Dr Grenfell, whose books and lectures had
brought them on the cruise, would dearly have loved to meet
him. Wyman Shaw, whose growing attachment to his daughter
Grenfell had noticed, was kept busy holding away autograph-
hunters and keeping Grenfell from being pestered.

He was given a royal welcome when the ship arrived at St
Anthony. Dr Curtis had warned the people there not to do
anything that would excite their visitor, and the welcome was
subdued though no less warm. He was escorted on shore and
under a triumphal arch of evergreen tree-boughs with WELCOME
on it, its builders, knowing how he disliked having the trees in
St Anthony cut down, explaining that the boughs had come
from a site being cleared, and not the settlement. Mrs Curtis,
Lady Grenfell's schoolmate and closest friend, took charge of
him and protected him from any over-enthusiastic callers. Old
friends came to see him, Edgar MacNeill, still the Mission's

Admirable Crichton, his old servant Reuben Sims, his ship-mates from the *Strathcona*, Will Sims and Albert Ash. Dr Curtis took him round the Mission buildings, the now enlarged hospital, where the equipment equalled anything in the outside world, where 200 patients were housed, and to which up to 100 people came for treatment with every steamer. He saw the farm Curtis had developed, now with huge barns for winter-ing the pedigree herd, where crops were grown successfully. He saw disabled fishermen, who would have starved without the Mission, carving ivory and cutting and polishing labradorite, women and girls shaping and embroidering garments from deerskin and from the famous "Grenfell cloth" he had sug-gested to a British manufacturer years before. The Mission's repair dock held a schooner. Children poured from school and orphanage to see this man they had heard so much about, watching him with shy, wondering eyes.

"Truly," Grenfell wrote afterwards, "it was to me a joyous, uplifting and inspiring occasion"; and he moved contentedly among the people, his smile gentle and happy, his eyes alight as he recognized those he had known as children and who were now grown men and women, aged fishermen he remembered as sturdy young men he had sailed with. He had missed these people, those places, so much. He could see how the work he had begun had grown, until now the Mission made a small town in itself and the homes of those who had come from out-lying ports to be near the schools and hospital and the work the Mission provided were scattered round the whole harbour. To know that St Anthony was only one of several, if smaller, settle-ments created by the Mission was enough reward. He was humble in gratitude.

From St Anthony Grenfell sailed north to Cartwright on board the mail-steamer *Kyle*, his party added to by an old friend and comrade, Dr Norman Stewart, who had been in charge of Battle Harbour for five years thirty years previously and who was now visiting his son, the Mission doctor at Cart-wright. At each stop the steamer made Grenfell was welcomed by his friends. "They will believe in the Resurrection now," he remarked jokingly to Wyman Shaw—and, indeed, he seemed to those people, for whom he had done so much, their special saint returned from the dead. For many who had heard

of him but were too young to have remembered him, to have
seen "Dr Grenfell" was an occasion to talk of all their lives.
They had heard so much about him from their parents, such
stories of his daring, his kindliness, his fight for their welfare.
Now, in this white-haired, sweetly smiling man they saw their
champion. They fired off their guns and cheered him to show
how much he still meant to them.

He stayed four days at Cartwright, finding this Mission
station grown as had St Anthony. He found an old sweetheart
there, in charge of the industrial department—Mrs Keddie,
who had been the three-year-old daughter of the Hudson's Bay
post manager at Rigolet forty years before, and his devoted
admirer. Sketch-book in hand, he wandered along the shore, or
into the woods behind the Mission buildings, more contented
than he had been for many years. His happiness was increased
when Dr Paddon and his son, Anthony, who was, in time, to
take up his father's task, arrived at Cartwright on board their
vessel *Maraval*. Dr Paddon was to die suddenly in a few months'
time, but he had done noble work in the twenty-five years he
served the Mission. His hospital at North West River was now
the centre of a prosperous settlement, his farm and gardens
teaching the people that they possessed more than fish and pelts.
Paddon covered the coast and country from above Nain to Cartwright, a distance as the crow flies of 300 miles, but much more
by ship and the dog team he drove during the winter. They had
much to talk of, those two missionaries of the past.

Back at St Anthony Grenfell had two more pleasures to enjoy.
Dr Curtis gave him the Mission tender, a small vessel named
Northern Messenger, and once again Grenfell was captain of a
ship. He crossed Belle Isle Strait to Red Bay, accompanied by
Wyman Shaw, Professor Frederick Sears, of Massachusetts
Agricultural College, who came north every year to advise the
settlers on their gardens and crops, an engineer, and, "owing
to my ageing memory, but nevertheless resentfully," a pilot.
He met Will Pike and his sister, and saw the co-operative still
flourishing and the people of the bay, whom he had found
destitute, now prosperous and healthy. On the way back to
St Anthony the vessel called at several small settlements, people
coming to Grenfell for advice as of old. Back at St Anthony he
was invited to another cruise, on board a trading schooner. In

R

her he went south, crossing Hare Bay, where he had lived through his ordeal on the ice pan and where memories came thickly. Everywhere he went there was a heart-touching welcome, and Wyman Shaw had a difficult task in protecting his charge from over-excitement. The fishermen wanted to show how happy Grenfell's coming made them, and would have entertained him too royally. But he was still as innocent as ever. His fishermen hosts added to their celebrations surreptitious visits to cached bottles, and one old fisherman who had made rather too many of these visits insisted on escorting Grenfell and Shaw back to their ship. He took Grenfell's arm to help him down the steep path to the harbour, but stumbled several times and finally fell to his knees. When Shaw got his charge safely on board the schooner Grenfell said with no small pride, "Poor old chap. . . . He is younger than I am, but his legs aren't nearly so good as mine."

Late in August Grenfell boarded the steamer, his visit ended. The whole population of St Anthony came to say good-bye. There were tears in many eyes as the Mission staff and fishermen sang him away with Auld Lang Syne, for no one believed he would ever return alive. He would come back, his ashes at least, to be laid beside his wife's by the granite outcrop high on the hill behind the Mission buildings. In spirit he would never be away from this coast and its people.

Fourteen months later he died. His health and mind seemed to improve even more after his return to the coast; he even lectured again. He attended the Grenfell Alumni Dinner in New York in 1940, where 250 men and women who had been Wops and who now supported and conducted the Mission's affairs and finances gathered to see their beloved 'chief.' He travelled across America to receive a degree from the University of California and carried out a leisurely lecture tour of the western States. He visited Utah and liked the Mormons. "Creed does not matter," he said. He was interviewed by "two huge Mormons from a Utah newspaper, but when they learned I had played football for my varsity, they forgave all my sins."

The outbreak of the Second World War upset him, but he had never trusted Hitler and believed he would have to be destroyed. Neither did he like Russia, and he wrote to the Canadian Prime Minister, his friend of many years, W. I.

Mackenzie King, to suggest that Finns should be "saved from the claws of Russia" by being brought to Labrador, where they would make ideal settlers. In this same letter he mentioned another of his shrewd and inspired hopes: "I have often wished that Labrador and Newfoundland might unite with Canada," he wrote. This was to happen one day, as so much Grenfell had urged was to happen: airfields in Newfoundland and Labrador serving the world traveller, vast mining ventures. One of his last interests was to correspond with the president of a large hæmatite-mining company, urging him to exploit the Labrador mineral wealth.

It was as though his visit to the North had given him new life, soothed his restless body, and cleared his mind. He was closer to his children now, though as a wise and guiding father he was not always a success. After advising his eldest son not to marry too hastily and to wait until he had known the girl for a longer time he laughed and said, "I'm a fine one to talk."

On October 9, 1940, he was at Kinloch House and seemed in excellent spirits. That afternoon he challenged Wyman Shaw and Professor Sears, who was visiting him, to a game of his favourite croquet. He was beaten, and this, as defeat always did, upset him. He left his companions, to go to his room and rest before the evening meal. When Shaw went to call him he was dead. He had passed over to Anne and to the welcoming Christ as peacefully as though they had summoned him to be comforted.

Principal Sources and Bibliography

Sources

Records of the Grenfell Association of Great Britain and Ireland.
Records of the International Grenfell Association.
Records of the Royal National Mission to Deep Sea Fishermen.
Archives, Hudson's Bay Company.
Records of the London Hospital.
The Grenfell Papers, Yale University Library.
H.M. Colonial Relations Office Library.
City Public Library, St John's, Newfoundland.
The *Times* Library.
Admiralty Hydrographic Department.
Family papers.

Bibliography

Toilers of the Sea (magazine of the Royal National Mission to Deep Sea Fishermen), 1884-1957.

Among the Deep Sea Fishermen (magazine of the International Grenfell Association), 1894-1957.

In Darkest England and the Way Out, by General Booth (International H.Q. Salvation Army, 1890).

What Cheer O, by Alexander Gordon (Nisbet, London, 1890).

North Sea Fishers and Fighters, by Walter Wood (Kegan Paul, London, 1911).

Grenfell of Labrador, by James Johnston (Partridge, London, 1908).

Wilfred Grenfell, the Labrador Doctor, by W. M. Comber (Lutterworth Press, 1950).

Fifty-two Years at the Labrador Fishery, by Nicholas Smith (Stockwell, London, 1937).

Dictatorship in Newfoundland, by T. Lodge (Cassell, 1939).

Opportunities for Co-operative Organization in Newfoundland and Labrador, by Dame Margaret Digby (Horace Plunkett Foundation).

Books by Sir Wilfred Grenfell

Adrift on an Ice Pan (Constable, 1910).
Adventure of Life, The (Nisbet, 1912).
Attractive Way, The (Pilgrim Press, Boston, 1913).
Challenge of Labrador, The (date unknown).
Christmas at Peace Haven (Houghton Mifflin, Boston, 1923).
Christmas Voyage of the Handy Lass (pamphlet).
Deeds of Daring (Hodder and Stoughton, 1934).
Down North on the Labrador (Nisbet, 1911).
Down to the Sea (Melrose, 1910).
Fishermen's Saint, The (Hodder and Stoughton, 1930).
Forty Years for Labrador (Hodder and Stoughton, 1933).
Harvest of the Sea (Revell, 1905).
Immortality (Nisbet, 1913).
Labrador, the Country and the People (Macmillan, New York, 1910).
Labrador Days (Hodder and Stoughton, 1921).
Labrador Doctor, A (Hodder and Stoughton, 1920).
Labrador Logbook, A (Hodder and Stoughton, 1939).
Labrador looks at the Orient (Jarrold, 1928).
Labrador's Fight for Economic Freedom (Benn, 1929).
Little Prince Pomiuk (pamphlet, Philadelphia, 1906).
Man's Faith, A (Marshall, 1909).
Man's Helpers, A (Pilgrim Press, Boston, 1910).
Northern Neighbours (Hodder and Stoughton, 1923).
Off the Rocks (Philadelphia, 1906).
On Immortality (Pilgrim Press, Boston, 1912).
Prize of Life, The (Pilgrim Press, Boston, 1914).
Religion in Everyday Life (American Library Association, 1926).
Romance of Labrador, The (Hodder and Stoughton, 1934).
Tales of the Labrador (Nisbet, 1917).
Vikings of To-day (Marshall, 1895).
Way of Life, The (pamphlet, Pilgrim Press, Boston).
What can Jesus Christ do with Me (pamphlet, Pilgrim Press, Boston, 1912).
What Christ means to Me (Hodder and Stoughton, 1926).
What Life means to Me (Nisbet, 1913).
What the Church means to Me (pamphlet, Pilgrim Press, Boston, 1911).
What will You do with Jesus Christ? (Pilgrim Press, Boston, 1910).
Yourself and Your Body (Hodder and Stoughton, 1925).

Petit Nord, Le, by Anne Grenfell and Katie Spalding (Hodder and Stoughton, 1921).

Index